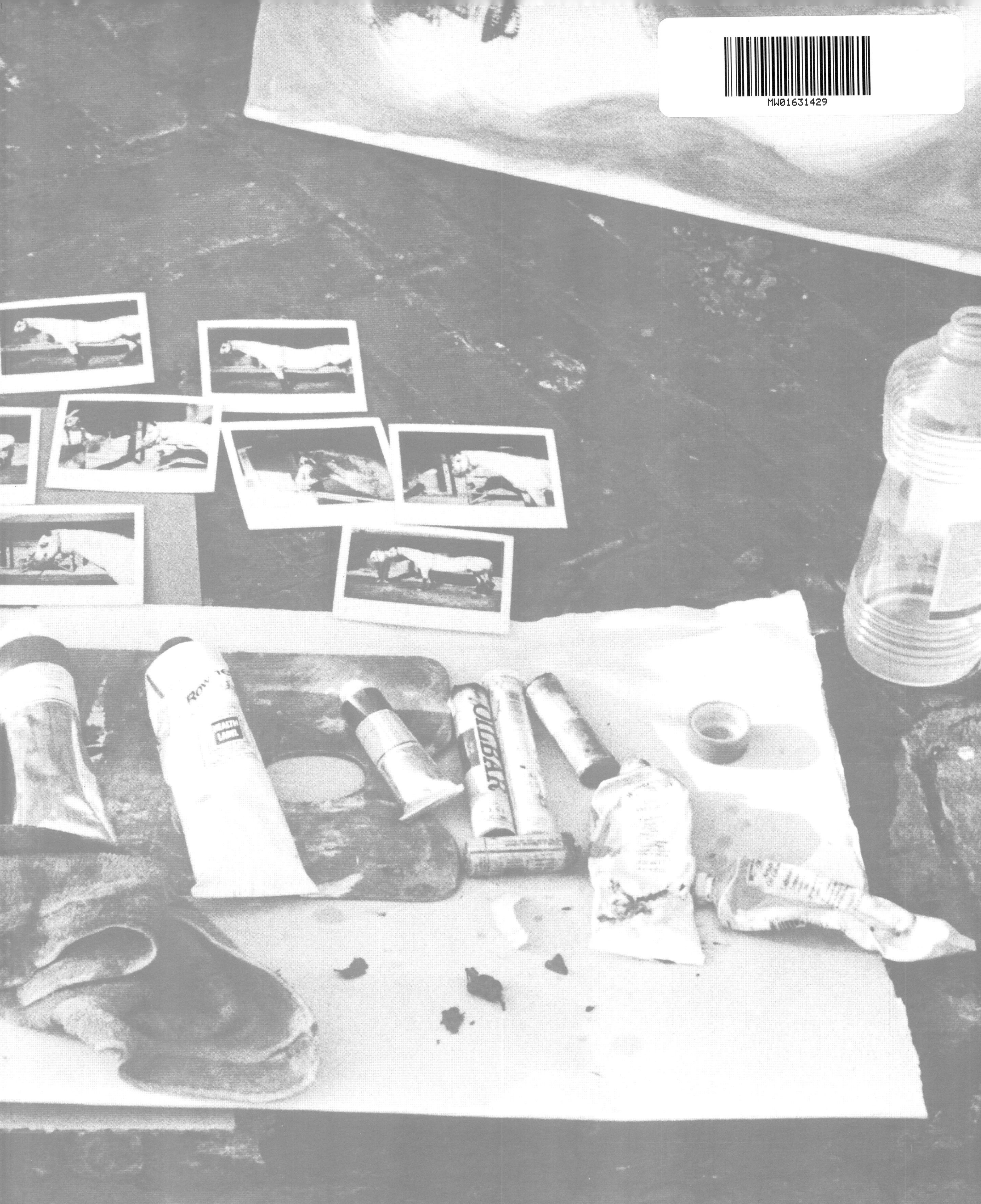
OILBAR

Paul McCartney

PAINTINGS

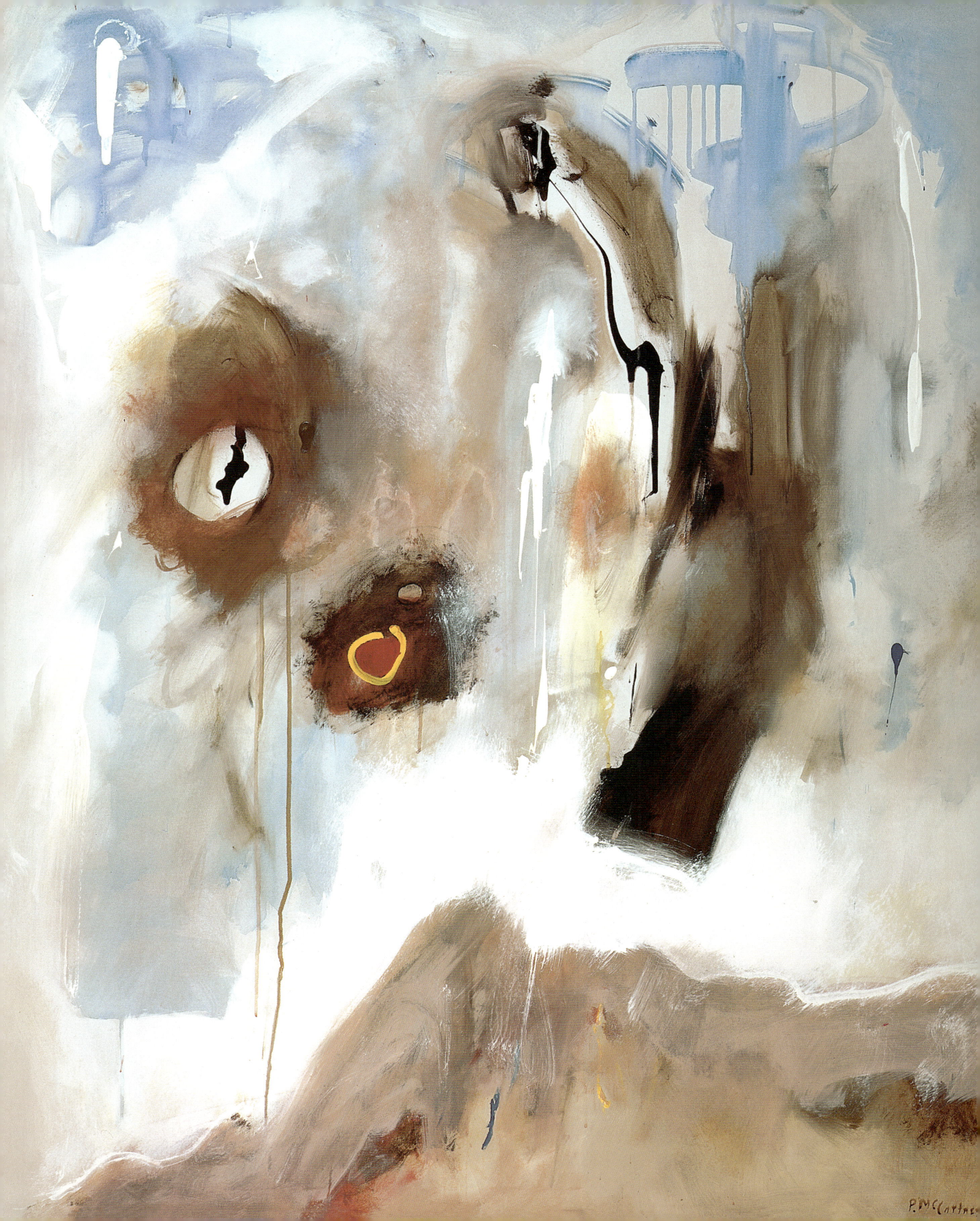
P. McCartne

Paul McCartney

PAINTINGS

WITH ESSAYS BY

BRIAN CLARKE

JULIAN TREUHERZ

BARRY MILES

WOLFGANG SUTTNER

CHRISTOPH TANNERT

AND AN INTERVIEW WITH PAUL McCARTNEY

A BULFINCH PRESS BOOK

LITTLE, BROWN AND COMPANY BOSTON NEW YORK LONDON

FRONTISPIECE:

Pintos in the sky with desert poppy, 1991

Translation from German: Alex Atkins

Translation from German: Fiona Elliot
Photographs of works by Nick Clark

This book has its roots in the exhibition *Paul McCartney: Paintings,* which was curated by Wolfgang Suttner and shown in the Lÿz Art Forum, Siegen, Germany, from May 1 to July 25, 1999, and the catalog, edited and produced by Mr. Suttner and Kultur!Buro, Siegen-Wittgenstein, which accompanied that exhibition.

FIRST EDITION

ISBN 0-8212-2673-8

Library of Congress Cataloging-in-Publication Data

McCartney, Paul.
Paul McCartney, paintings / with essays by Brian Clarke . . . [et al.] and an interview with Paul McCartney. — 1st U.S. ed.
p. cm.
"A Bulfinch Press book."
ISBN 0-8212-2673-8
1. McCartney, Paul — Catalogs. 2. Musicians as artists — England — Catalogs. 3. McCartney, Paul — Interviews. 4. Musicians — England — Interviews. I. Title: Paintings. II. Clarke, Brian. III. Title.

ND497.M49 A4 2000
759.2 — dc21

00-022177

Bulfinch Press is an imprint and trademark of Little, Brown and Company (Inc.)

PRINTED IN GERMANY

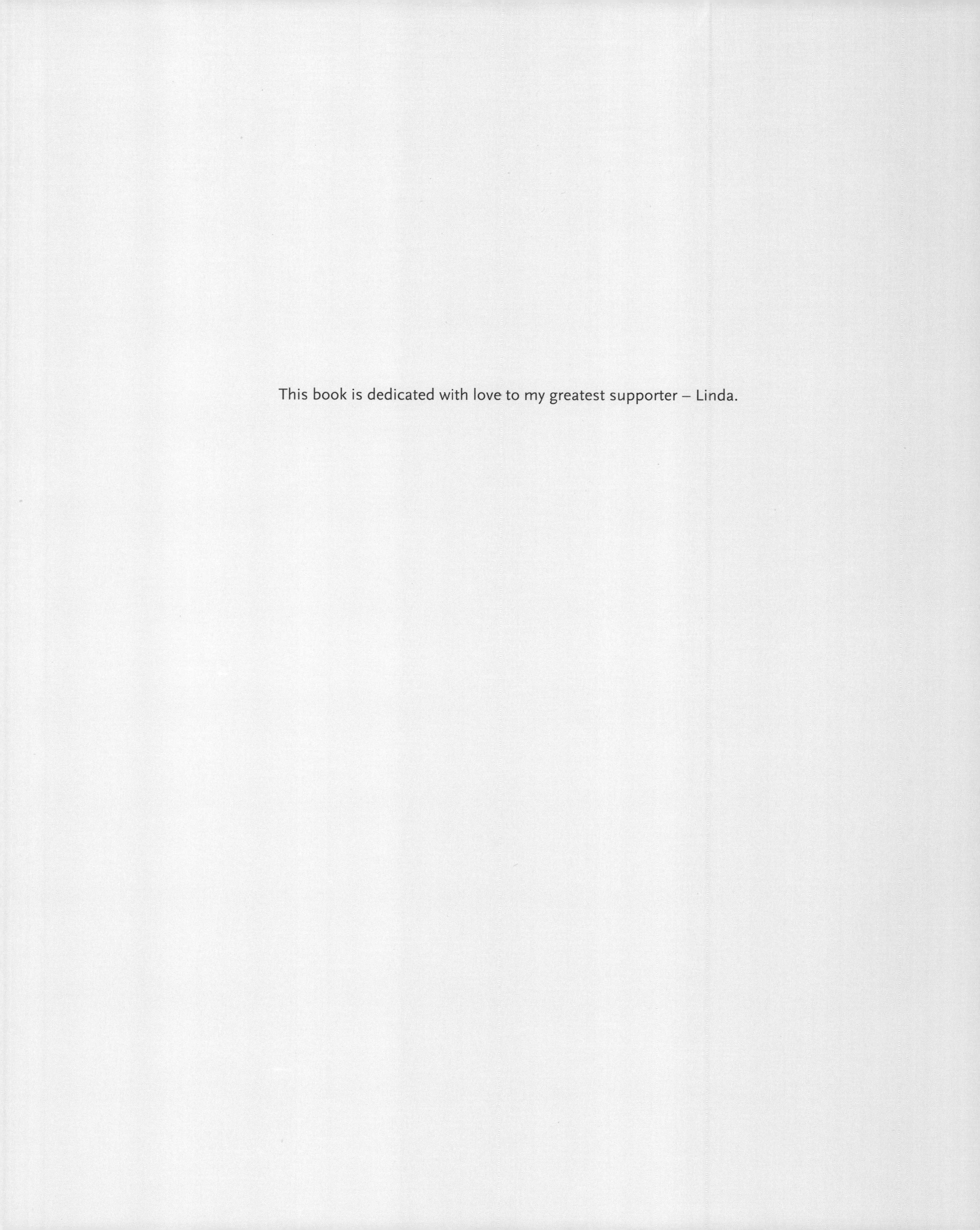

This book is dedicated with love to my greatest supporter – Linda.

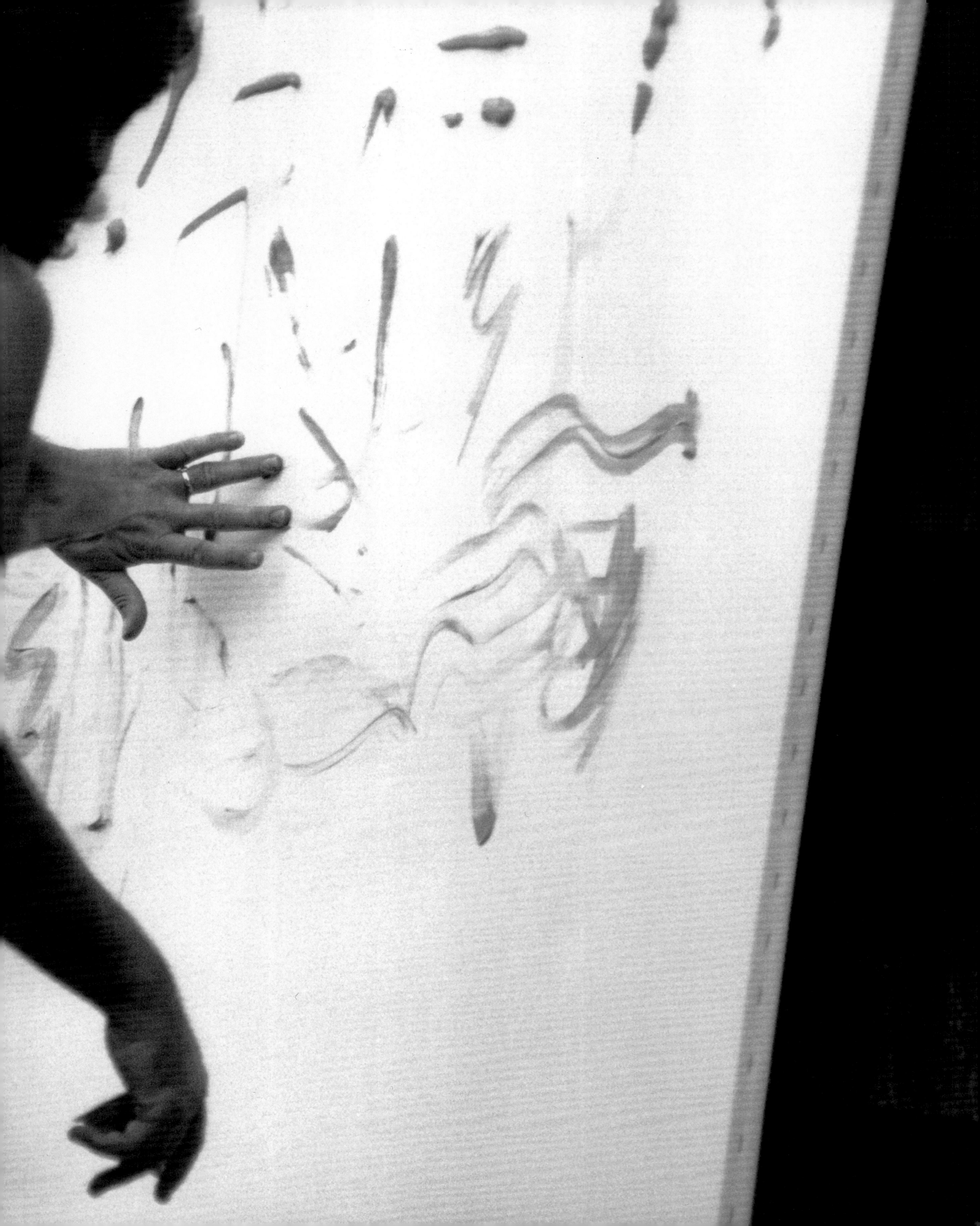

Contents

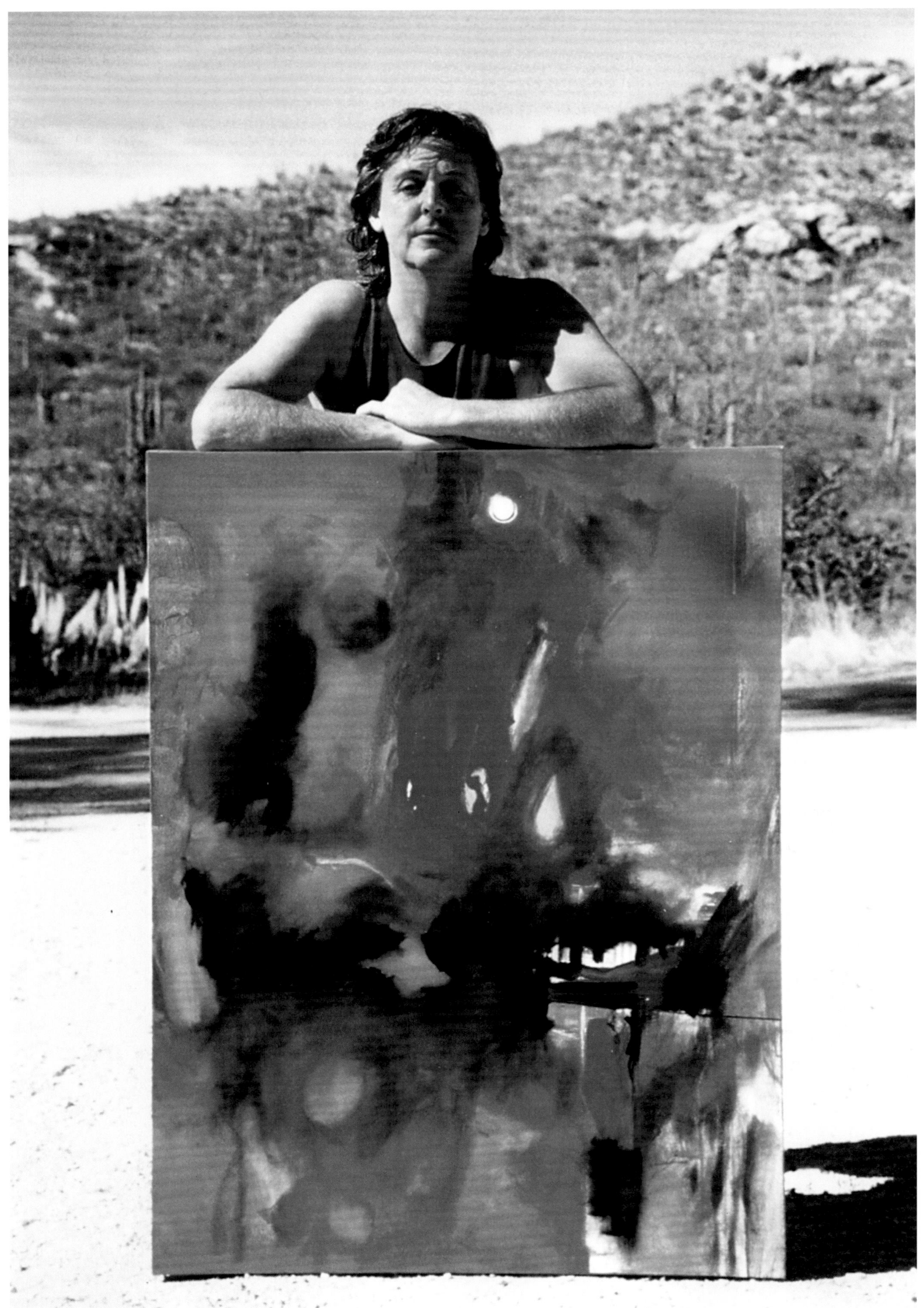

FOREWORD

Paul McCartney and the Courage to Get Lost

BRIAN CLARKE

One of the first things I noticed about Paul McCartney was his language. From the first conversation we had I was aware of the shared vocabulary of the painter. One of the most memorable conversations of my life took place in AIR London, the recording studios of George Martin. Paul went to great lengths to explain to me the detailed procedure of operating a mixing desk. Technologically uneducated and incapable of effectively operating a fax machine or TV remote control, I was astonished that I fully followed the lecture. The language he used was my language. In it sounds had texture, notes had color, tracks were applied in layers like impasto, sweeping strings were brushstrokes, and so on. At the time, I assumed that Paul had brilliantly come down to my level. As our friendship grew I came to realize that he always speaks in the language of the visual artist. It is his natural inclination.

Having distinguished himself as historically as he has in the cultural landscape of the century as a songwriter and performer, it's a brave move for Paul to share his paintings with us. Paul McCartney approaches his adventure in painting with the same characteristic modesty that animates his music. Painting, like music, is a journey for McCartney, a mystery tour that he allows to lead him where it will.

Over twenty-five years ago Paul and Linda, searching for a new home, decided consciously to get lost in the labyrinthine lanes of East Sussex, until by chance they happened upon the property that was to become their family home. On many occasions he has corrected me when I've described his long industrious days as "hard work." "I'm a musician; I don't work, I play." He is the ultimate amateur, the anti-professional, the intuitive, the subjective; he is, in short — by my definition at least — the genuine article, a real artist entirely fearless about getting lost. Armed with what must constitute one of the most full and varied lives of our time, with learning and experience that would make the most generous of us cynical, Paul McCartney, by some mercurial twist of fate and, I venture, gargantuan effort, has remained as an artist a humble, modest man. Nothing is too insignificant for his full attention; no little castaway item or urban waste lying on a beach escapes his creative eye. No idea in painting goes unregistered, and the great discoveries of artistic giants of the past are absorbed into his own vocabulary with the same gentle ease with which most of us might enjoy the scent of a flower. Robert Fraser described Paul to me in the late seventies as "that rare, exotic thing, a real artist."

Arizona, 1991, with
Red abstract white moon

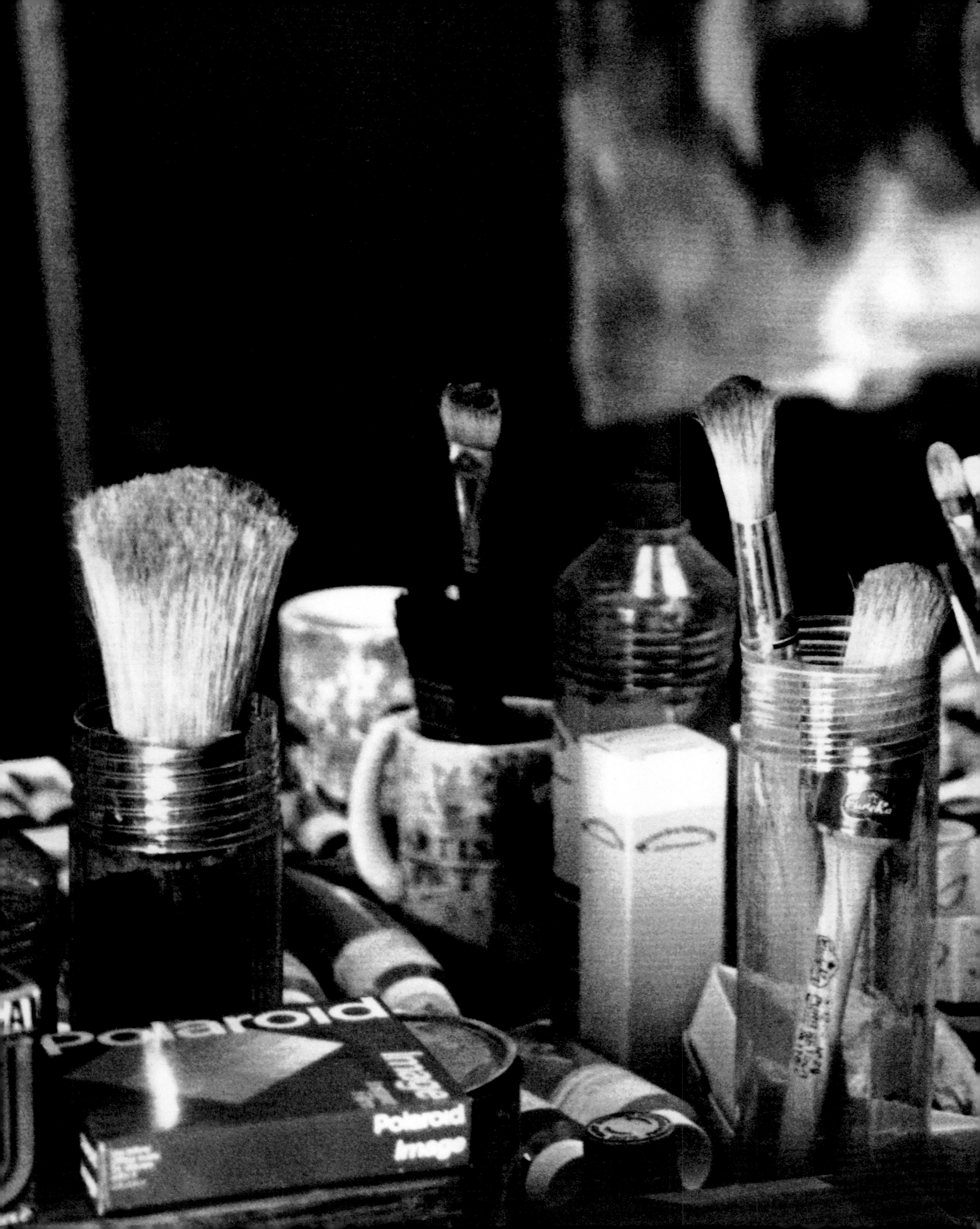
polaroid
Image
Polaroid
Image

Paul McCartney in Context

JULIAN TREUHERZ

When I first walked into a room of paintings by Paul McCartney, two of them seemed to sing across the room to me, asking me to come closer. They appealed to me on purely visual grounds, even before I knew the titles. One was *Mr. Magritte's ruler,* its translucent blue and yellow colors floating over the white ground creating an expansive air of serenity. The other was *Brains on fire,* a head exploding with agitation, hinting at a disturbed inner person behind the public face. Understandably, McCartney wants his painting to be judged like his music, on its merits, and not to be given special treatment as the work of a celebrity. But equally, it would be naive to think that we could entirely forget, when looking at these intensely personal works, who painted them. Does *Brains on fire,* for example, lay bare McCartney's own inner turmoil of creativity?

Paintings like these show that McCartney is a natural with paint, with the way it is applied to the canvas and with the expressive potential of different kinds of marks and colors. His paintings have a real sense of spontaneity. They are about process: they come from the way they are made rather than starting from an intellectual conception that is then realized in visual terms. Here is a clear parallel between the way McCartney composes music and the way he makes a painting. He has never made a secret of the fact that he has had no formal musical training and that when he started, he could not read a note of music. Far from inhibiting his creativity, this seems to have been a real advantage in that it gave full rein to improvisation and new ideas. Strumming a guitar until a tune or chord sequence emerged, or playing with musical phrases that gave rise to words that started off associations leading to a character or story — this is the origin of many of the classic songs that we all know. A big contributor to this process was also the group interaction with his fellow musicians, and of course McCartney's innate musical talent, which has developed and deepened with experience.

For McCartney, the process of making paintings has been very similar — minus the group dynamics, for painting is a lonely business. He talks of "killing the canvas," "exploring the accident," "following my nose," essentially starting a painting with random marks and working from them. Sometimes he has a subject in mind, sometimes he catches a subject as it emerges or even after completion — this is how he works. The method is not new; indeed, it has a long tradition in Western art. The Italian Renaissance artist Leonardo da Vinci recommended that artists seek inspiration by looking at cracks in walls or patterns in stones. In the eighteenth century the British watercolorist Alexander Cozens taught artists to take a brush loaded with ink and make a blot on the paper, which was then traced onto a second sheet as a starting point for an imaginary landscape. In the early twentieth century the surrealists preached auto-

Brushes in front of a painting (detail)
Sussex, 1996

matic writing not only as a visual device but also as a means of releasing the subconscious. The use of random effects of paint — whether totally unmediated, or shaped and manipulated by the artist — has been central to much of the art of the second half of the twentieth century.

In view of his lack of musical education, it is ironic that McCartney at first felt inhibited from painting because he had had no formal art training. At the foot of the stairs to his office hangs a large figure drawing by the Victorian painter Sir Edward Burne-Jones, one of the Pre-Raphaelites, whose work the young McCartney first saw at the Walker Art Gallery in Liverpool. The art of the Pre-Raphaelites may seem at the opposite pole to that of Paul McCartney and the Beatles — but Burne-Jones also never received any formal art qualifications. He took a few lessons from friends and fellow artists but found his artistic persona through self-exploration, experimentation, and study. The Pre-Raphaelites were impatient with rules and conventions, and as a result their art has a freshness and an arresting quality that makes it stand out from its contemporaries.

Another parallel with a famous artist presents itself: the French painter Ingres was an accomplished violinist, and it is said that he could have made an equally brilliant career as a professional musician. Now Paul McCartney has reversed the equation: one of the world's most famous musicians has shown us that he can paint. Just as he is still musically fertile, he is still painting, and his forthcoming exhibition at the Walker Art Gallery will demonstrate his continuing productivity.

In the second half of the twentieth century, Liverpool has been an exceptionally creative place; few cities in England can rival its distinctive culture, with poets and writers like Alan Bleasdale, Willy Russell, Roger McGough, and Adrian Henri as well as the Merseysound phenomenon. Liverpool has always had an artistic tradition independent of the rest of the country. In the nineteenth century the city proved more receptive to the innovations of the Pre-Raphaelites than London and produced its own talented group of Liverpool Pre-Raphaelite artists. Still earlier, George Stubbs, one of the most original of Britain's great eighteenth-century painters, was born in Liverpool. Yet, in order to make his reputation, Stubbs had to leave Liverpool, and this is also true of McCartney. Though he started out in Liverpool and latterly in such works as the *Liverpool Oratorio* he has returned to his roots, he needed to get away to release his creativity in full. Certainly his painting is as much the product of New York and his friendship with de Kooning as it is of Liverpool. Nevertheless, the city has left its legacy: its former position as an international port brought together a cosmopolitan and edgy mixture of people, which has proved to be a fertile breeding ground for creativity and original artistic achievement.

Brushes in front of a
painting (detail)
Sussex, 1996

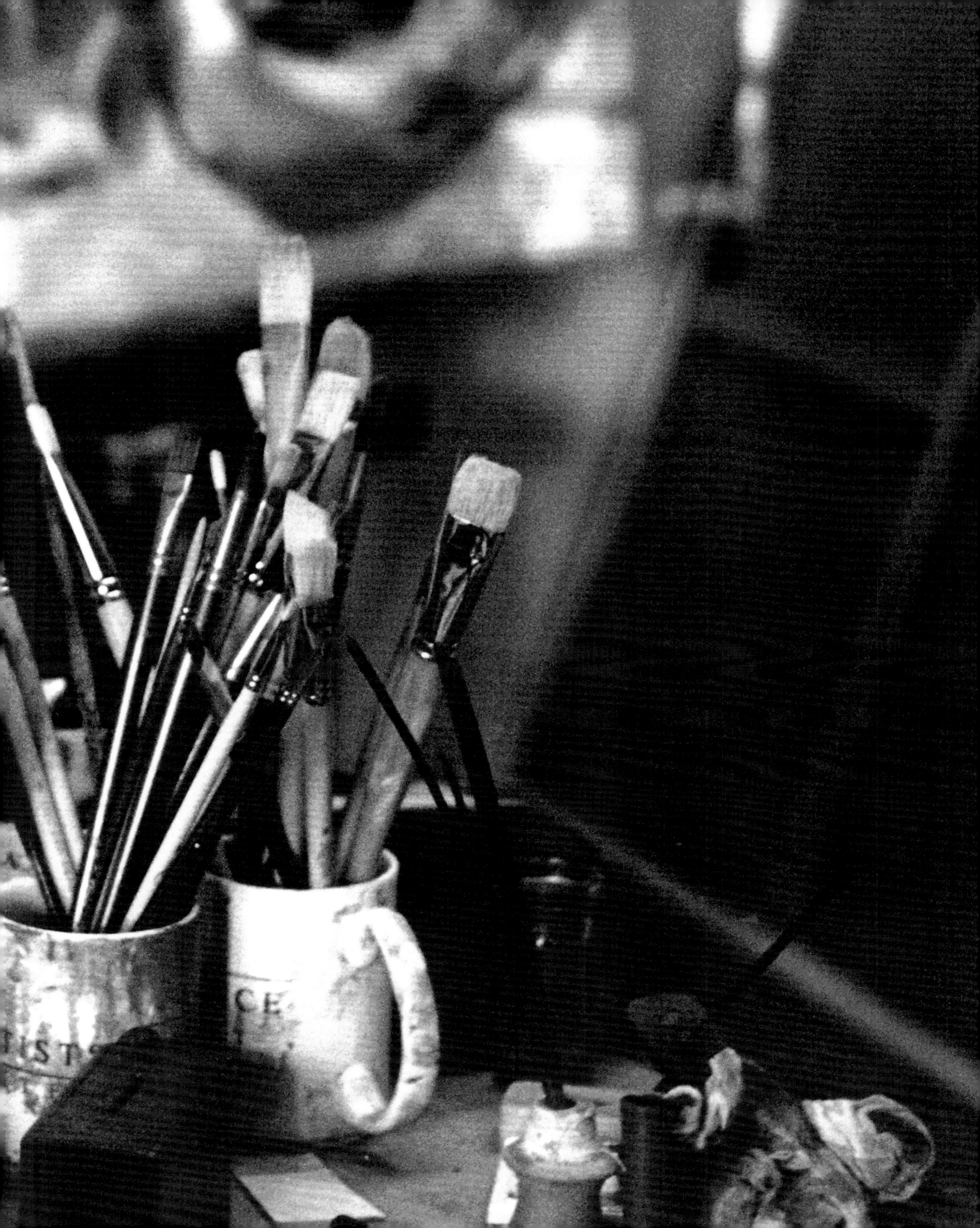

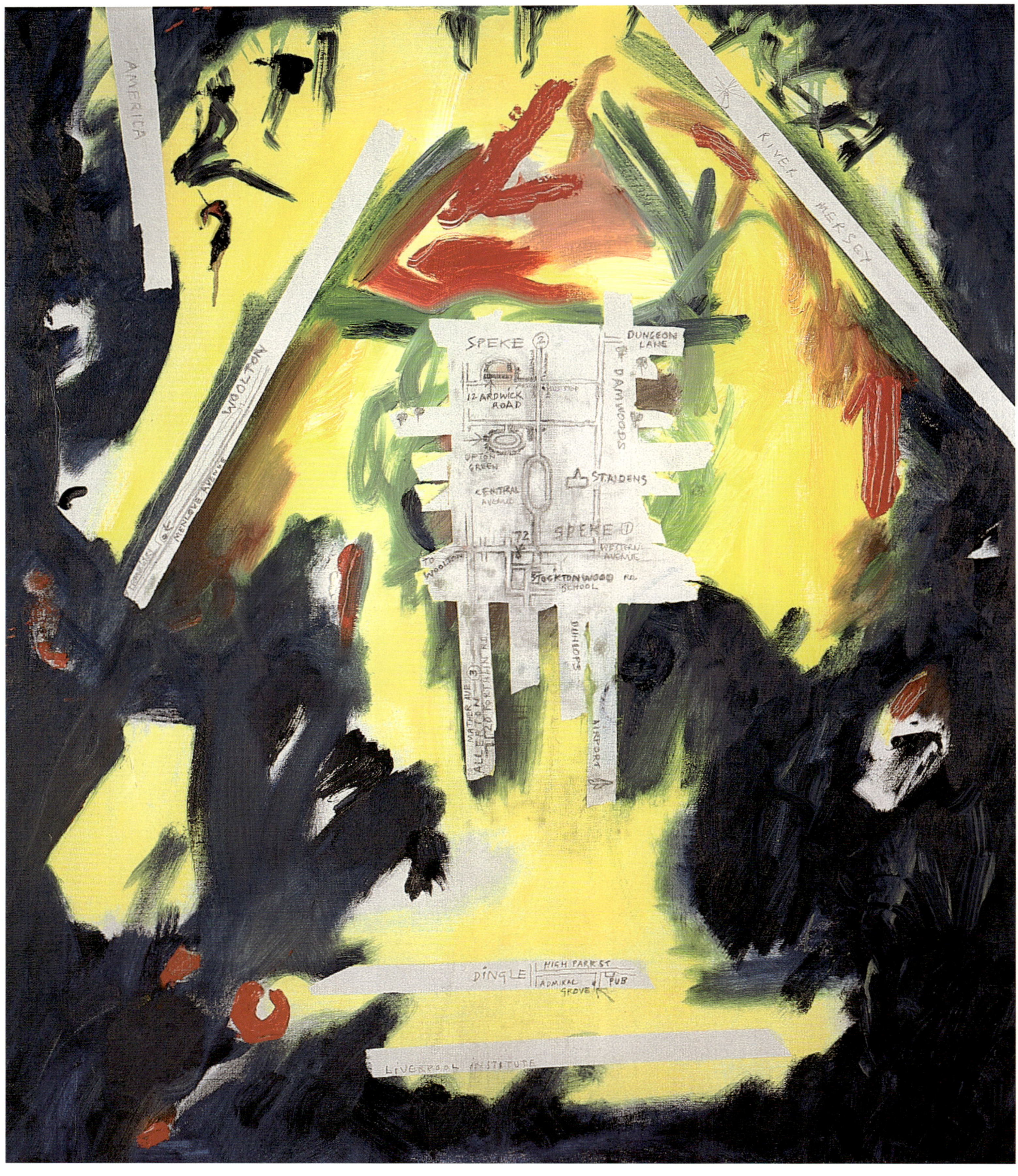
AMERICA
RIVER MERSEY
WOOLTON
MENLOVE AVENUE
SPEKE ②
DUNGEON LANE
12 ARDWICK ROAD
BUS STOP
DAMWOODS
UPTON GREEN
ST. AIDENS
CENTRAL AVENUE
SPEKE ①
72
WESTERN AVENUE
TO WOOLTON
STOCKTONWOOD RD.
SCHOOL
MATHER AVE ③
ALLERTON
20 FORTHLIN RD
DUNLOPS
AIRPORT
DINGLE
HIGH PARK ST
ADMIRAL GROVE
PUB
LIVERPOOL INSTITUTE

Exposure and Influences in the Paintings of Paul McCartney

BARRY MILES

Until the age of forty, Paul was always a little inhibited about painting, feeling that he was somehow not qualified or that he would be in competition with John Lennon: "I felt in John's shadow because I hadn't been to art college. This was one of my biggest blocks. I felt that only people who'd gone to art college were allowed to paint." In fact, Paul would have had no trouble getting into art school had he applied; there were no qualifications required in those days. All it took was the recommendation of an art teacher or headmaster, and a folio of work. Paul had always done well in art class at school, and even at the age of eleven he had won an art prize for a drawing of St. Aidan's Church, which had just been constructed on the Speke housing estate in Liverpool where he then lived. He used the prize book token to buy an art book and spent many hours studying the reproductions of Victor Pasmore, Dalí, and Picasso.

When John and Paul started the Beatles, the early lineup also included one of John's fellow art students, Stuart Sutcliffe. Sutcliffe was a talented painter but died before developing an individual style. His student work shows the undigested influence of Hans Hartung, Corneille, and, overwhelmingly, the then fashionable Nicolas de Staël. Sutcliffe admired de Staël so much that when the Beatles toured Scotland in May 1960 as a backing group for Johnny Gentle, he gave himself the stage name of Stuart de Staël. Paul saw the reproductions pinned to the wall of Sutcliffe's flat in Gambier Terrace, Liverpool, and listened to the art student's talk, taking it all in.

Home territory, 1990

During the sixties Paul was exposed to the full weight of the convulsive changes then occurring in contemporary art: from happenings to minimalism, abstract expressionism to pop and op art. Shortly after moving to London in 1963, Paul met John Dunbar, the art critic for *The Scotsman,* and through Dunbar met Robert Fraser, the gallery owner. Though he did not discover any artists of his own, Fraser had a brilliant eye and was quick to recognize quality among the younger painters. Among those shown at his gallery were Jean Dubuffet, Yves Klein, Matta, and Arman. He exhibited many American artists, including Ellsworth Kelly, Jim Dine, Claes Oldenburg, Roy Lichtenstein, Ed Ruscha, and Cy Twombly. Fraser very much liked the English pop artists and gave several shows to Peter Blake and Richard Hamilton.

Paul was always open to new influences and new information, and began to spend a lot of time at the Fraser Gallery: "Once I got to know Robert, a nice thing would be going to the gallery and helping install an exhibition. Just sit around and smoke a bit of pot while someone else was installing the exhibition. Helping. Play a little music for him. At Indica we did a lot of that, too, and a lot of fun we had."

Because of his friendship with the owners of Indica — John Dunbar, Peter Asher, and Barry Miles — Paul was actually involved in the physi-

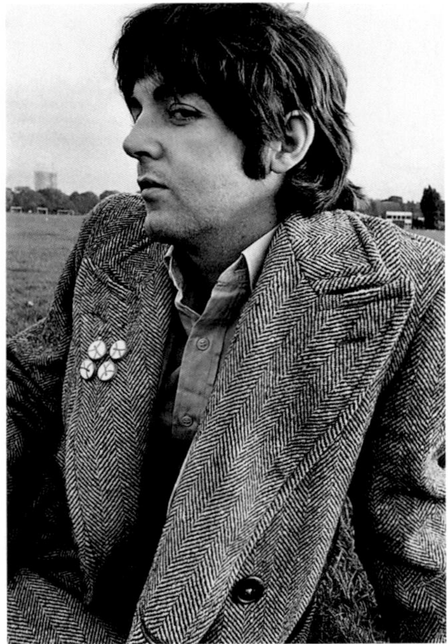

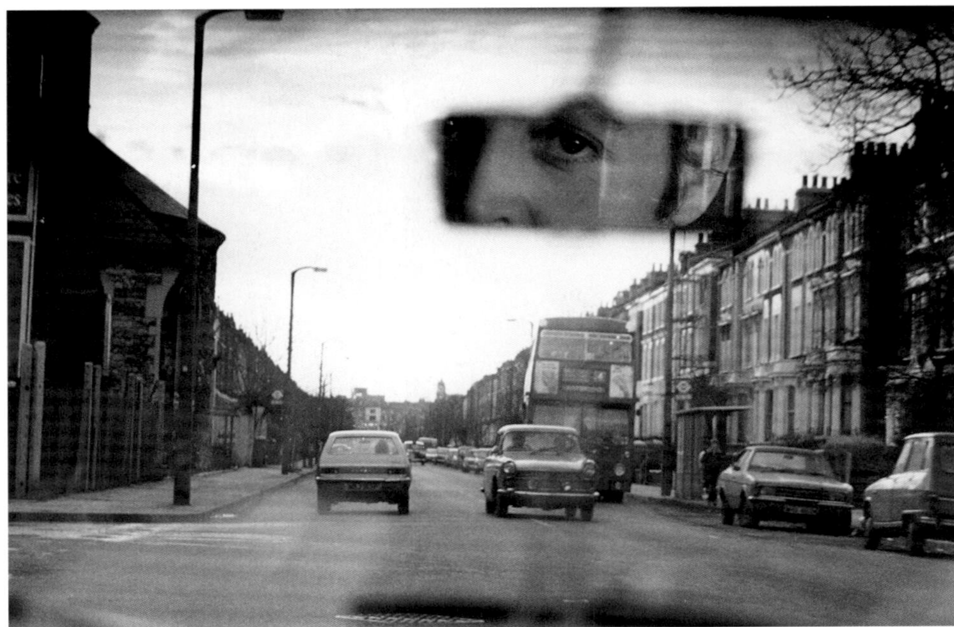

Paul – Regent's Park
London, 1968

My Love
London, 1977

cal construction of the gallery: literally helping to paint the walls and put up shelves. One of the pieces he bought from Indica was a sculpture by Takis, another artist he got to know. Paul: "The exposure was really the great thing. I bought one of his pieces, and I would kind of go as a collector in their eyes, I suppose, and as a Beatle, but in my eyes it was like exposure, it was great. Get down to Chelsea, sit around with this nice Greek guy, and ask him what this was about."

As a collector Paul quickly grew knowledgeable and at one point spent a weekend in Paris with Fraser, buying a number of Magrittes from his dealer, Iolas. Paul regarded Magritte as the premier surrealist painter, and his influence on Paul's own painting is considerable. Through Fraser, in 1965 Paul commissioned a painting by pop artist Peter Blake for the living room of his new house in London and was already thoroughly familiar with Blake's work when Fraser proposed that Blake do the sleeve for the Beatles' 1967 *Sgt. Pepper* album.

Though it was Lennon who was art school trained, it was McCartney who engaged the most with the art-related side of the Beatles: the sleeves of *Sgt. Pepper* and *Abbey Road* were both based upon his sketched ideas, and it was Paul who arranged the minimalist white sleeve for *The Beatles* (the "white album") with Richard Hamilton. Once again, McCartney was already familiar with Hamilton's work, having helped hang his *Guggenheim Museum* multiple show at the Robert Fraser Gallery (one of which he bought). Paul and Hamilton spent some time discussing the sleeve before agreeing on how it should be, and Paul then spent a week watching Hamilton assemble the poster collage that came with the album. After the breakup of the Beatles, Paul used two other British pop artists, Allen Jones and Eduardo Paolozzi, to provide artwork for the 1973 Paul McCartney and Wings album *Red Rose Speedway*.

In 1967 Fraser brought Andy Warhol to visit Paul, and they spent the evening watching one of Andy's movies on Paul's home projection system. Though Andy had temporarily given up painting in favor of filmmaking, Paul was very aware of Warhol's pictures. It is possible that Paul's decision to sometimes paint in series was in part influenced by Warhol.

Toward the end of the seventies, Paul got to know Willem de Kooning, who was a client of Linda's father's law firm. De Kooning was also a family friend, and Paul and Linda would always visit him when they were on Long Island. It was probably watching de Kooning in action that

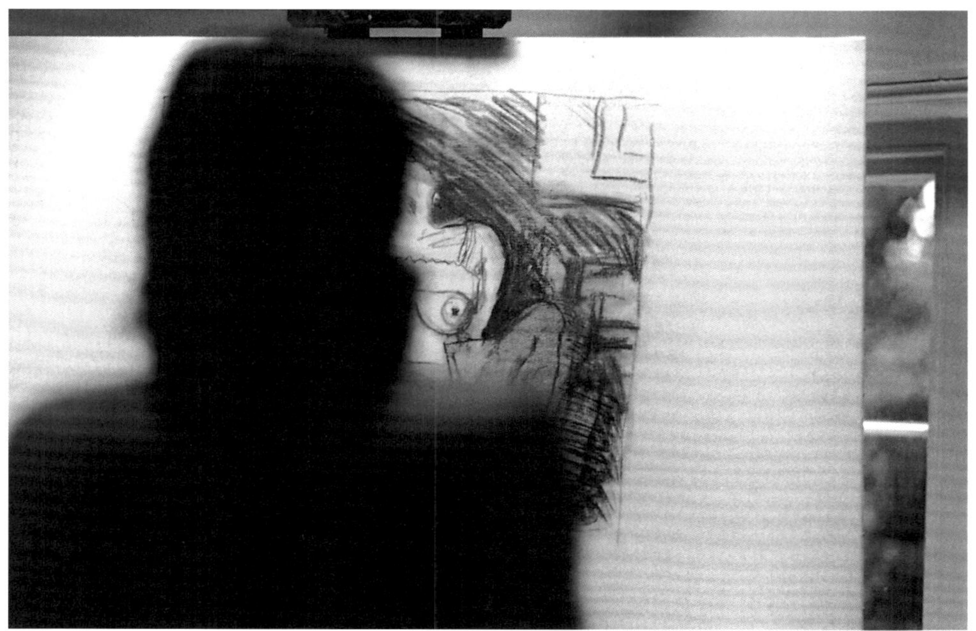

Paul shadow nude
Sussex, 1991

inspired Paul to do his first canvases. He and Linda had rented a house on Long Island, near de Kooning's studio at Springs in East Hampton, and the previous occupants had taken all their paintings with them, leaving large expanses of white wall. Paul: "There were these painting hooks all around the walls. I thought, 'A big red painting would look really good there.' . . . They were abstract. You have to paint abstract after you've been seeing Bill de Kooning."

In his conversations with me, Paul described how de Kooning had inspired him: "He has influenced me. Seeing someone like him draw, seeing someone like him paint, being there in his studio, seeing his attitude, has given me quite a buzz. After a visit with him I would often be so fired up I'd go along to the Golden Eagle Paint Shop where he buys his stuff and buy a big canvas. I'd go with paints from the shop that Bill used, canvases that Bill used, and then I'd go back and stick a canvas up on the porch."

Though he was not yet painting canvases in the sixties, Paul drew the sleeve for one of the Beatles' fan-club flexi-discs, designed and lettered the wrapping paper for Indica Books and Gallery, designed some of their flyers, and did the sleeve of his first solo album, *Ram*. His cartoonlike line drawings first appeared in public with the publication of the 1981 *Paul McCartney: Composer/Artist.*

From these myriad influences and much personal contact with well-known artists, Paul has evolved his own personal style. It is largely expressionistic, often abstract, owing more to de Kooning than to the British pop artists, and taking much of its dynamic from the actual act of painting, what Paul refers to as "applying paint." He told me, "I started to get quite interested in the brushstroke. I like de Kooning's work and I like free brushstrokes a lot, van Gogh and stuff like that. I am the exact opposite of Peter Blake. He said, 'I don't like loose painting.' I was telling a friend of mine, I had this bucket of paint just the other day and I was just about to throw it on the canvas when I remembered what Peter said: 'I don't like loose paint.' I put the bucket down. We were both laughing, you know. But I like that kind of big stroke." Paul brings to painting the same humor, enthusiasm, and enjoyment that is present in his music. They both stem from the same deep urge to create that has so far led him to compose classical pieces for a full orchestra, write poetry, direct films, design his own house, and write and perform the most successful popular music in history.

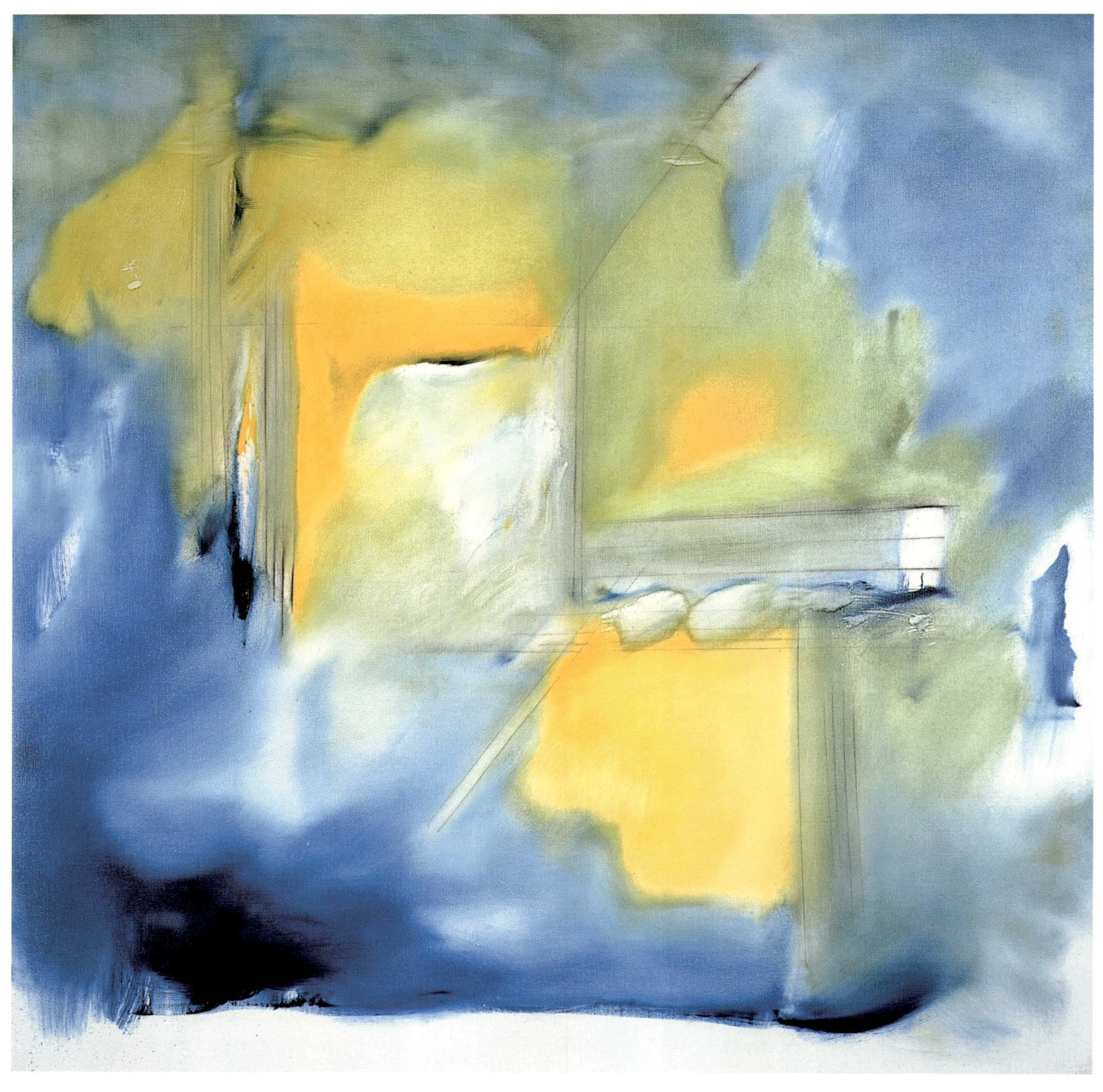

Mr. Magritte's ruler, 1995

From Line to Color – from Gesture to Picture

WOLFGANG SUTTNER

Paul McCartney has always been fascinated by lines: a line on white paper, idle doodling or a soberly functional sketch. He dashed off drawings for his children, drew designs for the *Sgt. Pepper* album, and in surrealistic or expressionistic caricatures has captured faces and people who have crossed his path. Spontaneous doodles, documentary sketches, studies in perspective, and the sheer joy of imagination: I draw; therefore, I am!

The urge to find himself on the white surface has all the symptoms of an addiction. The blank sheet and the material hold a magic attraction for McCartney, a fact that he likes to endorse himself with a little anecdote. He says that he remembers at school there being a cupboard full of paper and pencils, and every time he was sent to the cupboard to fetch the pencils, he had an overwhelming urge to steal them all. The white paper and the boxes of new pencils filled his head with dreams.

Although Paul McCartney is a painter who has made a principle of conversing with his colors, he still finds it extremely difficult — like practically all British artists — to conceal his love of lines. In the course of a conversation about *Mr. Magritte's ruler* (page 18), a wonderful color composition constructed around a system of lines, he said to me, "Drawing a straight line, it struck a chord in me. Underlining your name at school, if you get it right, it was quite nice, quite a satisfying feeling."

Nevertheless, McCartney does not bother with preparatory studies for his pictures, but sketches directly on the canvas with graphite or charcoal — if at all — because, especially in his earlier works, lines are themselves a central theme, lending expression and also acting as a fixative for the picture, whether it be a line of ornamentation or gestural expression. For example, *Brown man* and *Underwater man* are pictures that have strong lines, drawn with a brush on a colorful foundation. In *Reclining woman* (page 20) McCartney alludes clearly to Henry Moore's "shelter drawings."[1] Here it is the lines that hold the sculptural form onto the surface of the picture, giving it its horizontal and vertical structure; the composition is supported by ornamentation. Here the paint has rather more a coloring function.

The line marked on the white surface is McCartney's artistic starting point. It is with powerful, sometimes impulsive gestures that he brings the white canvas under his control. Especially his earlier pictures are based on lines, precisely structured and often quickly sketched. The caricature portraits are particularly eye-catching: McCartney's inner stock of images, emotions, and the many faces stored and remembered throughout a turbulent, multi-faceted life have found their way almost directly onto paper and canvas. Brush drawings like *Pigtail, Red eye, A handbag?* (page 21), *Potato head,* and *Ted Heath* are all complete pictures in their

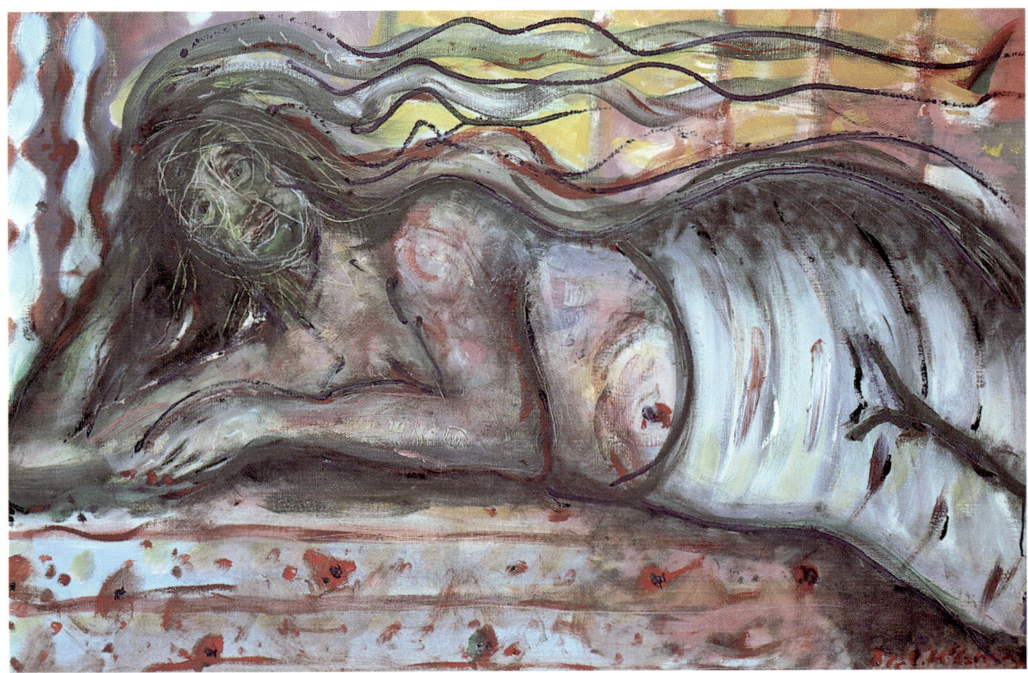

Reclining woman, 1987

own right. On the one hand, they are clear examples of McCartney's ability to come to grips with the blank canvas by using gestural lines; and on the other hand, they point to a technique that he later made much greater use of: scratching lines that cut through the layers of the picture. Often the shape of a line produces a satirical effect, like in the pointed single-line caricature *Patti Boyd* (page 100) or in *Yellow bow tie* (page 70), where the line provides a stimulus for the form-color relationship and lends it additional tension. Both pictures exemplify McCartney's great gift for drawing cartoons and caricatures, his lightness of touch in lending shape to the meaning behind the faces. "I find when I study it too much, it doesn't come out quite as well. Sometimes just to make a very quick line makes it more precise than a very slowly drawn, precise line. If this were drawn slowly, it wouldn't have the flow. I like the flow of things moving around."

In the four-part series *Kisses* (pages 120–21) the direction in which McCartney is developing becomes clear. The line in the center of the picture is the theme. Like in a picture puzzle it moves to and fro between the faces, while in *Green kiss* it melts into the picture to allow the color to control the structure. This becomes particularly clear on looking at two earlier pieces side by side: *Is this Bernard Miles?* (page 21), a very sparingly structured caricature that seems to make a second appearance in the small oil painting *Blue face* (page 21). Here McCartney applies the paint directly from the tube. The physiognomy in the foreground around which the picture is built up in shades of blue and white takes on a double meaning, suggesting a river course or a ridge of hills, like on a map. The abstracted physiognomy plunges under the surface and becomes a concrete element in the picture, an expressive focus for the lines of tension between content and form. The same development can later be seen in McCartney's "head landscapes," in which the use of color lends a physiognomy the features of an imaginary landscape. (Compare *Boxer lips,* page 129, a piece that alternates between a "head landscape" and a "color landscape.") McCartney has often commented on the tense relationship between painting and drawing. In this respect, the scratching technique he has since developed offers him a creative — even sculptural — solution, adding a dynamic element to his compositions and also paying tribute to his love of lines. He says that he often found himself faced with the problem of

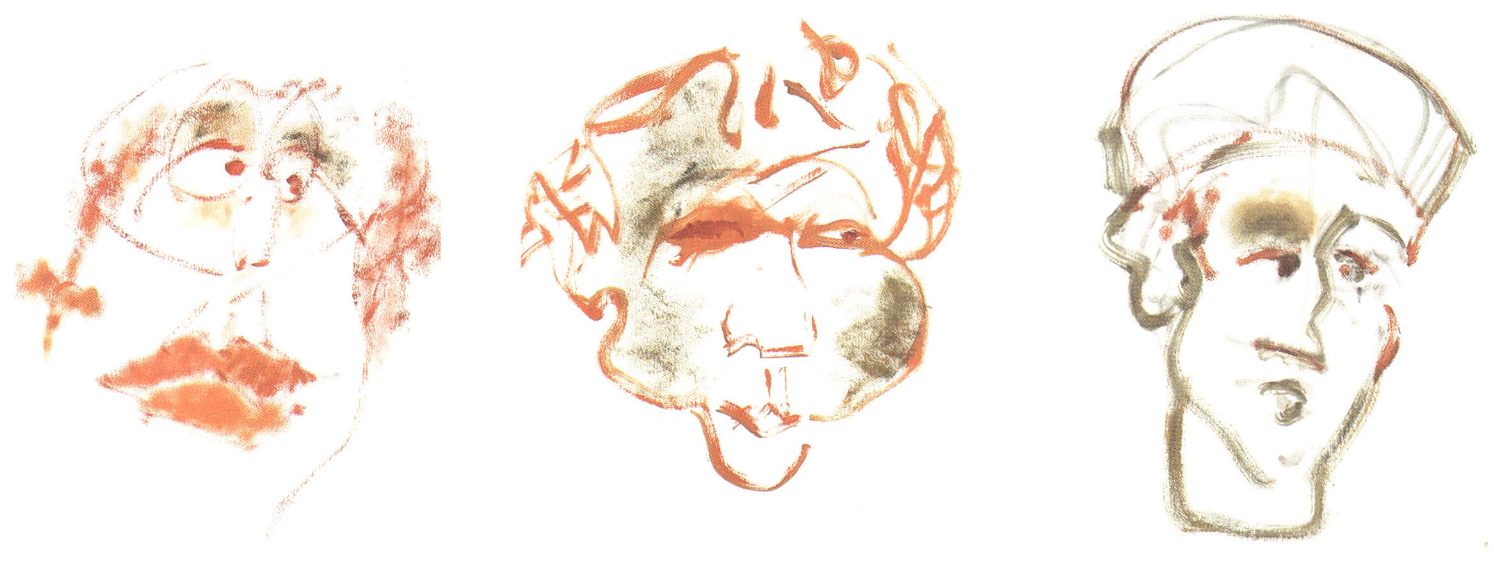

Pigtail, 1988

Red eye, 1988

A handbag?, 1988

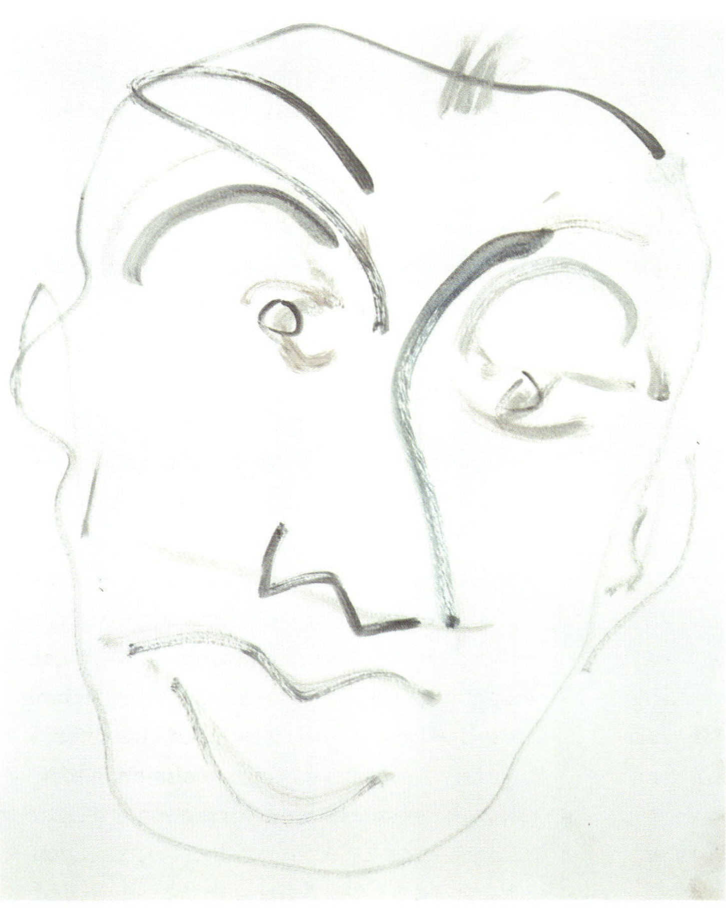

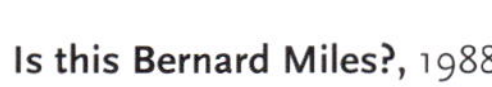

Is this Bernard Miles?, 1988

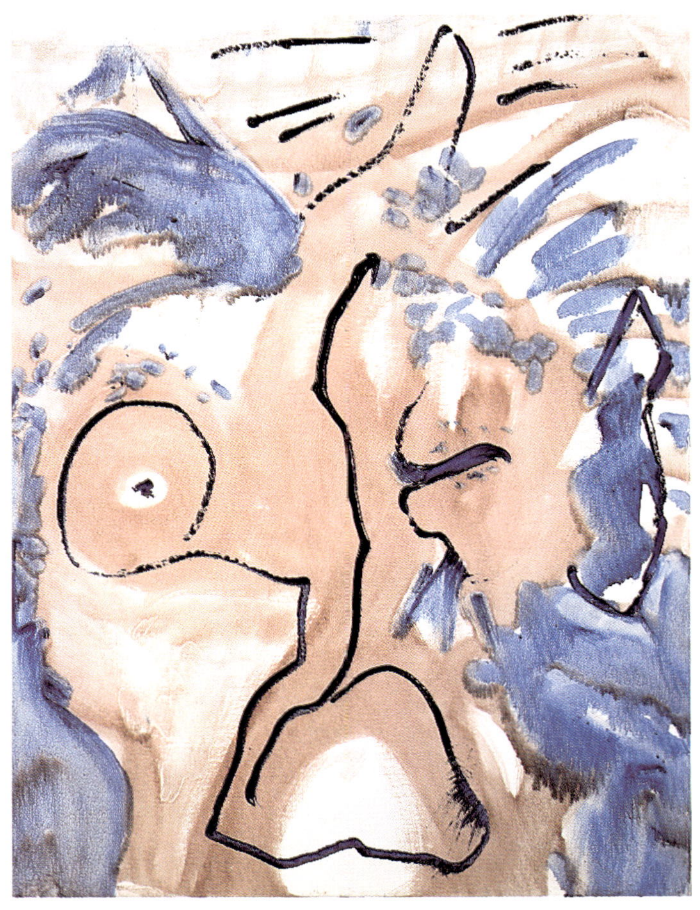

Blue face, 1988

whether or not to start with a drawing and then paint over it. For him scratching was the alternative because he could then at least do some drawing after the painting, by taking some of the paint off again. What was green before, for example, now became yellow, because the yellow was already underneath.

In pictures where the content is more strongly emphasized, like in the *Queen trilogy* (pages 98–99), a scratched line has a purely linear function, as a contour underlining the theme. In some of McCartney's other experiments with material and form, lines also appear as semi-controlled drainages of color, tracks left by the paint as it runs, as in *Big mountain face* (page 63). Here the lines document a process: painting itself is being demonstrated; lines appear to break up the sheer weight of the composition on the right-hand side; any illusion is retracted.

Since 1988 McCartney has intensified his painting output enormously, and the result has been a concentration on paint and process. In search of his own solutions to the color-shape problem, McCartney paints intensely and quickly, driven by the sheer joy of investigating the processes involving colors and shapes and also by an appetite for good art. The artist takes themes from nature: landscapes, still lifes, and surrealistic motifs. He uses Matisse, Magritte, and Hockney as points of orientation, although these are only moments and impulses in the forward movement of his fast and intense productivity. In contrast, the regular visits to Willem de Kooning have been decisive for his art, since they have influenced McCartney in his use of paint. De Kooning freed the process of a picture's development from any preconceived plan. The act of painting, the concentration on communicating with his paint became de Kooning's great theme, and for McCartney it became a stimulus and a challenge: paint as a material, paint as a communication partner, paint as a medium of self-expression. It is only now that Paul McCartney is painting freely from deep within himself, in constant dialogue with himself, but with his guard down, defenseless. He documents emotions and observations, unearths images that have long remained buried. He paints for himself and not for an art market. He does not pander to any trend or style, and says of his art: "I'm not trying to impress anybody except myself."

Through his painting he opens himself up, and elements of his biography become immediately accessible. Here the paint is his medium and its processes the catalyst. He arranges patches of color side by side; mixes colors on the canvas; brushes the paint on thinly, almost transparently; watches the way the paint runs; scratches paint off; uncovers layers that he has previously covered up. And yet the result is far from abstract: in the majority of his pictures, motif and subject matter are there to be discovered. The starting point may be Celtic motifs, for example, or associations arising during the painting process. The processes by which shapes emerge from the paint are always communicative, and whether they lead into or away from the actual theme, they give insight into the subject matter and offer the viewer a glimpse of the way in which the picture grew. But it is precisely this very personal style of painting, offering a key to McCartney as a human being, that has made it difficult for him — a musician who has become a legend in his own time — to put his work on public show: "I have never wanted to do that, because of the fact that I felt it would be depending on my celebrity and not on the pictures. So what happened was for years and years I just painted but always really wanted a little feedback. Then I started to imagine, What if I had been at art school when I started painting in 1983, and had been painting solid quite seriously for thirteen years? You know, in most people's lives, the guy would be thirty-two now and . . . he would have a lot of exhibits. So I wanted a little of that, not so much lots of exhibits but a bit of feedback. People might say to him, 'That is not my favorite bit,' and 'You see what you did there with that line, what you did there was good' — I wanted a bit of that."

McCartney needs to paint, and he needs the

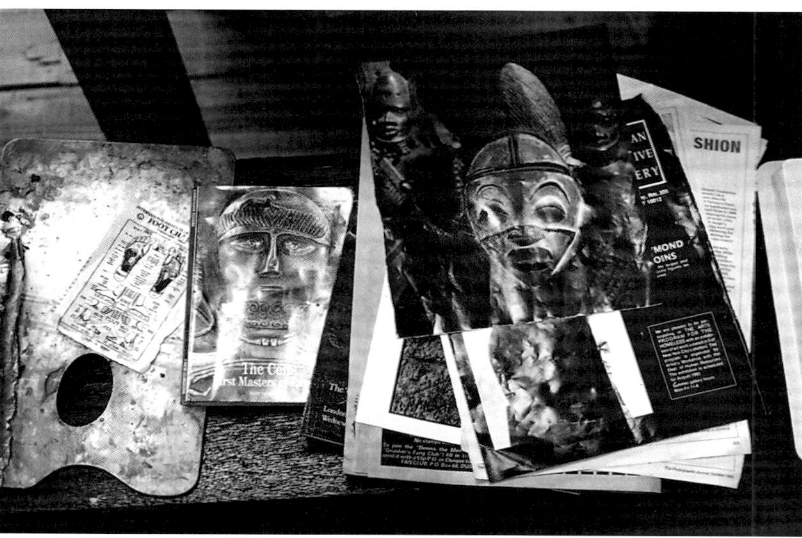

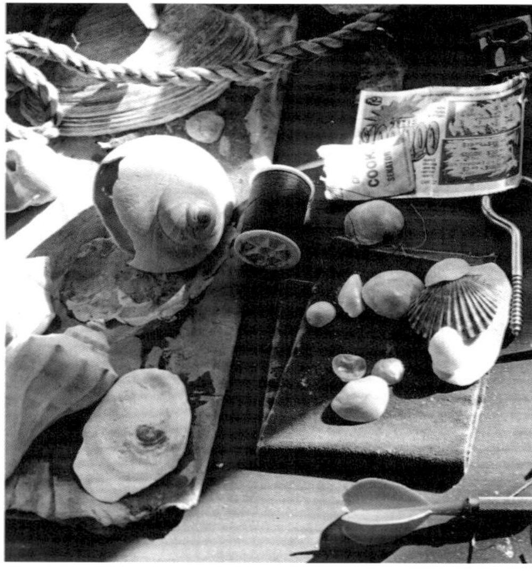

Celts/African/Aborigines
Sussex, 1996

Found objects (detail)
East Hampton, 1996

constant struggle with the white canvas. For the actual act of painting there is no lack of impulses or embarkation points. What is decisive is the right mood for painting. But then comes the blank, white surface, which may indeed cause a mental block. "Killing the canvas" is what Paul McCartney calls the first step in the struggle with the rectangle of immaculate white. Like de Kooning, McCartney may scribble a friend's name in charcoal on the canvas, or a fragment of a quotation or the hint of a face. Even a chance splash of paint can start off a picture. The random principle plays an important part in the free, communicative style of his dialogue with the canvas. So it could also be something he finds on the beach or a rusty wheel that triggers off the process, in the course of which McCartney tries to capture the structural features suggested by the object and, especially in his earlier work, at the same time give it a new value.

During the past ten years McCartney's oeuvre has been essentially dominated by two subject groups: portraits and landscapes. His "body and head landscapes" are where the two groups meet, blurring any apparently fixed thematic definitions. These are the works that indicate very clearly the real theme of his painting: the picture itself, pictorial essence. The decisive factor is the dominance of color processes in forming the shapes, whether self-determined or by chance. With many of the pictures in recent years it would seem that they painted themselves, as though the artist's part were only to assist in the act of creation, through close observation and sensitive reaction to what was developing before his eyes. It is often heads and human shapes that Paul McCartney chooses to paint, but the important thing is that they are first and foremost pictures. They meet the eye at one and the same moment both as heads and as pictures, as eruptions of shape and color, as paint running and mingling to form new colors. The viewer discovers objects, heads, and landscapes simultaneously. The painter loves his material, sometimes layering it into mounds, scratching it off again or scratching into it. A vertical gash, a line bulging horizontally, spots rising to peaks. Suddenly the picture becomes a head, not a real face (see *Black singer,* page 95) but a head forming a picture. One picture even shows its teeth (*Blue tooth,* page 124), another gazes expectantly, and a third one closes its eyes.

In pictures like these it is not, of course, a question of reproducing a real face or capturing a characteristic detail, even if McCartney's caricatures and portraits continue to arrest our gaze. They are about the painter's own emotions, reflected in the painting process, and about inner faces and obsessions finding pictorial fixation there, something stable to connect to in the physiognomic shapes in the picture. Or if not in the physiognomic element, then in the landscape

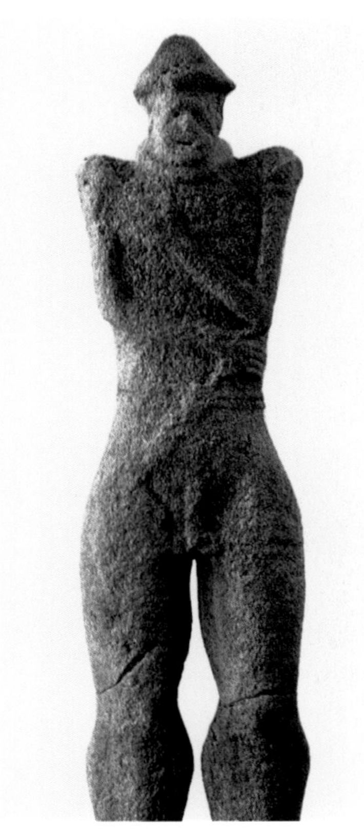

Warrior statue of Hirschlanden. Photograph by P. Frankenstein and H. Zwietasch, Württembergisches Landesmuseum Stuttgart.

character of the picture, the second central theme in McCartney's work. Here, however, it is often impossible to distinguish between landscape and physiognomy, since portraits spill over into landscapes, and landscape scenes are molded into physiognomic forms. As portraits or landscapes they thus provide only the thematic framework for what are realistic but nonetheless painted shapes, transformed by the painter's feelings into expressions of emotional states, into inner faces, landscapes of the heart and mind.

Paul McCartney's landscapes are the key to a particularly interesting and exciting chapter in his painting, misunderstandings included. Some pictures, for example, are so attractively colorful, like *Beach towels* (page 106) or *Pintos in the sky with desert poppy* (page 2), that what seems to determine the overall effect is the mood created by colors, lighting, and the landscape. In fact, they are anything but mere mood paintings. They play with the illusory effect colors can create within the scope of the picture and with a spatial perspective that points straight back to the pictorial level *(Beach towels)*. Or, in the midst of a picturesque and idyllic scene, like in *Shark on Georgica* (page 107), they may allude to the nasty surprises that life has in store, although maybe not at first sight. The eye comes to rest first of all on a sailing boat on Georgica Pond, an idyllic retreat of the rich and famous on Long Island. The artist makes his point by drawing the dorsal fin of a shark — an impossible idea! — which threateningly breaks the surface to upset the apparent harmony of the scene. The structural element allowing these two things to happen at the same time is on the one hand pure painting and on the other an ironic realism.

With *Red abstract white moon* (page 64), the picture assails the viewer without warning. It seems as though a cosmos of color is exploding. A dramatic mood sets the stage for the forces of nature, with overpowering reds, broken up by traces of blue and subtly highlighted with black. A mood reflecting both the glow of nature and the drama of war (and yet even here the act of painting being an autonomous process) establishes a physiognomic link, at least at a second glance. McCartney himself says about this picture: "I can see lots of stuff in it, not a lot of which I intended to paint."

One characteristic type of landscape in McCartney's oeuvre is the dream landscape. Although reminiscent of René Magritte's images with their mystical physiognomies set into landscapes, McCartney's pictures nevertheless establish their very own narrative theme and style. Typical of this variety is the series of Celts, pictures inspired by the illustrations of finds made at Celtic burial places in France and Baden-Württemberg, Germany. One such statue is of the "warrior of Hirschlanden" (depicted at left), now in the Württembergisches Landesmuseum Stuttgart. Here McCartney embarks on a journey into the fascinating history of the Celts and his own ancestry. His symphonic poem *Standing Stone story* (page 86) also revolves around this theme. Even if the pictures in this group never attain the status of an analytical search for roots, they are still typical and revealing. In poetic and almost playful manner they weave very modern references into the treatment of our early history.

Celtic eloquence (page 88) shows creatures communicating in a landscape made up of cool shades of gray and blue. And to form a contrast, there are the tree-of-life symbols. The picture is based on experiments with wiping turpentine and charcoal. The typically abstract face shapes and the ornament around the neck (called a "torque") are references to the finds made in Celtic burial places. A "chain of eloquence" linking a speaker with a listener symbolizes the development of language. The random trails of paint dripping out of the white cloud incorporate two apples as symbols of fertility. In *Yellow Celt* (page 93), the center of the picture is taken up with an oversize statuesque figure, whose physical features, almost expressionistic in form, especially the disproportionately long limbs, are taken from a Celtic relic: a figure that stands for fertility and strength, again embedded in an imaginary landscape. *Ancient connections* (page 89) is the link

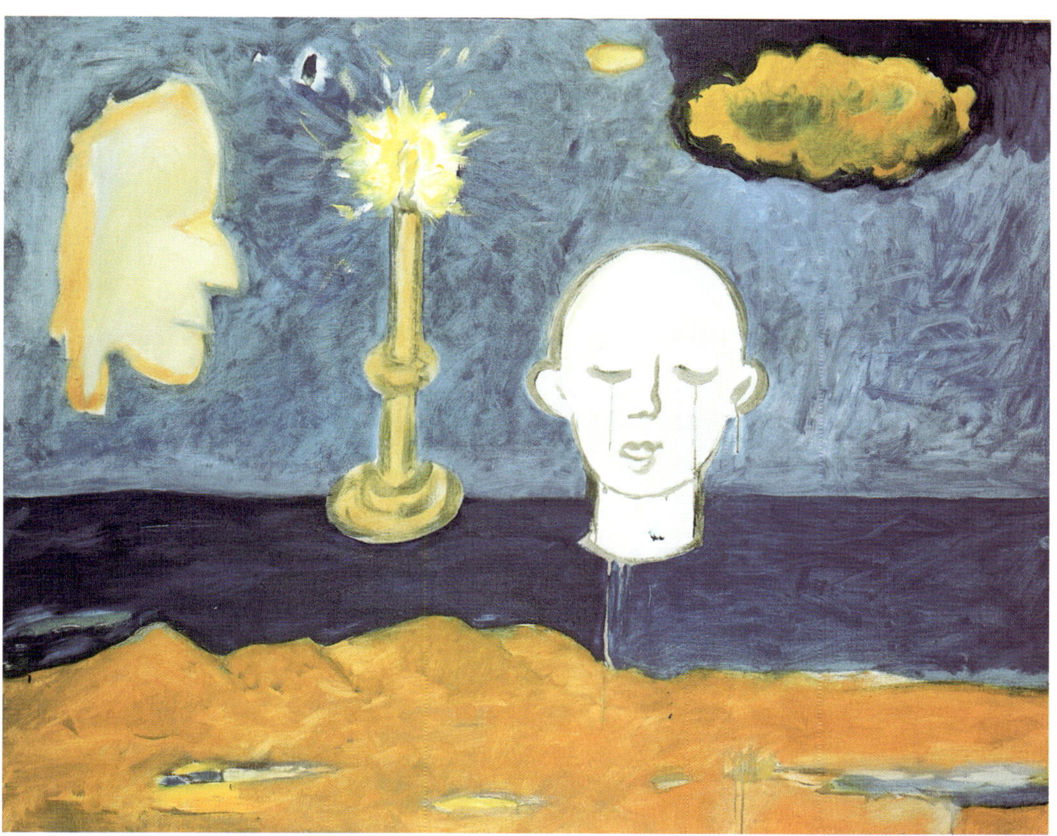

White dream, 1990

with the present. Partially superimposed over the Celtic mask in the center is a further, more differentiated physiognomy, which reminds McCartney of Charlie Watts of the Rolling Stones. The head symbols are arranged side by side but have no communication with each other. The only connecting element between the three heads is a sort of rod, which possibly symbolizes the unbroken succession of generations of humankind throughout the millennia.

Paul McCartney's painting is a product of the pure joy and enthusiasm he derives from gestural impetus and from the color processes that give structure to his compositions. Concrete elements come to the surface again and again, asserting themselves against a background of color. Abstract pieces are rare. With its great structuring power, the actual painting process remains McCartney's real theme. This is where he does his research, his investigations, his experimenting. McCartney examines lighting phenomena and studies physiognomies and Celtic origins, and the results of his investigations find their way onto the canvas as form and technique. He works his way under the surface; he scratches through yellow pictures to free the blue layers beneath; and carving through layers of paint, he hauls the white of the canvas back into the daylight. He uses a palette knife and even his fingernails: techniques that not only produce effects but are also vehicles for transporting meaning. A good example, and one with autobiographical references, is *Home territory* (page 14), in which McCartney draws sections of a Liverpool city map, his school, his friends' houses, the church, and the district of Woolton. He covers up the drawing with tape and paints abstract shapes in complementary colors all over it. Is this some vision of nature? A sulfurous, industrial city sky? When he peels the tape off again and returns to the drawings beneath, he is penetrating right through to the canvas, laying bare layer after layer, creating graphic shapes that look like the paths of childhood. This is art, his own art, bringing back memories, revealing life's layers.

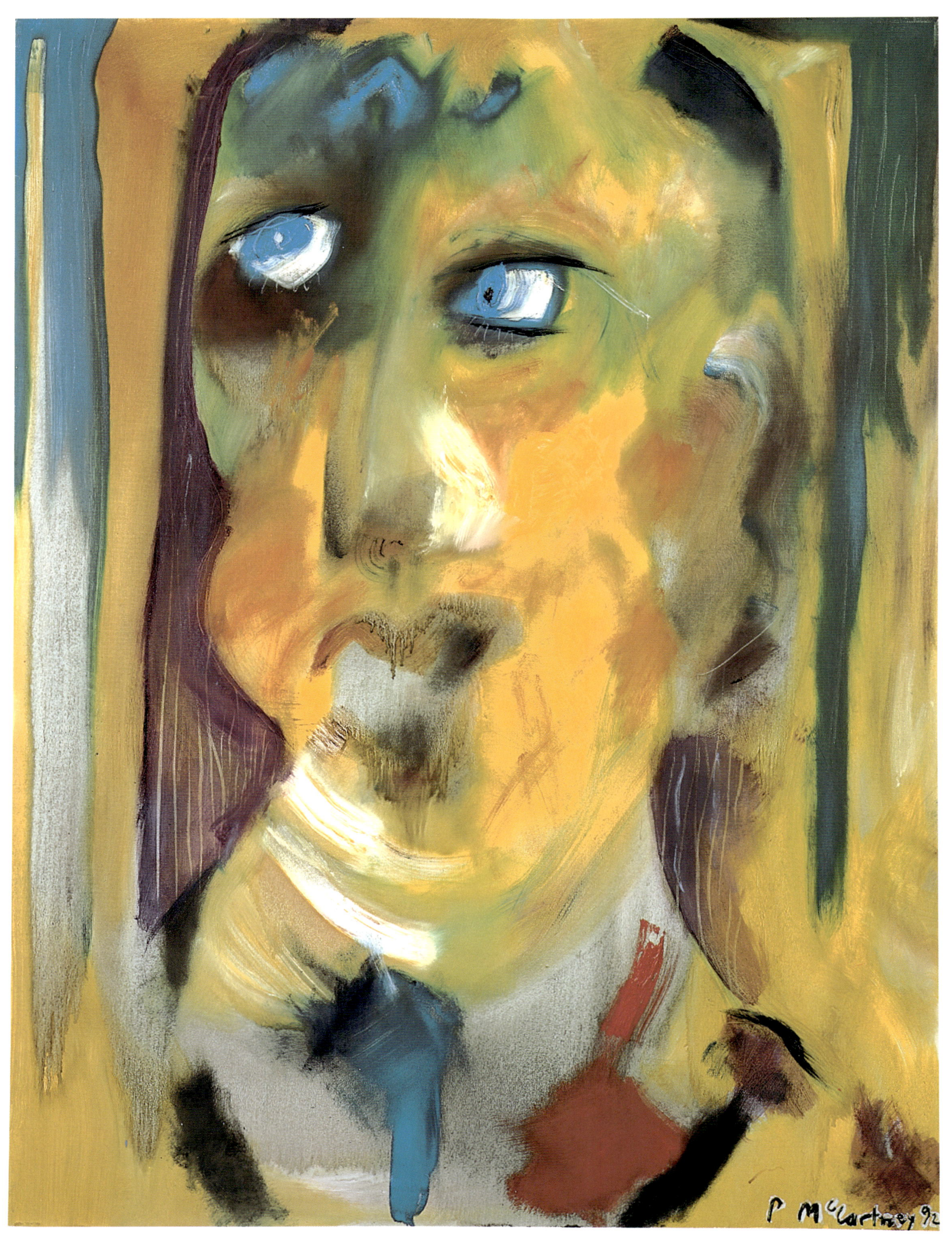
P McCartney 92

INTERVIEW

"I Don't Know – It Looks Like a Couch"

WOLFGANG SUTTNER SPEAKS WITH PAUL McCARTNEY

This text is based on eight interviews with Paul McCartney that took place between September 1994 and December 1995. The parts chosen for the compilation below are arranged in chronological order.

Wolfgang Suttner: How important was drawing for you before you started painting?

Paul McCartney: I used to draw a lot, not necessarily from life but from imagination. And all my days through school I could always draw quite well. I used to do drawings of women for classmates, but we shouldn't talk about that — I was the guy who could draw gorgeous naked women, you see, so for young boys this was a good attraction, and they used to ask me to draw for them. But I have always enjoyed drawing, often cartoon faces. I like the line, not necessarily the content. I like quick lines, very spontaneous lines. I like the circle, a couple of eyes, a mouth, and just characters in the faces, so I have done that quite a bit.

Do you now do drawings as a preparing process for your painting?

No, I don't normally; most of the story happens on the canvas while I am painting. It has to do with what the paint does, so sometimes I prepare a shape and a rough composition with some lines or with some drawing if I know I want a definite face or something like that, or I put that on with charcoal or a pencil. But then I used to find that the charcoal would pick up in the colors and it would make the yellow muddy, so I started to look for a little process to stop the charcoal moving, and I got interested in turpentine on it, which takes most of the line away. You wipe it away, the turpentine, but it does some interesting things and it stops it blending into the colors, so, yes, I do most of the drawing on the canvas.

Do you sometimes do drawings of certain things you come across?

Yes, one of the things I realized with a lot of painters many years before I started painting seriously was that they often didn't know what to paint and they did a lot of soul-searching about what to paint, so I tried to find a few tricks to get over this because I knew that if I just felt like painting, I did not want to stand in front of a canvas for three hours worrying about what it was going to be. If painting is to be fun for me, and for me it was necessary for it to be fun, then I had to get some tricks. So I heard things like de Kooning used to write his friend's name in charcoal and then he would make a big abstract over that, but at least he had made a mark, he'd started, and I met de Kooning quite often through the years. But he would always give me little clues with his naive disregard for the worry in painting. I don't think he wanted to worry, either. He wanted to get into "exploring the accident." One of them was if I couldn't think of what to paint, I would sometimes just go for a walk and find some objects that I liked. So, depending on where I am, on a beach some-

Father figure, 1992

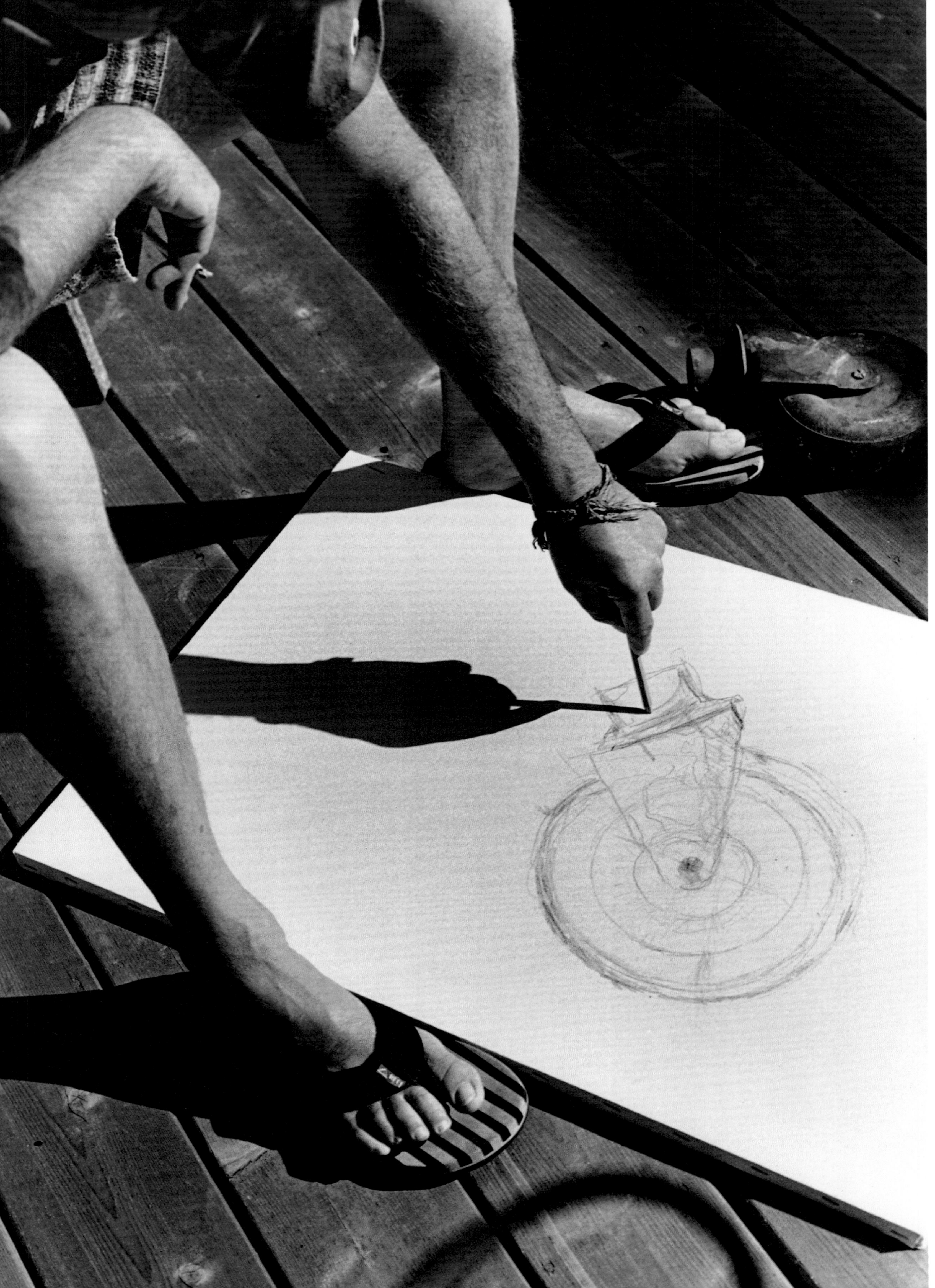

"I think that what I really enjoy is actually applying the paint, putting the paint on the canvas. Just the act of putting the paint on the canvas is enough sometimes for me."

where, or on Long Island I might be on the beach and find an old bottle-top or a shell or just a piece of driftwood that interests me, and I'd come home and just draw that, and maybe place it in the sky floating or something, and that would be enough. That would be enough because it would be something to do with me, so that is where the drawing comes in, but I wouldn't sit around and prepare how to draw it. I would try to just draw it straight on the canvas.

You don't prepare compositions with lines?

No, they either happen or they don't happen, on the canvas. It is just instinctive. Say, for instance, if I wanted to make one little brushstroke but it was a raw canvas, white canvas with no paint on it, then I felt it was a bit of a cheat because there wasn't really a background and a foreground, there was just one mark. So I then started this little trick of painting something on the canvas, maybe a pink or a brown, just a red and white together, or a brown or a white together or something, just to get started. I was talking to a friend who is a painter, and she said that is called "killing the canvas," and I loved that phrase. It seemed exciting and aggressive, the idea that if you are worried, then kill the canvas. If it is worrying you, kill it.

This killing the canvas is a kind of influencing the random principle. Have you got other techniques?

Yes, I just listen and read a lot and look at what people say. I mean, if I am getting a bit bored with a picture, one thing I do a lot is turn it round because I heard this is a good way of resting composition. I like to turn them on their sides, I like them to work any way as an abstract, and sometimes this is good because I will let the paint drip, and it will drip one way and then if I turn it, it will drip another way and it turns into a nice little shape. Then I work on that shape. But I am basically just following my nose, basically making a line. If I don't really like it too much, I will try and change it in some way, and nearly always something comes out of that and then I will follow that line. So it is like being a detective in some ways, seeing what clues I can get, and often as I am painting I think that what I really enjoy is actually applying the paint, putting the paint on the canvas. Just the act of putting the paint on the canvas is enough sometimes for me. It satisfies me intellectually, just because of the color or the blend with the next color to it, or the contrast with the next color.

You have been painting for a long time. When did you start?

Well, I started when I was forty. No, well, I have painted much longer, really. I have paintings going back to when I was a kid. The first things I ever did would be at school, and the first thing, I think, was when I won an art prize at school.

You won an art prize?

Well, yes, but it wasn't an art school, it was just at school.

I painted a little local church, that was the first time I had ever done anything like that. I had always liked that, the artistic ambience and the idea of being an artist. I was always attracted to the idea of being a songwriter as well, the idea of just going off on your own and creating some sort of illusion, some sort of magic. So I did this church, which was called St. Aidan's, a modern church in Liverpool. I must have been about fourteen, and that got a little art prize.

Has it been exhibited somewhere?

I don't know. I don't know where it is. But I used to do some paintings then; I was interested in modern art. I used to buy long rolls of paper, lay them out on the floor, and use watercolors or poster paints, something with water, and I used to blow the paint all over everywhere. That was the technique, blowing the paint, a bit like the dripping now, but instead of gravity doing it, I just blew it, and it would splay out like spiders' nests and spiders' webs, and the thing is that after blowing for five minutes, you get high, because of oxygen deprivation, you know. So I did a few of those pictures, which I'd hang in my room, just big abstracts, good for decoration. I did a few things then.

When did you start working in a regular way?

When I was forty, somebody said, "Life begins at forty," so I took them literally and instead of taking it as just a symbolic idea of a time to start something, I really wanted some-

Paul in the sun drawing a wheel
East Hampton, 1993

"My wife bought me Magritte's easel for Christmas from the sale of his studio, and that was an incredible thing. . . . I sat in front of it, thinking I must paint a picture of a man with a bowler hat and blue sky and some clouds, and they were the only thoughts I had for a little while. But then I pushed through that."

thing to start, so I took up a couple of things, and the main one was painting. I thought I would love to paint, I thought it would be very liberating for me, I had got a lot of visual ideas. Through the years you would work on album covers, you would work on films, and you would be asked to have visual ideas, and even in sound, in music, we would often talk in visual terms, about a sound being a little too dark or a sound being too light, or we would talk about a sound of monks on a hill in the distance.

It is like when artists talk in terms of music, the sound of colors, rhythm.

Yes, there is a big crossover between the two things, one the visual and one the sound, so I just thought, OK, if I am going to paint, what am I going to do? First of all, I just didn't know anything. I didn't know what kind of canvas I would want, what kind of medium I would want or whatever, so I just set about buying a few canvases. Until then, I had this silly idea that only people who went to art college bought canvases and that people like me who didn't go to art college, they painted on towels and bits of wood and toilet seats. No, I just had a feeling, an irrational feeling, like some people would, for instance, think, People like me don't ride horses, or People like me don't swim. For me it was that people like me don't paint. And I thought, Well, why have I got this idea? And I realized that it was just conditioning through society that if I didn't go to art school, I somehow thought it was not right for me to paint. I decided that that would be a good idea to get rid of. So I went into a shop and bought some canvases, started to get some good linen canvases occasionally, and then started to look at things like charcoal, and watch what other painters did, painters I admired. I would visit de Kooning's studio, and I would see him playing with the charcoal and stuff.

There is so much to learn, that is half the fun for me. I realize when I bought charcoal, for instance, I would normally just buy charcoal and not specify whether I wanted hard, medium, or soft, but I see that now. My wife bought me Magritte's easel for Christmas from the sale of his studio, and that was an incredible thing.

Very inspiring for you?

Yes, it was intimidating. I sat in front of it, thinking I must paint a picture of a man with a bowler hat and blue sky and some clouds, and they were the only thoughts I had for a little while. But then I pushed through that.

I think you know there are a lot of connections for me with the music. Maybe the first one would be that not having been trained in music but having come through and learned it all by myself and with the Beatles, you learn certain tricks. You learn that it is good to be spontaneous, it is good to be thorough, it is good to have something that inspires you, it is good to be in a great mood, and all these things cross over into something like painting. And this idea of not worrying too much. If an idea doesn't come, you can just go for a walk, you know, not be too intense. So I think a lot of these things that I use for songwriting I felt were able to start me a little bit down the track of painting. I wouldn't need to go through some of the worries that people go through in the early days; I felt I could lose some of those. So that was one of the good things. And then as I get on in painting, and it is not just the confidence, the courage that knowing what I know from music gives me, sometimes now there are actually crossovers with music.

Do you think it has something to do with making a composition of a picture and making a composition for a piece of music, the process?

Yes, I think so. You learn little things like economy, you know. Simple economy is very good. Space is very good.

What do you mean?

Spacing. You know, if you have a piece of music that is all just [sings a few bars of continuous music] it is no good, mainly because there is no space in it. But then you can have [sings the same bars of music with spaces in between]. These spaces are very important; negative space is very important, and that comes into painting. I did one of these cross-references when we were

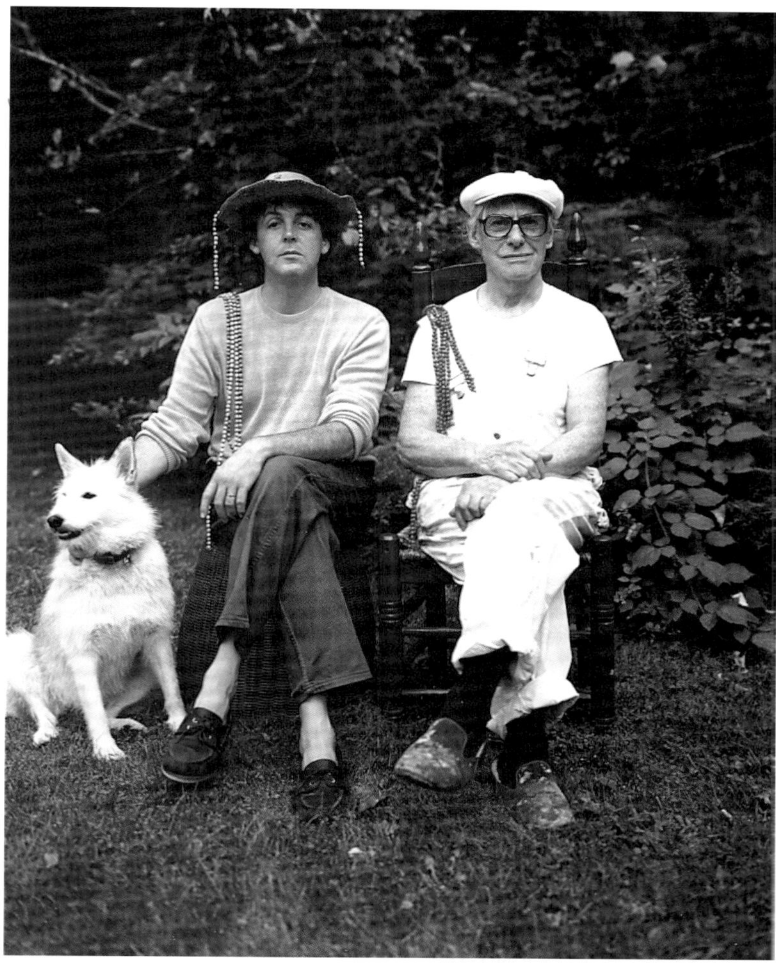

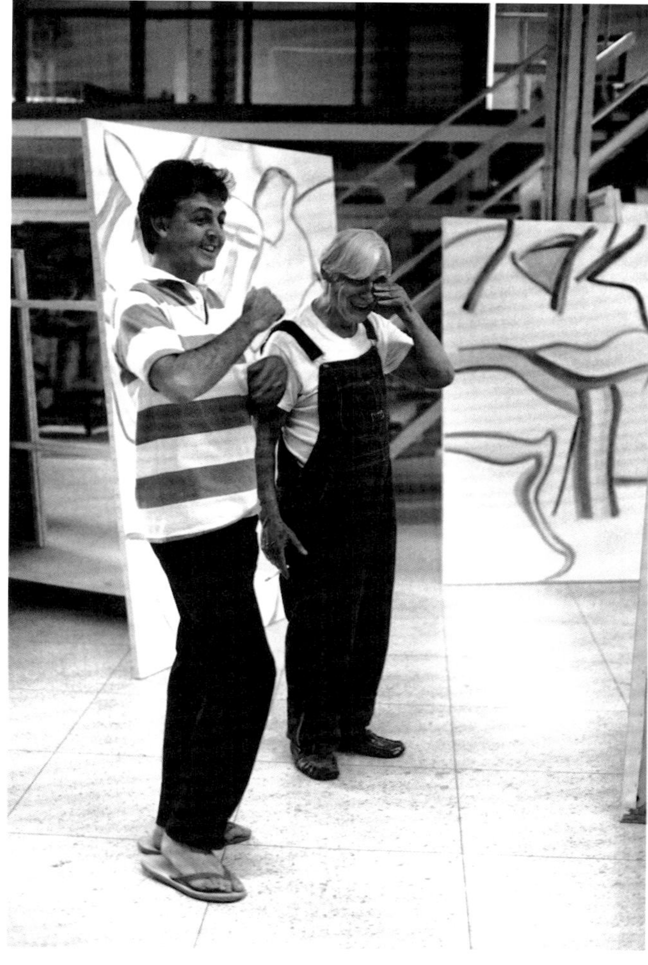

Paul McCartney and
Willem de Kooning
East Hampton, 1983

Paul and Willem laughing
East Hampton, 1984

making the Beatles' "white album." I spent a week with Richard Hamilton, the painter, the British pop painter, who was going to design the cover and the poster inside. It was very designed, the cover; it was just white but it was still a design. . . .

Monochrome . . .

It took a lot to arrive at that design. It is a negative kind of design, it is almost anti-design. But the collage inside, the photo collage, that makes the poster. You know, you get those moments that inspire you in your life and one of them was working with Richard that week. I was bringing in photos and sitting there, just he and I sitting in his studio. First of all, he selected the favorite photos that he wanted to use, that meant something to him, and he cut them up and he started to arrange them. And when I thought he had it all done, when the whole board was filled with pictures, I thought, That's fantastic, he's finished. But I came back in the next day and he had cut out pieces of white paper and put little moments on the things that weren't doing anything. He put the white in and he said, "Now you can see through the picture. There's space, there is a distance in it." And these are just things that I picked up, very informal lessons, you know. Of course, he was a great person to teach me, really. When I visited de Kooning in his studio, he gave Linda and me a picture, because he had known Linda a long time, and we were offered the choice of any picture in his studio. We could have had one of his big, big canvases, but we thought because he was a friend, we would just take something meaningful rather than expensive, so we took a little picture that he had framed himself. And it was a "pull"; with the *New York Times* he often used to pull the excess paint off his canvas. He would put a *New York Times* on it and pull it all off. And he would lay that down and sometimes he liked the "pull" better than the painting. He had framed it and we were looking at it, and it looked like a big purple mountain to me. I said, "At the risk of seeming very naive, what is it, Bill?" He said, "I don't know, it looks like a couch, huh?" The lovely naïveté — he wasn't bothered [about] what it was, he thought it might look like a couch, and then he said, "huh?" like, Your guess is as good as mine. So I thought, This is great: very liberating, that moment for me. He makes either a good picture or a bad picture, and if it is a good picture, he then doesn't worry, and your guess is as good as his as to what it is about sometimes . . . so that was great, I learned at moments like that.

Do you think other artists — for example, expressionists, fauvists, cubists, Magritte, Klee — are artists who influenced you?

Klee, actually, I like him, but he has not inspired me. Matisse very much. Van Gogh is very powerful. Picasso, Magritte, de Kooning, very much in abstract expression.

And would you say you like more spontaneous artists, not like Magritte, more like de Kooning?

I think as far as what I do and what I enjoy in painting, the de Kooning approach, the very wild approach, the spontaneous approach and "exploring the accident," is more interesting for me. It would be difficult if I was choosing which picture to buy, because I would like them equally well, but if I was going to choose either style to follow, then I would have more fun with the de Kooning thing.

Do you have a special English painter you like?

Bacon. Bacon is the English painter I like best. Peter Blake is very good, and I have liked a lot of Peter's work, but Peter once said something about a Monet exhibition that came to England, and he was asked to look at it and review it, and he said, "I don't like loose painting." I thought that was a little . . . it seemed to sum Peter up, but he is a fantastic painter. He likes "tight" painting; he likes it very precise. He doesn't like abstract. He has done some fantastic pictures.

Paul in front of canvas
(low diagonal perspective)
Sussex, 1992

But let's come to your paintings. We saw some really outstandingly good pictures you did in Arizona. I think that for your work, the place has something to do with it.

Yes, I think so. Yes, it does because I am painting spontaneously; my mood has much to do with it. If you are somewhere where the light is very bright and the vegetation is very different — cactus, and the soil is desert sand — it is quite exciting. I find it exciting.

Does it depend on your mood, for instance, having holidays, or do you also paint while you are working?

Yes, I did actually. A lot of pictures you are looking at were done on tour, if we had a few days off from working on tour. I just wouldn't have the time if I was actually working on the tour. But we would often have three or four days off, and I found myself painting. I paint in my special West Coast place. Then I paint on Long Island, on the east coast of America, which is again another special place where I have paints and canvases, and then I paint here at home. . . . In my studio and sometimes at the house, but normally here now.

But your working process is that you come here for two or three hours and you paint?

Yes, that is normally what it is. Normally I will just select a day when I have time to paint, and it would normally be in the afternoon. I would nearly always do something recreational first, but I don't just come to work — it's not that kind of thing. If it is a beautiful day and I notice, say, that the horizon is very little and there is this massive sky, I might want to make this great big blue painting with a tiny little thing at the bottom. I would come normally in the afternoons until the light starts to go, so that would be normally about five or six hours, and I would just paint straight and I would say that this was "alla prima." If I go back the next day to a picture, which I sometimes do if there is something I don't like about it or if I think there is something I can fix, then I might paint over it and do something else to it to try and fix it. But quite often it is just "there," it just appears, and I like it or I don't. And if I like it, I just stop. Then the final act is to sign it. Once I have signed it, then I think that is it, I am just signing off.

You talked about some incentives you have for

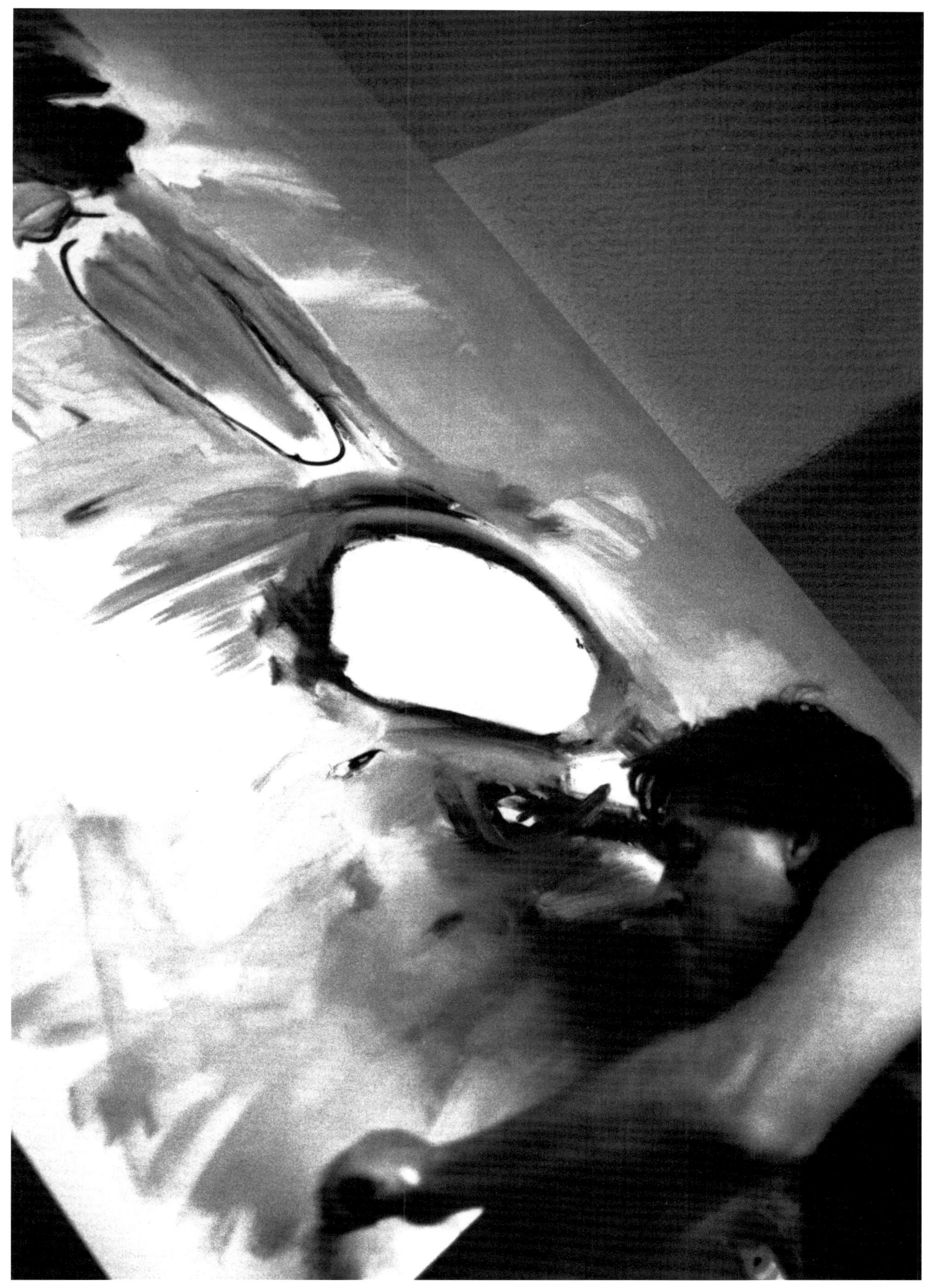

"I have this fictional person in my mind, who is Luigi and he owns a restaurant. He has this alcove in the middle of the restaurant, a little alcove, and he needs a painting. He has asked me, 'Please Mr. Blendini, please make a painting for Luigi's alcove.' So I always think, 'This is for Luigi.' "

painting. Is it possible that you have an incentive from special materials or special feelings? Other pictures, photos?

Yes, I like stuff I find, because of the random aspect. I like a random aspect in life and I am interested to see now that modern science is beginning to look at this, the chaos theory. We thought that everything was mechanically perfect and there was some definite explanation and these results could be repeated endlessly. Now I am much more free in myself.

Sometimes painters are influenced by photos?

Not too much by photos, no, unless it is stuff I have taken or a Polaroid that Linda has taken or something that might help me. With one or two items, the Celtic things that I did, I was just looking through a book and I saw these faces that were done with hardly any lines, and yet they were not modern cartoonists. It wasn't Disney, it was a Celt knocking into a piece of stone thousands of years ago.

But you are looking for pictures and further ideas, you are not looking for Celtic history, only for iconographic things?

Yes, that is right, and the thing that interests me about Celts is that it isn't written down, they didn't write anything down. And nobody knows quite who did the pictures. I like that, the air of mystery, because sometimes when you know too much about a thing, it spoils it. When you are a child, you don't quite know how things work and they have a magic to them. You grow up, you learn exactly how it works, and you say, "Oh, how boring." You know your imagination is better. For instance, I like earthy things. When I was on Long Island, I was driving along the road and I noticed all the cars were swerving to avoid this thing in the road, so I swerved and looked to see what it was, and it turned out to be a wheel off a big industrial thing, a metal wheel. It was a caster, all metal. It was just a big, rusty wheel. So I stopped, went back, picked it up, and took it back with me, in the same way that I would pick up a nice piece of driftwood. It was just a nice shape, and it suited my random feeling. You know, I thought somebody should take this, this should belong to someone. So I just took it back and did a painting of it, tried to get the color of the rust. And so I just put that in a blue sky, just let it hang there, which would be a Magritte kind of echo. That is a kind of trick. Just a very simple trick, it's nothing clever, but just to put it out of its context. It was more noble for it to fly; it was like a heroic wheel.

I'd like to ask you about two people you mentioned. The first is Blendini, and second is Luigi. I think Blendini is your alter ego?

Yes, he is one of them — there are a few in there. You know, I was talking about the fear of painting, the fear of creativity. One of my aims, as I say, is to enjoy the painting. I like blending, to take a color, mix a couple of colors and blend them through, and so when I am doing that, I always imagine myself as Mr. Blendini, and this is the whole thing. You will see it a lot in my pictures. Certain areas are not blended in, they are just left; but if I blend in to try to get rid of any brushstrokes and any joins, it becomes a big blend of color and then I often think in my own mind that this is Mr. Blendini. The Luigi thing has to do with when you are thinking to yourself and you can't help the conversations that go on in your head. For me, if I ever get stuck, and think, Why am I doing this? Why am I standing here putting paint on this thing? Do I want to sell it? and if I can't think of any reason, again I have this fictional person in my mind, who is Luigi and he owns a restaurant. He has this alcove in the middle of the restaurant, a little alcove, and he needs a painting. He has asked me, "Please, Mr. Blendini, please make a painting for Luigi's alcove." So I always think, This is for Luigi. Making something for Luigi is a trick. You have seen the famous film scene where you have a novelist in front of a typewriter and it's a blank sheet of paper and he types something and he takes it out, screws it up, throws it in the wastepaper basket, and you pan down to the wastepaper basket and there are millions of bits of paper, and you pan back up and you realize that he is very frustrated about what he is doing. That is when you need Luigi's alcove. If you can't think of anything to do, you think, Well, this would be OK for

Luigi, he likes this kind of thing, he wi l like just a simple blend of colors. So it is a freeir g device.

Do you think Damien Hirst feels like this at all?

I don't really know about him. I think that a lot of young artists, when they look at what has gone before, must be very daunted, confused, at the thought of picking up a brush. Because they must look at Rembrandt and think, Well I am sure I am not going to get as good as him. They must look at all of Picasso's work and think, Well, maybe I am not going to ever be as good a draftsman as him. So if I was trying to be different and I was in that state, then the whole thing would become much more conceptual. I could think of taking a monkey and skinning it, then putting a nail through its head and then nailing it to a bathtub and then filling the bathtub with pink water, so that the monkey's feet just float out of the top, and then I could attach balloons to its feet. You can think of this, and many people would think this is a good idea!

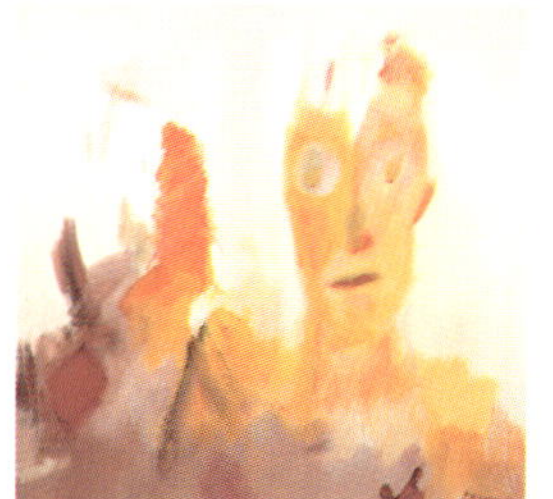

Large yellow face, page 80

Is it true, that you have problems with "celebrity paintings"?

Yes, I noticed over the years that many actors, singers, and people paint. People like Tony Curtis, I am thinking of. I have known Tony awhile and I realize he paints, he really likes painting, and he is a serious painter. To me there was always a problem because it was "Celebrity paints!" He is not a painter, he is a celebrity who paints. David Bowie is a singer who paints, and to me if I were to paint, the only interesting thing would be for the paintings to be seen on their own without this celebrity thing. Now I know I can't escape that. You know, just to say "Paul McCartney paintings" brings up the Beatles in most people's minds. But that is why I didn't do it for so long: I have never wanted to do that, because of the fact that I felt it would be depending on my celebrity and not on the pictures. So what happened was for years and years I just painted but always really wanted a little feedback. Then I started to imagine, What if I had been to art school when I started painting in 1983, and had been painting solid quite seriously for thirteen years? You know, in most people's lives, the guy would be thirty-two now and possibly a well-accepted painter; he would have a lot of exhibits. So I wanted a little of that, not so much lots of exhibits but a bit of feedback. People might say to him, "That is not my favorite bit," and "You see what you did there with that line, what you did there was good"—I wanted a bit of that. I don't know what you do about critics, and critics are in anything I do. I generally don't read them. I don't, because I feel that often people are enhancing their own careers. It is not really about you, it is about the critic himself.

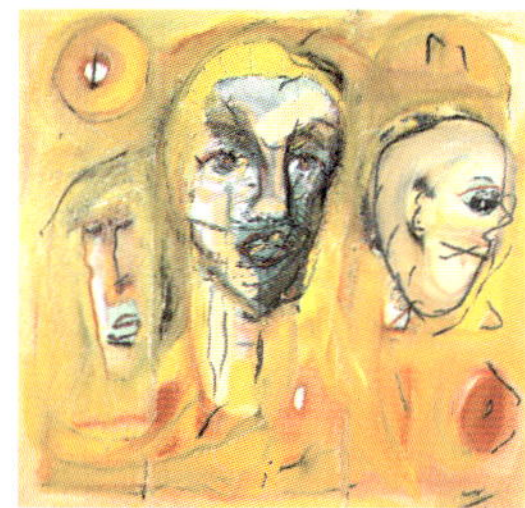

Unspoken words, page 108

Large yellow face

This picture has a lot of light in it.

Yes, I thought for a while it was unfinished because it is pretty luminous, but I left it and I am glad I did now.

I like this head coming out of the depth.

It was based on Linda; it started to look a bit like Linda to me, but it was not a portrait.

I think you painted it very quickly. It looks very fresh, lively.

Unspoken words

This is 100 percent composition—it isn't in every picture.

As you can see, it is very spontaneous and I didn't really have any preconceived ideas when I started it, but I started with blue behind it and then I drew some faces on top of that and then just worked on them, just the three faces, and turned it round a lot when I was working. I turned it lots of ways, upside down often.

You turned the canvas upside down?

Yes, I turned it on its side and upside down, just to get a look at the composition, to see if it worked. A lot of the drawing, these blue marks, were done from the upside-down position, and then in the end I decided it seemed like a

"I like the word *primitive* because a lot of what I do is primitive. Because when I started out in music, I never took lessons but I learned in a primitive way to make music. I learned the piano, the guitar in a primitive way."

woman. It had a kind of grille across it, stopping it from talking, so it was something to do with forbidden speech. And this guy definitely has a cross, the face on the right: his mouth seemed to pick up the same theme, something forbidden. And then this face on the left has got an *S* mouth, which is a similar thing, so that became the theme.

Can you say something about the scratching here, scratching the color out on the left-hand side?

That is something I started to do a few years ago. When I put the paint on, I sometimes wouldn't be quite satisfied with the effect or how it was lying there, so I took a palette knife and scratched some lines, just to improve the drawing. So it has become a thing that I like to do a lot, and it is normally in areas where I am just not happy with the way the paint is lying there. The hair in the middle face, that would have been just a long yellow brushstroke, but to break it up, I put a little bit of drawing in there.

The left-hand face comes out from behind — did you paint it later?

No, it was all painted at the same time. I think I have always liked drawing faces and heads since I was a kid, as caricatures of people. So it is very deep in your psyche, a head, a face: it is something we all have, and so I just find myself doing faces and heads a lot and just making them up; it's like inventing people. Some of these faces might as well be landscapes because a lot of the time all I want to do is apply paint, so sometimes just putting the paint on is to me more interesting than actually thinking what it all means.

I can see that that is a very important principle of your work, that you start out from the process of painting and not from the process of thinking. Special compositions or subject matter you would like to paint come from the process, from the interior.

And in the end that is based on the theory that whatever you do, there must be some sort of meaning. There will be some sort of meaning, because it is like you are unloading your mind's computer, you are printing out your psychic computer, whether you know it or not.

For me it is very fascinating how in a lot of pictures you play with the process of painting. You go under the surface of the color and you show, "This is me, I took this color away, this is canvas, this is dripping, this is random." In the later paintings in recent years, I think you have used faces and portraits for doing something abstract, as a way through.

It's like we were talking about Peter Blake before: he needs an excuse to loosen up, so this was to get free.

So you start with something you know and then you step back from the special person you are also painting?

Yes, that is right, I think I always liked abstract painting, but to do it, I feel I would have to ask myself, Why would I do it? I think I was looking for doors through to abstract painting and this is a transition. This is not really a face or an abstract, it is somewhere between the two of them, and these bits of painting along the side are just painterly things. The sky isn't really attempting to be anything except a nice shape.

It is very interesting for the public, for art viewers, to go with you along that road. "Oh yes, it's a head," and then you recognize that is what painting can do.

Yes, it is really true. That is the painterly thing about it. That has to do with painting rather than content.

It was the same with Picasso when people said, "Oh, he paints eyes and noses, but that isn't an eye or a nose." But for Picasso it wasn't interesting to paint a nose in the right position; he wanted to develop something.

To move the idea more into the abstract dreamworld.

Oak apple twenties man

I was looking for some ink to write a letter and went into the shop, but they hadn't got any. And an old man in the shop had overheard me not being able to get the ink for my fountain pen, and as I came out of the shop, he took me to one side and he said, "If you want ink, you can make

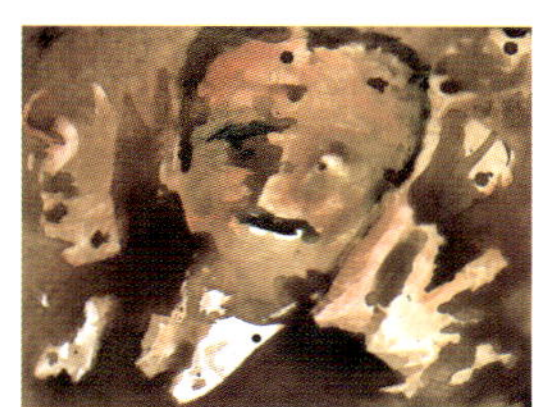

Oak apple twenties man, page 82

it out of oak apples, those little things that grow on oak trees. When a bug attacks the oak tree, it encases the bug in a hard cork ball. If you take them and soak them in water, they give off a very powerful dye that you can use as an ink. They used to use it in the old days for ink." So I did that and made this brown ink, and then to experiment with it, I did some monochrome canvases with a bit of red to add a bit of warmth to it, but it is mainly this oak apple ink.

It is a very specific kind of brown.

It is a nice brown, isn't it? I love it when it gets very dark, a deep brown, and it is all oak apple. That is a little bit of green and red, which is to stop it [from] being completely monochromatic. And the man to me looks like he could have been a friend of my father's in the 1920s, down at the dance hall or something. Because my father used to be in a jazz band in the 1920s. . . . The little mustache reminds me of the period, the oak-apple mustache there. So he had a certain freedom to him, and this was almost a hand, fingers, a strong little hand. It seems like he has a little Band-Aid on it; it is crazy, that, in the detail. Like a dirty old one, or a bandage, he looks like he has got something wrong with his finger. But I just find that happens, so I would leave it as that, and there is no way I would go over it and formalize it and make it look more like a Band-Aid or more like a bandage by adding some identifying lines. It would completely lose all the scale. If I added another line, it would all go wrong.

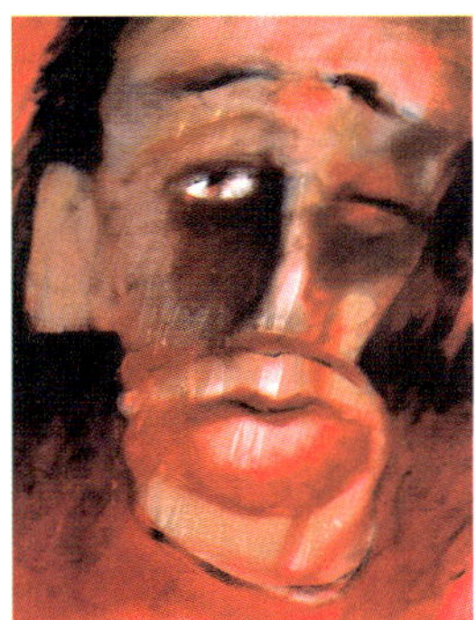

Boxer lips, page 129

Boxer lips

I like this. It has an absolute richness in red colors, bright and earthy colors, and those colors give us certain meaning.

What kind of meaning do you think — hot, sensual, violent?

Mystic . . .

The shape of the head is a bit improbable . . . and again you have the two sorts of eyes. It wouldn't have been as interesting to me to just have the one eye, or both eyes closed, or both eyes open. He looks like a boxer possibly after losing a fight; there is a bit of a battering in that left eye, isn't there? So he is a sort of hero figure, a warrior figure, like comic-book heroes. I could almost imagine, like Marlon Brando. But I like these white streaks behind it, like highlights, like lighting on him.

Do you remember when you did this picture?

No. What I will do with all of these things is I will try and guess; I can often figure it out. The smaller canvases tend to be a bit earlier because probably at this time I wouldn't have a big canvas, just do lots of little ones, but then I felt more comfortable with the bigger canvases.

He is really perfect.

He is really nice. There is something of me in this, I don't know why, I don't know how to describe it, but a lot of these ideas you can see the germs of back in my schoolbooks, old schoolbooks I have: little scrawlings, rude ladies, naked girls, things I was awakening to, and the thrill was being able to conjure them up like an illusionist. I like the word *primitive* because a lot of what I do is primitive. Because when I started out in music, I never took lessons but I learned in a primitive way to make music. I learned the piano, the guitar in a primitive way. So when I do things like sail a boat, again it reminds me. I imagine myself like the first man who had a boat and put a sail up, and the same wind that blows me is the same one that blew him. I like that ancient connection. It is like your heritage going right back. And in the same way in painting — the rock painters, cave artists, I love their work.

We find a lot of things where you are influenced by modern art, but I think you have found it for yourself, you have found some principles and repertoires because you are painting a lot.

Yes, that was my plan. I thought, I shouldn't paint because I haven't been to art school. Then I thought, That is irrational and stupid. But then I thought, I will paint, but now I will have to get over the blocks, and I discovered the blocks myself, and it was very interesting talking to other painters because they said, "Oh, I have that same fear," and I thought that was just me being frightened by a blank canvas. My most frightening moment was when Linda bought me Magritte's easel, and I actually had one of his canvases on it.

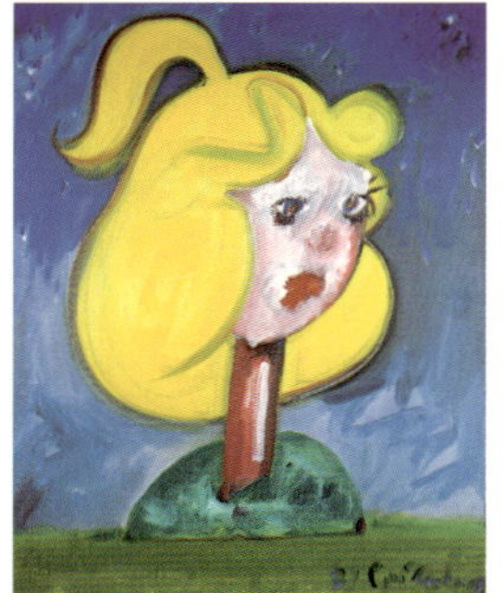

Patti Boyd, page 100

"Sometimes just to make a very quick line makes it more precise than a very slowly drawn, precise line. If this were drawn slowly, it wouldn't have the flow."

Patti Boyd

I like the color of this picture. It is named *Patti Boyd* — your girlfriend?

No, my fantasy perhaps, at one point. The painting itself is a caricature and is just of any woman with blond hair, the neck is more abstract and the body becomes like a hill, with a red pole for the neck, and you get a little bit of painting on the face. But after I had done it and I was looking to title the painting, just for my memory, it reminded me of Patti Boyd. It had a look that Patti had. It does look a little bit like her, actually, if you see her.

What do you call this kind of nose?

Like a button nose. Sometimes when I am painting faces, I enjoy the fact that I am making the person up. You know, for a second it becomes like you are putting makeup on them. So she had a kind of white makeup. It has a kind of sixties fantasy quality that in some way captures the image that Patti Boyd had. We first met her when we did the film *Hard Day's Night.* We were young guys, and she was one of the models who were hired to play the schoolgirls on the train, and that was when she and George met; they married, and she later married Eric Clapton. She was a very good looking girl. So it is not from life, or from a photograph, it is more a fantasy. But, as usual, it provided me some excuse to put paint on a canvas.

I like the hair, good motion.

I think one of the things I have enjoyed since I was a kid is drawing little caricatures. So it follows through into the pictures. I find when I study it too much, it doesn't come out quite as well. Sometimes just to make a very quick line makes it more precise than a very slowly drawn, precise line. If this were drawn slowly, it wouldn't have the flow. I like the flow of things moving around.

Sea god

This is one of your very important pictures.

I like the colors. There used to be things that children could get to draw on, in the sixties and seventies. I have just put all the paint on as a background, and started to experiment with getting a bit of paint coming out of the surface.

You put the colors on the canvas before, and then you did it?

Yes, this was at first just colors, like an abstract, and then I wanted to draw on it so then I used the scratching technique which —

Are there three different kinds of noses . . . ?

This is a bit sexual to me. . . . The beard looks like a vagina, too. This is almost another mouth here, below the mouth, that line here. It is just loose lines, not a lot of precision, but I think it has a nice movement to it.

I think this picture has three movements: one movement is the brushstroke, and this is a movement here, and the scratching, it goes back and forth.

You know, what happens to me is that I have seen pictures with a lot of buildup of paint. That might be something I would try today, to lay some paint on there. And all this toward the top of the picture, where this rough surface is, where the texture is, I play with that and try to get things to stand out, this eye. And that is a separate idea from the scratching, which is more of a drawing technique. I often feel sorry when some great drawing gets covered by paint. Sometimes I like to buy an artist's drawings rather than his paintings.

Like Daumier . . .

Like Daumier or Tiepolo, because those are his original little pen marks or pencil marks. That is him actually making these marks, and even though it is him when he paints over them, I

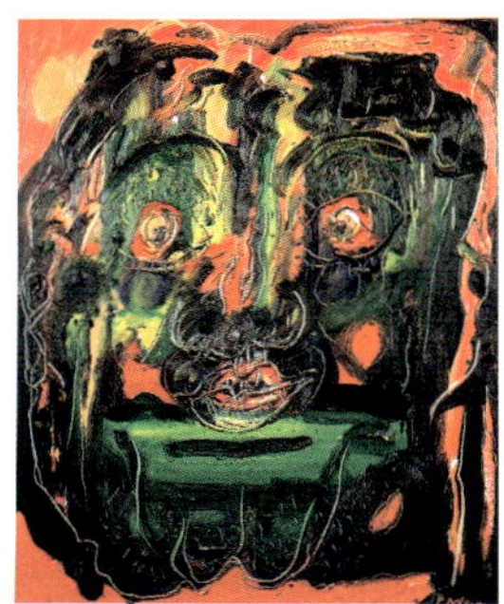

Sea god, page 68

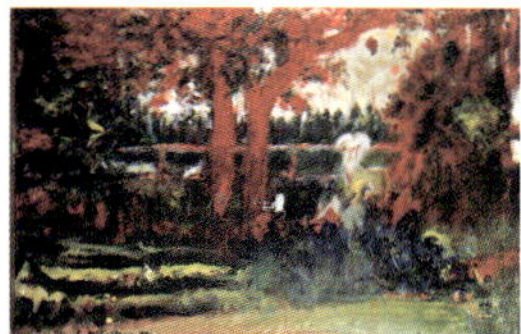

Andy in the garden, page 67

kind of regret the loss of these lines, you know. So one of the little problems I was always working with was whether I should put drawing on it and then cover it, and this became a bit of a solution because you could draw after you had painted. And in pulling the paint away, where it was green you get a yellow, because the yellow is behind it. And so that became one of the techniques that I have got very interested in, and I find it very helpful. It is the same with music. When I write a song, I don't know what I am going to write, I don't know how I am going to write it. Or a poem; I don't know what is going to come out, and that is the thrill.

But you start with an idea for a lyric?

I start with some sort of idea, or just a notion, like "Eleanor Rigby." I just had that first line. I didn't think, That will be a character, as I was mumbling [sings], "Eleanor Rigby picks up the rice in a church where a wedding has been." Well, that is a whole story: a woman picks up the rice in a church where there has been a wedding. Right in that first line we know there is a woman, called Eleanor Rigby; we know she picks up the rice, so she is obviously a cleaner, or she is not too important a person. And if she is in a church, why is she in a church? She is an old woman who hangs around churches; it gives me a lot of her character. And "where a wedding has been" — well, maybe she wishes she was married, and so we start to see her as a spinster, because she is picking up the rice like a souvenir. In that one little line, you get a lot of information if you care to analyze it, and so that was the mystery of writing that song. I didn't mean those words to come out. It could suddenly have been [sings] "Charlie McWilliams picks up the bat that the cricket player has just dropped." And we would have a completely different story, so out of this mysterious chant I just listened to myself to hear what was going on: what did I just say? Good, I have the clue. Then the rest of the tune came and the rest of the lyrics came, and we followed her home then, and it is the same process for the painting, where there will be just something there I am messing around with, and suddenly a character will start to be there and I think, Ah, because this is reddish and this is greenish, and I just follow the paint. These are very reggae colors — red, green, and gold.

Andy in the garden

This is the view from our house where we live, and there are a couple of interesting trees in the center of the picture that I was painting. It was a sort of golden evening, the sun was coming through onto the grass, which is the yellow. And on those evenings you often get balloonists coming from behind the clouds, and the wind comes this way, out of the picture as it were, so that you often see them start here, and over the next half hour or so these balloonists come over. Just as there is a balloon over Andy's head. And as I was just painting the picture, just getting a kind of landscape, messing with colors like Nolde did — not necessarily the correct colors of the trees, just the shape, so these are the evergreen trees at the back, these are the forestry, this is the fencing, which goes into a paddock — and I was just playing with a little white when Andy Warhol appeared, sitting in the garden, as the paint was being put on. I was just putting on some white, and his likeness appeared there, and so I just left it and finished off other bits of white in the picture and filled in other bits of white. And the more I left it, the more it became Andy Warhol, which is a paradox that might have amused him. I had heard about the Velvet Underground, and I was listening to a program where they were saying that one of the great things about having him produce a record for them was that they would ask, "How was it, how did it sound?" and he would say, "Oh, great." And then they would ask, "Shall we do this with it, should we just vary it a little bit here?" and he would say, "Oh no, leave it, it was very beautiful, what you did." And they said it made him the greatest producer ever because anything they did, he allowed them complete freedom and he just enjoyed it. It is very interesting because it is almost the opposite for me in painting: his coming into music and just allowing it, following what he saw, is the same journey as I am doing into painting, only in the opposite direction. The paint makes Andy appear, so it is just a magic moment, a lucky moment. It is great to get a bit of magic like that at any time of your life, isn't it? I have another picture called *John's room* where John Lennon just appeared in it. And that is a wonderful moment for me, just like, OK, I didn't mean to do that . . . it just arrived.

I find pictures very interesting — and this is one of them — that tell me the story of a painting process. Some pictures have a painting process, some pictures are good and they are painted, but you can't see the process. Here it is like a film. It is not one picture, it is a picture at different stages.

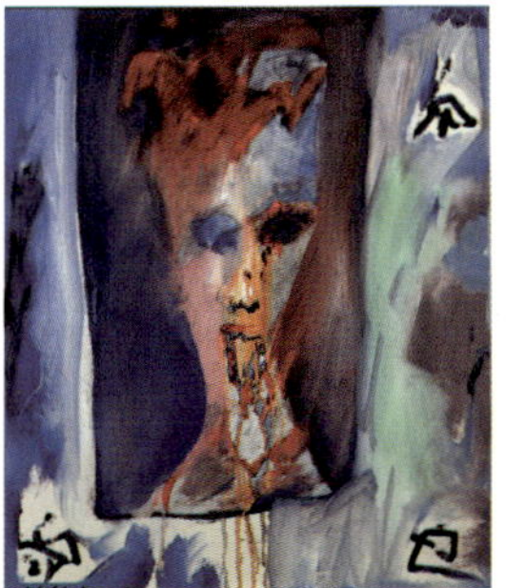

Bowie spewing, page 97

Bowie spewing

Which means being sick.

It is the random principle here? You took a lot of turpentine.

Yes. This was started off with some drips. As I say, I like to just observe the motion of paint dripping down the canvas. And in experimenting, it was only at the end it struck me that it looked a bit like David Bowie as Ziggy Stardust, in that period, and it looked like I put little Oriental characters round the edge. This lower left one became a little figure, a person with a little head.

They look like Japanese characters.

Yes, this was arrived at by my usual method, which was just to let the paint lead the way. This one eye is very blue; the eyes are different. I don't know much about this picture; it just arrived and it amuses me because it looked like David Bowie being sick. Linda had taken a Polaroid once of him backstage somewhere, and this reminds me of that Polaroid.

I think it is a very interesting picture because it is a frame within a frame, with different kinds of blue, and this flowing of color gives a connection between the two realities within the picture. Outside the picture is a certain reality, and that comes second. This is the first reality, and these are writings or figures. This picture has two realities, and that is perfect, too, and it is all connected here.

Yes, I can see I have gone in and painted in some of these little things. They dictate the shape, and I have gone back in and painted in some bits.

It looks like color is flowing out of the picture, and it looks, in a second meaning, like he is spewing. The technique and meaning mix together. It is a really dramatic, perfect picture. It has a lot of different levels.

Yes, you can interpret it in a lot of ways. My main intention is just in remembering it, so the image I got was of David Bowie spewing. Somebody else might look at it and think it is their young cousin eating a chocolate cake!

It looks very broken up here, as if you wanted to push the picture toward the abstract.

From looking at so many of these faces, it seems to me I agree with what you have been saying, that I am using the faces just to get through to an abstract thing. It is a means to an end, so that anyone looking at them as faces is really getting only half the point. Half the point is to ignore the face. It was Khalil Gibran, in his book *The Prophet,* who said something like, "Half of what I say is meaningless, but I say it just to reach you." It was something John used in a song called "Julia" that he wrote: "Half of what I say is meaningless, but I say it just to reach you." So in a way, half of the painting is meaningless, but I paint it just to reach somebody. It is a variation on the old quote.

Mr. Kipps

He is a little bit like the earlier brushstroke portraits you did.

This is a humorous face. He is a definite kind of character, and I always enjoyed the old John Mills film that they did about Mr. Kipps, where he is a young shop attendant. And this fel-

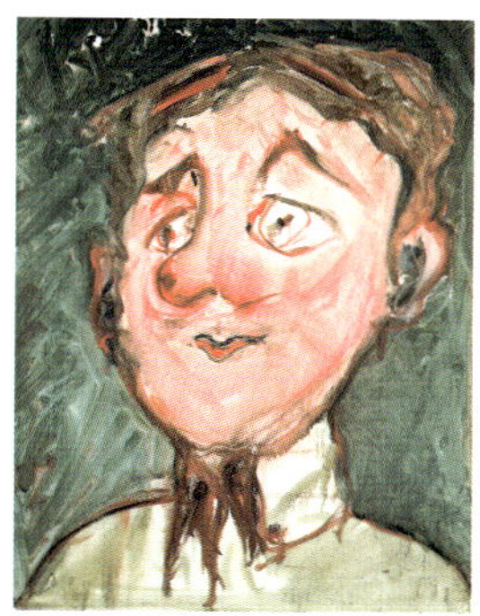

Mr. Kipps, page 100

"I always liked that word *play:* it is an interesting word because in English when you make music, you call it playing music; when you make a painting it is a 'work.' People don't say an 'art-play.'"

low always seemed to have that character to me, with his high collar, but he looked slightly old-fashioned, and his haircut looked a little old-fashioned, from the nineteenth century. I like his humor; he has a nice humor. It is very lightly painted, quite delicate, with a lot of white.

It looks like the skin of someone who drinks a lot — the red and the fat nose, and the eyes are very narrow.

Yes, he is the kind of person you could almost imagine you have met. I am always very attracted to him. I liked him; I would like to take a drink with him.

I think he has a quality of painting like the Patti Boyd picture has — more caricature.

When I am on the phone, I will draw little faces. I won't really doodle like people make little crosses. I will do little faces and shade them in. I will always do that, like in school exercise books, so having done it for so long, it is very natural. If you put a pen in my hand or a pencil, that is where I go to immediately. It is like a bad habit, so that was what I had to decide: whether I would try and break that habit, or whether to allow it to be and to carry it into the painting and let it be a source for some of the paintings. So as you can see, I did allow it to be and didn't worry about it. Although, you know, the criticism could be, "Well, it is a little young, a little caricature, frivolous." I thought through that and thought, It doesn't matter. I don't need my painting to be serious; there is no requirement for it to be anything. Its only requirement was that I should enjoy it, so he comes out of the caricature tradition and he has got a special look.

Did you have a special intention in mind?

No, I often don't have a special intention. Just sometimes I will get an idea and say, "OK, that is what I am going to paint," and that starts me off. But very often it is just the colors. I will often just start with a mood and the colors, and sometimes if I paint fast, then I wish I could go on painting longer. At this stage I really enjoy putting the paint on, and so one of the nice things for me is doing all of this here. I spend much longer on these bits, just forming them and blending them. That's Mr. Blendini here. And I take more time just because I enjoy doing it, so I don't want it to be over too quickly, like sex. You know, if it is over too quickly, you think, Oh, I wish that had gone on a bit longer, it felt so good. So with the painting, this would have been the quick bit, and that would have been first, to frame it. And I have taken more time on these bits; I can see I have taken longer. It is something I enjoy a lot, the blending; it is a very pleasant process. It is a magical process because I would put some paint on here and then I would decide whether I ought to try and get this purple in here or not. It actually just stays on its own, the purple. I'm just playing.

I always liked that word *play:* it is an interesting word because in English when you make music, you call it playing music; when you make a painting it is a "work." People don't say an "art-play."

The actor and musician play onstage . . .

We "play," which is frivolous, but "works" of art. So for me I think I bring the play from my music back into the art. This is playful, the freedom of playing. . . .

One of my great beliefs in the world is "less is more," and the more I read and find out about other artists like de Kooning "exploring the accident," things like that, that kind of theory, the paradox . . . You know, you would think that if you studied for millions and millions of years at music, you would therefore be the finest musician in the world.

But I don't actually believe that. My most-known song is called "Yesterday," and I woke up having dreamed that song. I didn't sit down and think about it, and it is the one out of all my songs that people have played. More than three thousand people have covered that song, so I must start to think that there is a paradox here. You know, I should have sat down for three weeks and slaved over something that successful, but I just woke up one morning and had dreamed it. So this is where I talk about freedom in art. If that little piece of string gets caught in the paint as I do it, I just think, Oh, that is OK. I certainly didn't think to do that. You know, if I had thought to do that, it may be it wouldn't be good, but because it was an accident, it finds its way in there organically.

But what you say about your music, and it's the same with pictures, it isn't that you are dreaming this, it's that you are doing a lot of music, doing a lot of painting, and sometimes it comes together, like a bang, a lot of influences.

Yes, and I value that, I really value that moment when a little organic accident happens. I value it more because I didn't actually mean to do it. It is like Shakespeare says, "There are more things in heaven and earth, Horatio, than are dreamt of in your philosophy." And it's true. There is just more in that little finger than I am ever going to know about: there are bones, nerves, capillaries, blood cells; there is a nail growing out of it. I could spend a lifetime studying how that happens. I am a great believer in that; I believe that there is so much magic around that it may be it isn't necessary to study, study, study. I think sometimes you lose the magic that way. You study so much that there is no room for magic.

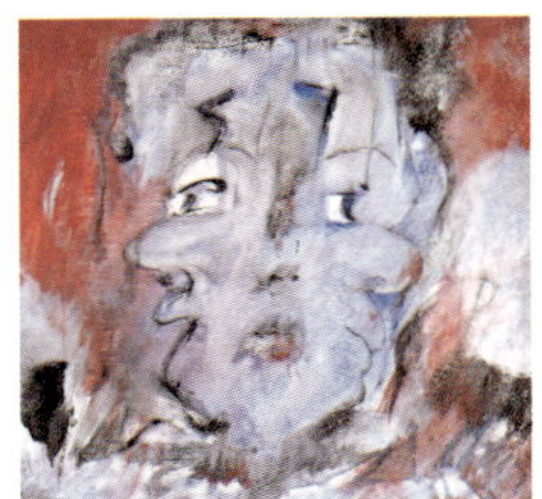

Three blue faces in red sky,
page 125

Yellow Linda with piano

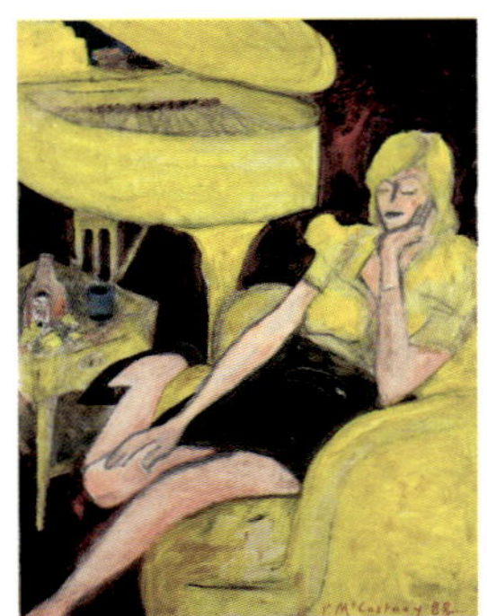

Yellow Linda with piano,
page 79

A couple of people who have looked at my book singled this one out, a couple of women who said that is the picture they would like, and I am not sure why but I like it. This is Linda relaxing in my room at home where I have the piano, and she is sitting on the couch and she was in yellow. So I made everything yellow. The piano isn't really yellow, but I just thought it would be nice. Her hair was yellow, her blouse was yellow, so I made them all yellow. So it became a very yellow picture. It didn't need brown or any of their real colors. This is interesting because this little stool here, this little piece here, was René Magritte's. That was in a sale of the contents of his studio, and in this little thing here are his charcoals and his drawing pens and pencils exactly as he left them, including his spectacles. Maybe it was the atmosphere they liked. It's very peaceful. I enjoyed making it. It is a very typical pose of Linda's: the legs — this foot is slightly strange, but I like it — this shoe.

Three blue faces in red sky

I don't know where I have seen this idea, but over the years I have liked the idea that out of one face you make a few faces, so the eyes work for the central face as if someone is turning. You get two profiles and a front. So it is like a three-sided portrait. But it isn't an actual portrait of someone. I like the lines; the lines are quite free, particularly this side. I like spontaneous lines. When I really take a lot of time and study the lines, they get a little bit too wooden, they lose their freedom, and they lose their life. This is an idea I have done a couple of times — two-sided things, or the kiss where it is two faces, those kiss pictures. So this has just three sides, three imaginary faces; the one in the middle looks rather a beautiful face. This is quite colorful, the cheeks, quite glamorous. Then this is more like someone out of Leonardo's time. . . .

It changes completely if you block out the other things. . . .

More like a country person. It reminds me of W. C. Fields's nose, a lot of character there. Then this is a crazier face, more aggressive, this one over here, but I like looking at it all in one. We had a crazy idea in the sixties, a friend of mine and me, that you could make an album, a record, with two pieces of music playing at the same time, for instance, a Beethoven symphony and a Ravi Shankar piece. It is crazy because it is like three things. You don't really hear anything, but our idea is that you would ignore one of the pieces of music and listen to the other. Then play it again and ignore the other piece of music and listen to that one. And we felt that this was a very good idea because you had the two together, or just one or just the other. So you had three goes at the record! The only thing in people's way is that they would only perceive it as the three: they

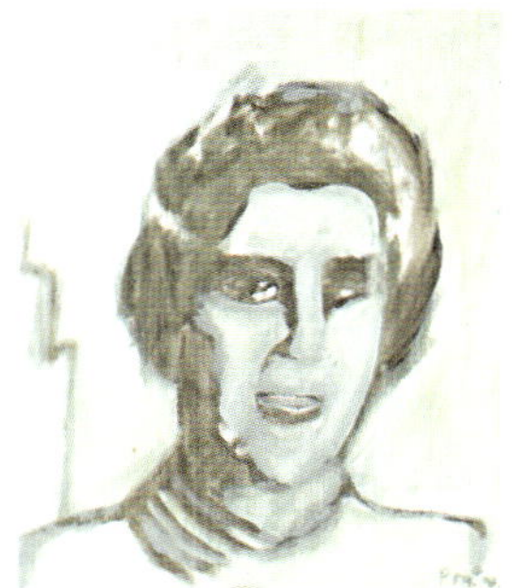

The Queen after her first cigarette, page 98

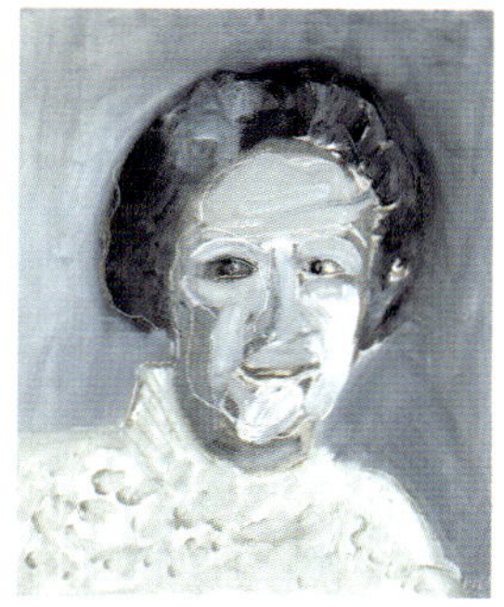

The Queen getting a joke, page 99

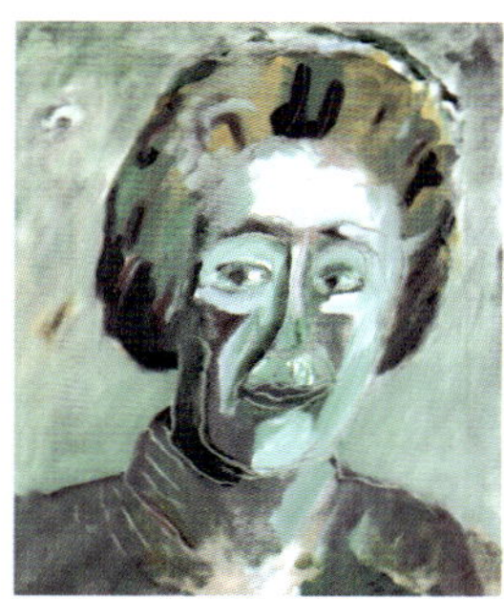

A greener Queen, page 99

don't have the ability to do that. But mentally I like the idea.

It gains much more three-dimensionally, but it becomes quite a beautiful face.

I think I don't like to have a formula. It is the same with music. People used to ask John Lennon and me, "What is your formula — who writes the words, who does the music?" Because traditionally there is a formula. You know, Hammerstein writes the music, and Rodgers writes the words, or whichever the process is. But we used to say, "No, there isn't a formula; we don't want to find a formula." But in doing it a lot, you inevitably arrive at some sort of formula, just out of habit.

So the nearest thing to a formula, I would say, is that my painting falls into two schools. One is that I know exactly what I want to paint: I have found some leaves and I want to paint them. If I don't know what I want to paint, I often just do the "toothpaste" thing, and often just find some colors that I am in the mood for. You know, maybe I am in a fiery mood, just something to start. Just to get some sort of inspiration. I am not a great person for sitting and looking at a white canvas for hours. I don't do that, I just come in and I think, Right, let's just start. It reminds me of people I read about recently who have bad Parkinson's disease. A friend of mine used to have it, so I know about it. If they are walking, they will sometimes freeze and they just cannot think how to get walking again. They just cannot understand it until someone walks in front of them, or if they can touch a leaf or a tree, touch something, then they fall into it again, and their body remembers how to do it. So I need something like that, some sort of impetus, some sort of catalyst. So the catalyst for me is nearly always the paint itself, the color. For instance, that is a Prussian blue we are looking at in this picture. I like Prussian blue a lot; it has something exciting in it. I like watering it down; there is something very exciting that happens in the mid area there.

Queen trilogy

That is the first time and the last time Paul McCartney painted Her Majesty.

Growing up in England, one of the strong images, particularly then, was the Queen. And when I was eleven, she had her coronation, and it was a very big event. They did a lot of work in the schools, and I won an essay competition in Liverpool. It was my first prize ever. I had to go up, and the Lord Mayor gave me the prize. It was the first time I ever felt my knees go to rubber; I had never experienced anything like that. Later I would feel it with my music. But it was interesting for us, because the Queen's coronation was very big news then.

With the prize money I bought my first modern art book, a beautiful book that had all the modern art of the period, and I was particularly keen on some of the English people like Victor Pasmore, some of the artists of the time, so that was the connection.

The other book you were given with it was a book on the Queen. It was probably a very big public-relations exercise on the coronation, but it worked. So the Queen has always been an important figure. With the Beatles I met her once and I have always liked her. I always thought she was a reasonable person. And in some ways I felt a bit sorry for her, because she is trapped inside her celebrity. My celebrity, unlike royal celebrity, carries with it freedom. Like sitting here now, we didn't have to have elaborate things: I can just sit here, I can drive a car. Whereas their celebrity doesn't carry with it freedom, so I often feel sorry for them. Anyway, in this case I saw a picture of her in a magazine, very queenly, looking very royal, and I was attracted to this picture, to this image, so I thought that would be a fun subject. So I started off with the gray one and just used the magazine image as a starting point, just to paint. And I liked it very unfinished like this and this eventually got the title, *The Queen after her first cigarette.*

That is the gray one? She looks very flat.

"If you dream of someone, if you dream of your father and he is dead, in your dream you meet him again, and if it is a good dream, it is a wonderful moment because for two seconds you are with him again and you don't think. 'Oh, he's dead, I can't enjoy this moment.' You accept it."

She looks flat, but she also looks as if she has gone a bit pale — you know, how people do when they have their first cigarette: it can make them feel a bit sick. And she has got a crazy look in her eye. The right eye as we are looking at it looks as if it has gone a bit crazy, so that is a slightly irreverent portrait of the Queen. You know, the Queen after her first cigarette, as a young person. Then the second picture — they are all based on the same image — so the blue one, the second one, is most like the image, that is the nearest to the actual image. But this time I did it in blue. And then, when I'd finished and used the scratching technique on her face, it looked a little like her, but it seemed like she was just getting a joke. So that is *The Queen getting a joke:* it is like someone has just told her a joke and she is just about to laugh, Mona Lisa–style. She is just about to get a joke, so that is the second one.

And then I did one more, which is the green one. And the double meaning there with the word *green* is ecological, so that one is *A greener Queen*. So really they are a little series.

What is very good is you see the stripes on her collar, that is in every picture.

Yes, that was the outfit she had on; it was a particularly interesting collar on the outfit.

But it isn't an antiroyalistic act, to paint her like this? Involving her like this in the process?

No, it is the opposite; it is affectionate. It is slightly irreverent, but I don't think she would mind.

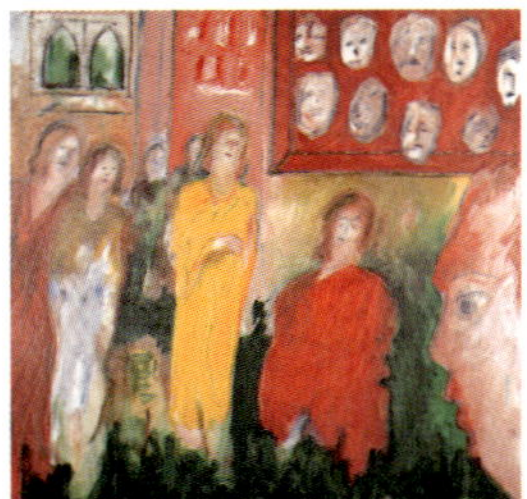

John's room, page 115

John's room

To me this picture looks like it is in a church, or a monastery, a sacred, religious room.

I remember the process with this one. Sometimes I get an idea of what I want to do, but I don't hold to it religiously. If something else happens that I prefer, I am happy to destroy the first idea and move on to something else if it seems better. The original idea for this was started with the central figure in the yellow, and I was going to see if I could paint folded clothing, like in the great tradition; folding is a great painterly thing.

It was one of the most important things in former times that you had to paint.

So I was going to see if I could get into the great depths of the shadows. So I blocked her out, the middle figure in yellow there, to start with. Then I was going to put in a couple of figures to really get into doing their clothes, there to the right of the woman in yellow. So I was just sketching, blocking it in quite roughly, and I was going to make another character there — the first sketch was done in the blue, to get the composition — but as I started to fill in a little bit, I got a very strong feeling that that was John Lennon's face. The one with the face on the clothes, sitting down. It had a look that was John Lennon. Just in a moment, it reminded me — it may not remind anyone else of John Lennon, but for me it reminded me of him. I then had an idea for his clothes; instead of material in the medieval tradition, I made his clothes, his toga, into one of his faces. When John used to draw, that would be a typical face on the right profile.

Do you know his drawings?

John's drawings? Yes, I know them quite well, of course. Well, I saw him do a lot of them, and I obviously saw all his books and stuff. So that became the fun of it then — it was now John, so now the picture centered on him. So instead of the yellow person becoming central, it suddenly all seemed to me that everyone was now focusing on this John Lennon figure. And obviously, as John is a very strong, important person in my life, I always enjoy getting an image of him. It's like if you dream of someone, if you dream of your father and he is dead, in your dream you meet him again, and if it is a good dream, it is a wonderful moment because for two seconds you are with him again and you don't think, Oh, he's dead, I can't enjoy this moment. You accept it. So in painting, this sometimes happens to me, and this was a bit like that, meeting John again, drawing his face. It was a great

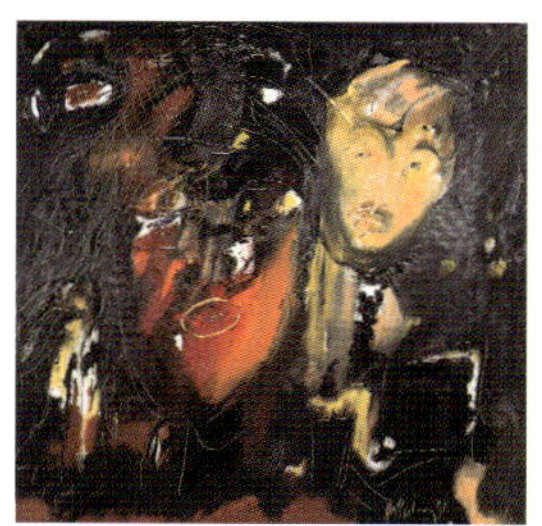

Dark faces, page 109

pleasure to do it and then to draw this face here. And then the big face on the side, the large profile looking into the picture, looking in at John, again reminded me of someone I knew, so I filled that in like that.

Do you know who?

Yes, it was a manager called Brian Brolly. The face was meant to be very unfinished. I think if I finished it, it would lose: it wouldn't look like him. I know if I put one more piece of paint on that face, it would suddenly look like someone else. So I made the rest of the picture unfinished-looking in order to fit with that. So these faces up here that I was going to get great detail in, that was my intention, on the upper right-hand corner, they just become strange little people that come out of the frame, almost floating, slightly dreamlike.

There are nine faces in here — very symbolic. Actually nine was one of John's favorite numbers, funnily enough. I hadn't noticed that there were nine people, but he would have taken that as being very symbolic. And seven figures in the foreground; that is another good number. You know he was into all that stuff.

The yellow figure is well painted, I think, the clothes and the hand holding the clothes.

It has got a very unfinished look. I like the unfinished look. The more I see the painting, the more glad I am I didn't try to get any more detail into it. I think I would have had to make the whole canvas more detailed; I couldn't just do one little bit. So I left it with this kind of rough look, and it is called *John's room* because John is the central figure in it.

It is wonderful because of the contrast of the colors in it, the red and the green and the yellow and the orange.

Dark faces

This is one of my favorites. There is a lot of black in it and the right amount of red contrasting. The motion and composition . . .

And the signature is more unusual; for me it is more like an autograph. That scratching was all done very fast.

It is part of the composition, the signature.

I like the idea of dark canvases. Some of the old Dutch canvases and some of the Old Masters used to use dark canvases very effectively, so that is probably what attracted me to it in the first place. It's not a color I often get involved with, black. It is a difficult color I find; it can have no life; it can be a little too dark. But this was an experiment with black, and the best thing about the black was the fact that when I scratched through it, it gave a really good contrast with the canvas underneath. And because the contrast was so immediate from scratching out the black, it seemed to me it needed to be done quickly, with a lot of emotion and motion. So that is what I did.

I always used to draw little circles, little cartoon faces. Doodles. And I always did those — and I still do sometimes — on an autograph, or on a letter to someone if I want to be friendly. So I always thought there was something strong in that, but I couldn't ever find a use for it. But when I started painting, I did get into faces because I felt quite at home with them. I felt that any lines I made with them would be fresh and immediate, rather than taking out a ruler and drawing the lines very, very carefully, which to me often loses the spirit. They then look like lines that have been thought of, and I get a feeling that it looks like the artist has tried too hard. Like Sunday painters. And I remember someone talking to me about my painting — it was Brian Clarke, actually — and he said the difference in his mind between me and a Sunday painter was that theirs looked like they'd tried too hard; it didn't come off, it stayed wooden, it remained stiff, and it didn't have any life.

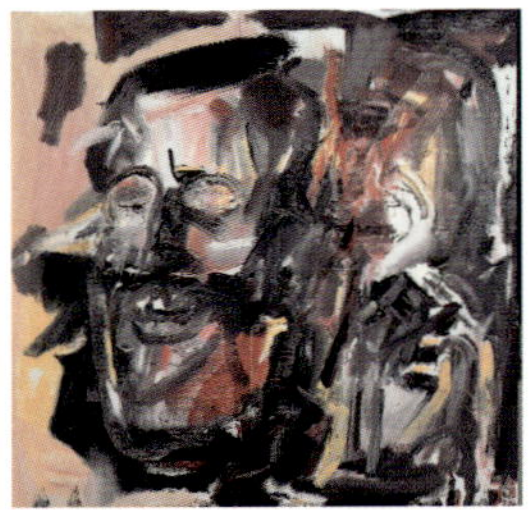

Brains on fire, page 133

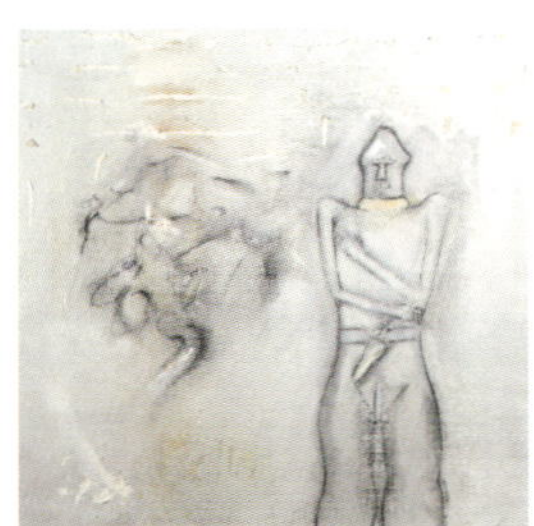

Celts, page 91

Brains on fire

There is a lot of black, white, and gray.

Yes. What it reminded me of in the end was a large face with some black hair, a big nose. A large face on the left of the picture, and then toward the right-hand side it explodes. To me the picture is less figurative. It becomes more abstract out of the right-hand side. And so I called the picture *Brains on fire.* You could imagine that the face on the left is maybe overworked, has got one of those moments when his brain has exploded or something. There is a lot of activity, a lot of excitement in that picture. I like the grays and black, and I like these pinks behind it, to cool it down a little bit, make it more delicate toward the left of the picture. A big fire up at the back there. Another thing I enjoy you can see in that fire, to the right of it: I have scraped off a bunch of paint with a palette knife. And it is as if I have put sticky tape on things, like when they wax women's legs and pull it off, and it reveals a millimeter beneath that layer. It is that sort of contrast. Just with a palette knife I lift off that thickness. I have done it there, too. I like that look, and then against some of the real paint.

For me one of the important things of your process is going back to the surface, the layers. It's something to do with painting on the surface of the world or surface of your thinking and feeling and breaking through layers.

Yes — different layers. I have a friend who is very interesting, a psychiatrist who says that all of the people he has met — and he has met some people who were so crazy they were like the devil or something, that you would think that they were bad people — he said that his theory was that as he peels off the layers of the onion, however many layers people have put over themselves, everybody underneath is benign and all these surface things are laid on by childhood, by abuse, by crises and stuff. That was quite reassuring to me. So the idea of layers is important, psychologically as well as with paint.

Some people think that if painters don't paint every day, it isn't right. But if you do paint every day and you don't enjoy it, or you don't paint well, I think it's probably better not to paint. I don't think there is any great heroic act in going in slavishly every day and saying, "I must do this." So what I find is that I do it when I am inspired. And it's how I can combine it with music. Some days the inspiration is a musical one, and other days it has just got to be painting.

Celts

Celtic images refer to pictures you have found?

I got the idea of looking into the Celts because the obvious question to me is, Where do I go back to? And I think the answer in my case is that I go back to the Irish, and to the Celts. So I started to read about the Celts. Of course, the history is very complicated and we tend to have a romantic view now about anything that is historical, but apparently some of the Celtic tribes were a pretty bad lot and were very warlike, but I don't really get heavily into the history; it is more of a romantic look at the past.

So I picked up a small book, *The Celts: First Masters of Europe,* that I happened to see, and I found this image of a statue that appears in this first picture. This is a statue found in Baden-Württemberg, and it is a life-size ithyphallic sandstone statue. So I was taken by that image. I just liked the look of that image; it excited me. In many ways it was phallic. The image itself is like a phallus, particularly the top of his little hat; it all looks very phallic there. And I noticed as I was painting it that the man has got an erection — fertility. In those days they used to have offerings to increase their fertility and the fertility of the crops, that was what was important. So I like the fact that they were not ashamed of erections. Thousands of years later we have come a long way, and yet a hundred years ago people were having their pictures confiscated because they showed an erection or pubic hair, like it didn't

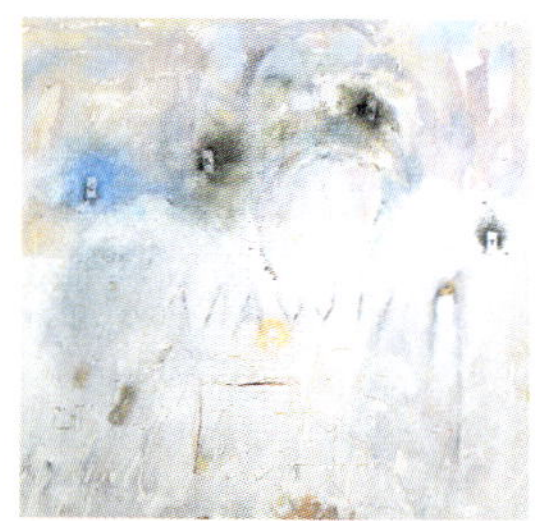

White Celts, page 90

"I don't think there is any great heroic act in going in slavishly every day and saying, 'I must do this.' So what I find is that I do it when I am inspired. And it's how I can combine it with music. Some days the inspiration is a musical one, and other days it has just got to be painting."

exist. So I am always happy to find that in ancient Tantric art or in Japanese prints or Celtic things they have no shame.

So I started with him, the statue, and started to just draw him in charcoal. And the thing with charcoal for me was, how to fix it? I had one method that was to get a fixing spray so it became stable, but another method I started to experiment with was using turpentine, which would move the particles of charcoal, the little specks of dust. The liquid would move them and do interesting things to them. So I kept this picture white, very pure, just drew the character pretty much straight from the thing, got an idea of the character, and to the left of the statue figure there is a symbolic thing from another story that I loved, and it carried me through this series.

The Celts didn't write their history: it was an oral tradition. They just spoke it to one another, but we don't know a lot about them. Most of what we know about them is from the Greeks and the Romans, who would visit them and write about it. I am not sure who it was, but a Roman writer was visiting the Celts and writing about them, and he described a scene with an old man. Because the Celts had an oral tradition, they prized eloquence, the art of being able to speak well and use words well; that was very important to them. So this image was of an old man in the middle of a group of figures, and he was the eloquent one and he had a ring in his tongue [that] was attached to the ears of his disciples, of his admirers. They had either a thin gold or an amber chain from his tongue to their ears, which was an incredibly modern, surreal image to me. It was an immediate, very visual image, tongues connected to ears, so symbolic — that is what I like about it, that you are scratching right through history going back thousands of years and you are finding something that is appealing to us today as a modern symbolic image. It is every bit as appealing as it must have been then.

They are interesting symbols because now you are connected with telephone lines, cordless.

That is what I mean. The idea fascinates me because we are so interested in the spoken word, the sound, and all of those years ago they chose this great way to symbolize it. Like a telephone line, cables, the whole world is connected.

This is wonderful, this reduced drawing.

Yes, it is very reduced, isn't it? I rubbed at it a bit to try to get a little bit of movement. This was the first thing I did in this series, so that started me off really in this Celtic vibe. And these straight from the tube, that became a theme, the way I did it here; I did a lot of them. It became a way to represent the sky with some lines.

These Celtic images are like a circle, because this is like continuing the white thing, the white part. That is more concentrated on the figure.

White Celts

I overpainted this. It was a figure of a horse in the middle there, which you can still just about see. But I wanted to overpaint it and get this white ghostly look, so it then started to turn into more like a wall of graffiti, scratchings on a wall. In the book it gives a very simple language of letters the Celts used for the Celtic inscriptions, in the Lepontic alphabet. So just for a bit of fun I worked out how I would do the word *Paul.* That actually says "Paul" in the middle of the picture, the *V* shapes. So it was like graffiti; the idea that the Celts wrote on walls, in caves, and so on. Then I was imagining myself as some guy messing around on a wall, and then I started to try and get something like a logo, as if imagining the Celts would do a logo. So I wrote the word *Celts* a lot and started to try to make it into a little logo, very minimalist. And I found this little set here, an antique sign-writing set that I picked up in an antique shop, with all the numbers and all the letters.

It is interesting, the contents of the picture, because when we talked yesterday we didn't know our signs for our letters.

These are our words, and these are their signs.

It is a good conception.

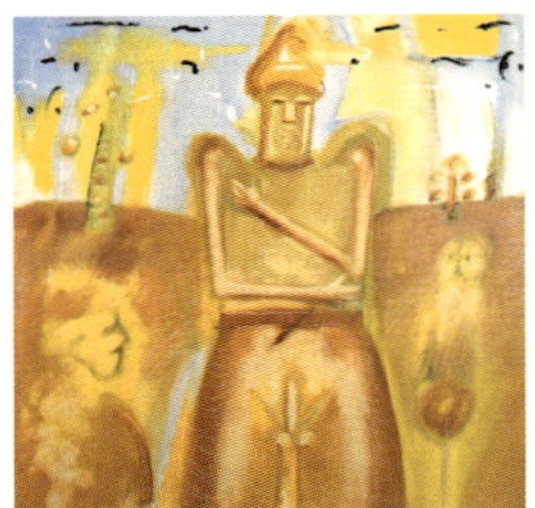

Yellow Celt, page 93

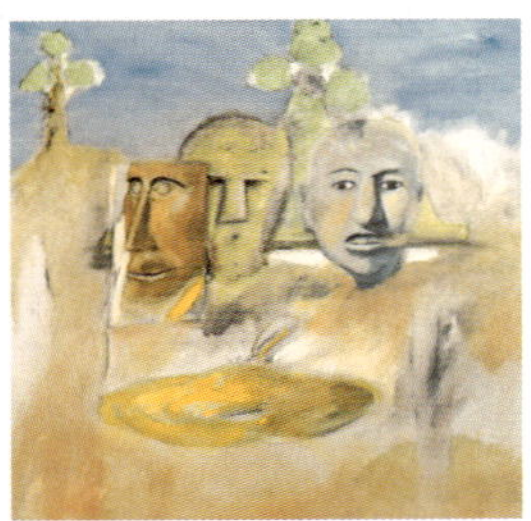

Ancient connections, page 89

Yellow Celt

This is another representation of the statue from the first picture, which started the Celtic series. I like this statue: I like the skinny arms; I like the erection, the fat thighs, the strange little hat; and I like his face. And the dagger in this one gets a little bit more symbolic; his dagger just becomes a line, instead of a knife there. And I used rubbing-out in this, on the arms; that is rubbed back to the canvas. It is a nice way of getting highlights there. It looks like this is a shiny shoulder, with that little rubbing-out on the arms. So I put him in a landscape. The others had not been in landscapes yet, so I put him in a horizon and made some symbolic trees, which are these things here.

It comes back on one of the other pictures.

Yes, and then a couple of other things happened around him. To the left of him there is a strange figure. I wanted to convey religious mysticism, with the statue having something to do with fertility and so on. So when I started thinking about these people and how they might have lived, I imagined they might have been priests, like the equivalent of our modern bishops, things like that. So he seemed a little bit like that to me. He has got a strange little face, but I quite like it. It seemed to me like he was wearing bishop's gowns or something, and then his hair became very un-bishoppy, more like a punk rocker. So I was quite happy with him, a mysterious little figure. You don't really know what he is doing. But it suggests to me religion, which I think would have crept into the civilization at some point or another — probably fairly important, as it was in those old civilizations. And then to the other side of the figure, on the right, an owl appeared, so I made it look like he is trying to fly, with his wings either up or down. There is movement in his wings, and he is perched on a golden or brass orb or sphere. They use that kind of thing in Parliament a lot; they have a sphere and a rod. These things get handed down.

Then I put them in a landscape, and while the paint was still wet, I put some thumbprints on. I quite like this. If I like them, I leave them.

Ancient connections

So — starting in the center with the Celtic face, the symbolic Celtic face . . . That is like a mouth.

That was one of the pittings in the stone. I was drawn to that little mouth thing; it is like a funny expression. To the left of it is another piece from the book, another face, which reminded me of Charlie Watts of the Rolling Stones. He looks rather like that.

Is he so old?

He is older.

It is a very sharp cut.

It was something about the mouth and the nose that reminded me. So I imagined that that was another tribe: the Celtic man was one tribe, and this was another tribe. And these were the connections between all the ancient civilizations, but as the painting started to develop, the one on the right started to look quite modern, so I think of him as a more modern face, with these ancient connections in the background there. The rod almost goes through his mouth, like a cigar or something; it comes out of his mouth. So that is quite nice, pretty.

It is delicate, gets a lot of form here.

A little bit of pencil there, rather than charcoal, and then this shape here I painted as a cymbal, a drum cymbal. Like a joke. With all this talk of symbolism, symbols, symbolic, finally I had to put a cymbal in there. For one of these ancients to play. A couple of symbolic trees in the background.

Why did you take three heads? It looks like three really different heads: the one in the middle is very reduced, the one from the side is a profile, and this is more detailed.

It is really an idea of the tribes being connected by something, the thread or the rod that connects us all. So he is us now, this is us in ancient times, this is middle times or before;

they are all different peoples, all joined with a similar idea.

You know, whereas there was always a mechanical universe, this is the random chaotic universe. That is definitely what they are thinking about now. There is something that appeals to me about random things. I often use it in music, too, just throw some elements together and stand back and look at how they are joined to each other.

Do you remember in music where you used the random principle?

Yes, in some new stuff I'm writing, particularly. But, for instance, in the Beatles, the orchestral surge in "Day in the Life" was random principle. That was from telling the musicians that they should start at the lowest note on their instrument and progress to the highest note on their instrument over twenty-three bars of music, but at their own speed. If they wanted to, they could sit back for the rest of the time, or they could spin it out; it was up to them completely. That was the random element, and that is why it's such a powerful noise. Random is powerful, but is well established, too; it is not like it is anything new. For pop music it is new, bringing it in was a bit avant-garde for that time, but it worked well within the context of a strong pop song.

Shark on Georgica, page 107

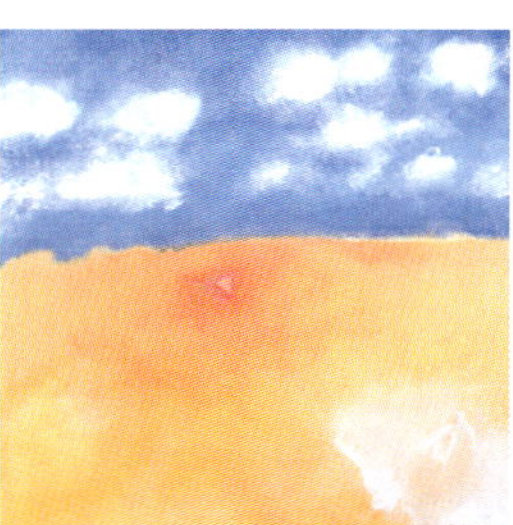

Red triangle sand, page 105

Red triangle sand

This is painted on Long Island; it is three years old.

It is a beach, sand; it looks like skin, too.

This is just a "summer in Long Island" feeling; this would have been painted after a visit to the beach in the morning. It looks like a beautiful day. When I am swimming, I just look around and I always like that horizon out there; it is a very low horizon, because it is really a big sand spit; Long Island is just a big piece of sand, a sandbar. I am always fascinated by the color of the sand, so this is a very simple picture. The red thing is really to break it up, just to give it something else. It would be a bit boring without it, so the red is a point of interest, really.

It gives a different meaning to this association, an ochre brown and a skin color.

Yes, it could almost be a torso lying down, with that as a nipple or something. I didn't think that, but I see it now [that] you mention it. That is an old tradition, isn't it? With people like Bill Brandt, the photographer — nudes as landscapes.

You know his work?

Just a little through Linda.

Shark on Georgica

There is a large pond in East Hampton on Long Island where I kept a little sailboat. People sail on this pond and it is a very wonderful place and there are lots of big houses around it. This is a very rough representation of the pond; it doesn't really look like this, but there is an area over to the right where I start from, this right-hand bottom corner, and I sail out here and up to there, which is the sand spit.

So this would be me on a sailboat; the red piece is me on a sailboat, and it goes down there — Spielberg has a house in the left-hand corner. Calvin Klein has a house rather near the blue object, which looked to me like a shark. So this is a very posh residential area where rich people live, and the idea that there might be a shark in the pond is amusing. A shark on Georgica — that is a joke, that is the last thing you'd ever hear. The sharks you might get out there in the real sea — up there in Montauk they do actually get sharks. So this is me on the red. I sail up there; I nearly always park there, go for a swim, go for a run along here, come back, and bring the sailboat back. It is a very beautiful summer activity for me, very private. A small fifteen-foot Sunfish, it is a very basic boat, a little boat, and I have had many great summer memories.

Do you have a house there?

No, we don't, actually. The Eastmans have a

house here in East Hampton, but we visit every year, so this is a memory.

There is some nice movement; I like the movement in the water. It almost looks like sperm or something. So to me it works on a couple of levels, so that I can just remember my sailing: that I know I started off here. I came off here. I hit the wind there always; it is shallow here, and I'd sometimes go past Calvin Klein's or Spielberg's and wave and say, "Hey, Cal, be a pal, get us a drink." And he never comes out. I do sometimes wave up to their houses and have an amusing moment for myself: there is me in my little boat, and they are big rich people. It reminds me of when I was a little kid. I like that because I don't like formality, and you know that with money, you can get formality. So I have little tricks like this that allow me to go down there and get my boat out. A childhood thing.

I think the sky looks quite nice there; there is a nice sky effect, and the sea is quite effective. Some kind of light in the sky, and the sea looks a bit sealike; the color is quite good.

When I look at the pictures, I do feel that they are painted in the summer.

These are definitely summer pictures. And it's the same fascination with just the sand. You see in the summer there, the good thing is that life simplifies, and there isn't much more to life than sand, water, sky. So that is why it crops up a lot.

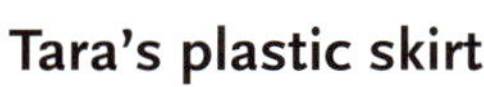

Tara's plastic skirt

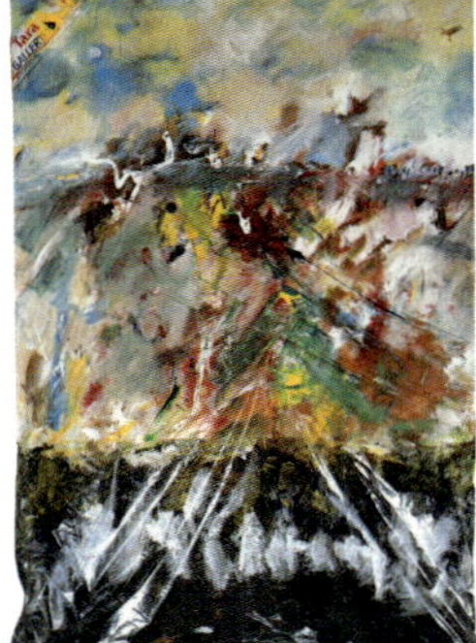

Tara's plastic skirt, page 76

The picture with the plastic sheet.

Yes, I am always going around art shops to see if there are any canvases or paints that interest me. I like shopping; it is nice. There is this particular shop I go to that has this Tara Gallery Wrap, which is a commercial canvas. Because it wraps around. And I had seen a Rothko painting at my father-in-law's house in New York, and I was looking at it from the side and I noticed that he had painted around the sides of the canvas and not framed it, and I thought that was a good idea. So I was looking for wraparound canvases and I found them in this shop in Arizona, in the West. And normally you just used to take the plastic off to put on the floor to stop spoiling the floor. And I would normally take the Tara sign off, but I started playing around with this because as I got the wrap halfway off, I thought this might be quite nice to have a skirt on a painting, a little bit of Christo, a little bit like wrapping something. I thought it would be nice, instead of leaving the plastic all over it, to expose some of the canvas and work on that normally but then just keep dropping paint down behind the plastic and making the plastic stick. So that is what I did with this one.

I would work on the top bit and then occasionally throw bits of paint behind the plastic and stick it up. And [I] started to work on the front of the plastic to get these pleats and these folds in it, which just gave it a more lively surface. The idea would be to hang it on a white wall so that the skirt would hang down, looking almost like a dress: a canvas with a frock on. So it developed into a kind of experimental landscape piece. With the canvas in my mind, the sky, and all this stuff being the foreground, it looks quite violent, quite chaotic.

I used to have a very good friend in the sixties, who was the son of the Irish Guinness family, the son called Tara. He came up to Liverpool on a visit with me, and that's how we knew each other. He came round to my house in London a lot, and we would sit and talk and get a bit stoned together and he was a really nice friend. It was very sad that he died in a car accident in London. Many people often thought the words to the Beatles song "Day in the Life" — "He blew his mind out in a car" — was about Tara. I don't think it was, but I have heard that John even thought it was. Since John was half writer of that song, it may be true.

So when I was leaving the plastic on, I thought I would leave the sticker on because it had this nice name that I like, the name Tara. So that became a little tribute to him in the top left-

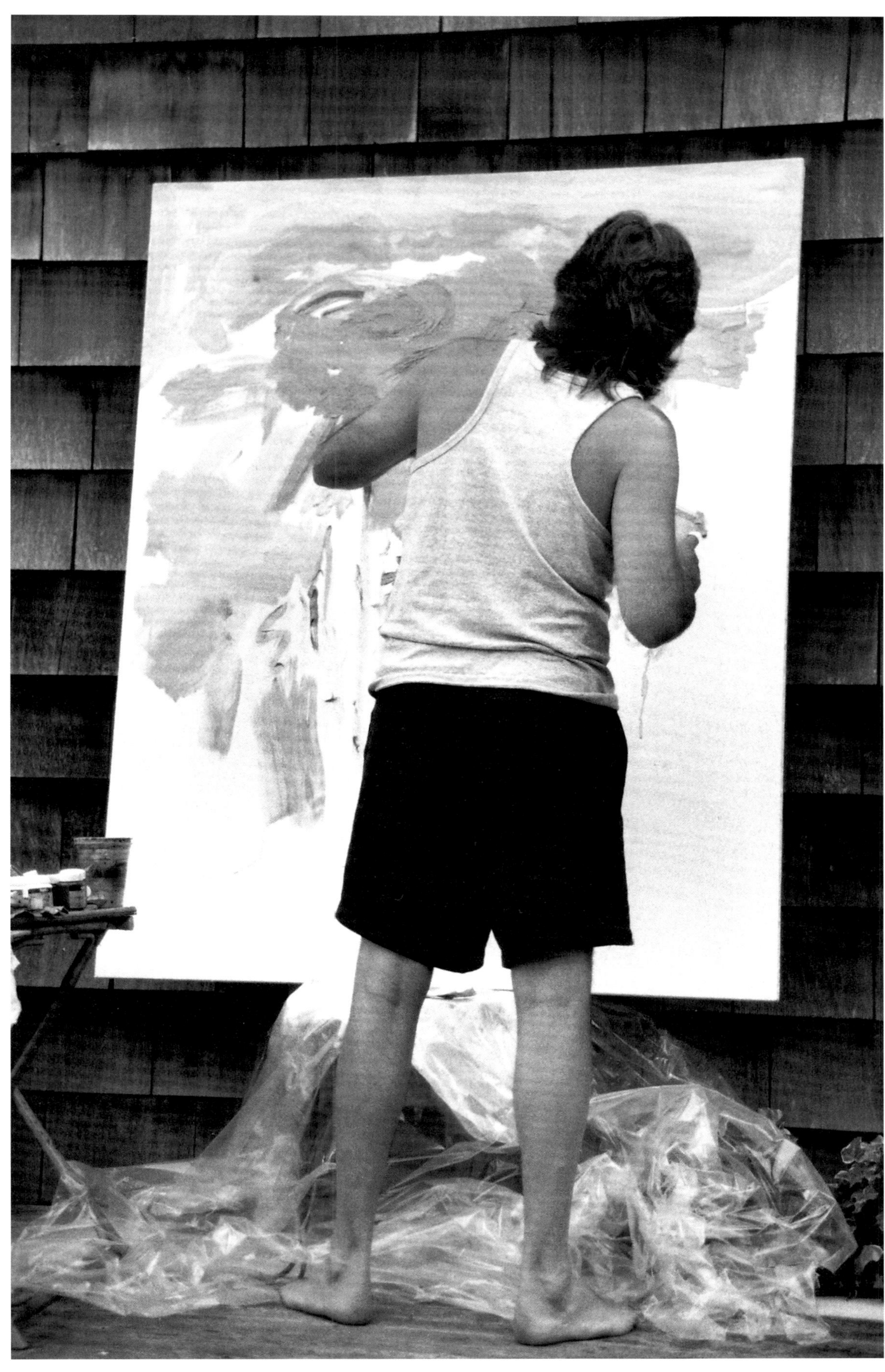

Paul – Long Island painting
East Hampton, 1990

"I would have liked to have been able to do this in the early days, but my attempts at this have shown me that you have really got to learn the process, you have just got to learn it; there is no substitute for time. You know, I said to you before, when I used to ask painters what their advice would be, it was 'Paint more.' And it was the best advice."

hand corner, and I signed it up in the middle so it almost became part of the landscape.

This signing is very integrated in the picture, and the level where the sheet begins looks like a horizon in the picture and then comes a second surface, like a relief.

It is almost like a perspective thing, like it is coming toward you where the relief begins.

It wouldn't be good if it was only a painted sheet, but there is a second meaning in this picture. The picture comes out into reality, like a symbol of a picture, like we talked about. It is one of the elements of your style to play with surface, going under the surface.

Yes, this was a way of getting a lively surface without putting on masses and masses of paint.

This picture is very modern.

Because my whole thing over the years has been an experiment, it is all one giant experiment, really. And because I am so interested in stuff that other people do, I am sometimes influenced. Linda asked a painter the other day who he was influenced by, and he said, "I am influenced by everything."

It is an enormous and very interesting way of painting, when you see your first pictures, the horses and the ships.

Very figurative, straightforward.

It is really coming out.

I would have liked to have been able to do this in the early days, but my attempts at this have shown me that you have really got to learn the process, you have just got to learn it; there is no substitute for time. You know, I said to you before, when I used to ask painters what their advice would be, it was "Paint more." And it was the best advice.

Sometimes we can see if you paint in the USA on holiday, the pictures are much lighter, and bigger; every picture is a part of your life, and it is a process.

I think it affects you where you are. It is like recordings, recording a moment, a feeling; it is like taking a snapshot of your inside.

Black scratch I

I like this picture more and more.

It grows on you.

Yes, it grows.

I like that; it is a great compliment if it can grow. I was saying before with the last picture, [Red triangle sand], that there was no idea in my mind when I painted it. With this one I did have a definite idea. Sometimes I would wake up in the morning with some kind of an image, and here I was imagining something like a prison wall with scratches on it. Somebody had scratched maybe trying to climb out or something, but I imagined three or four fingers scratching down. I imagined three first of all, just these scratches, and the image I had was of a completely black canvas. But I wondered whether I would get a little bit bored with completely black, and sure enough I did. As I was starting out putting black in there, I started to want a bit of blue in there, too. And in the end this big blue phallic shape here emerged.

So I let that happen and did the picture, which was mainly a black canvas but with this big blue shape. I was working the blue into the black first of all, to try and get a bluey black, rather than just a straight black, but then the blue took on its own shape. It wanted to not just be part of the black, it wanted to be separate. So I allowed it to be. I said, "All right blue, you shall do what you want to do," and so this big phallic shape came in the middle of it and a couple of little spirals. And then eventually once it was drying as a finished thing, I took my fingers and just scratched down on the paint, like trying to climb out of a room, to get back to my original thought, the scratch idea.

It is like a curtain in front of the picture.

And there is almost a figure walking here in the center, and the blue, the classical figure with a little head. This I suppose must remind me of a great penis. . . .

Or an asshole . . .

Yes, also this could look like someone bend-

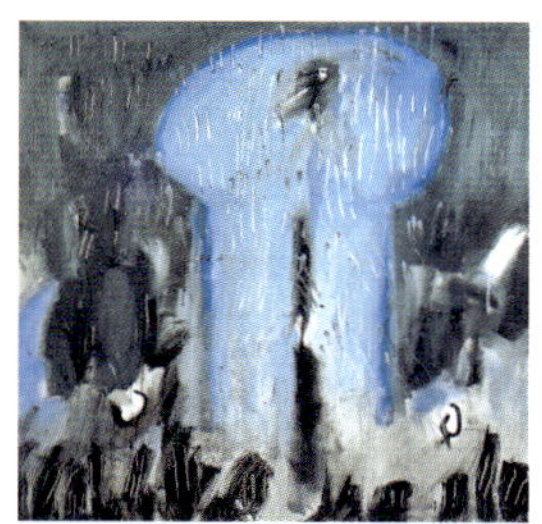
Black scratch I, page 73

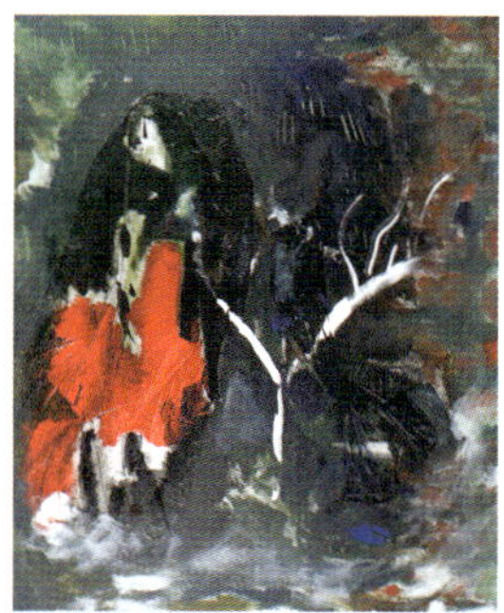
Black scratch II, page 74

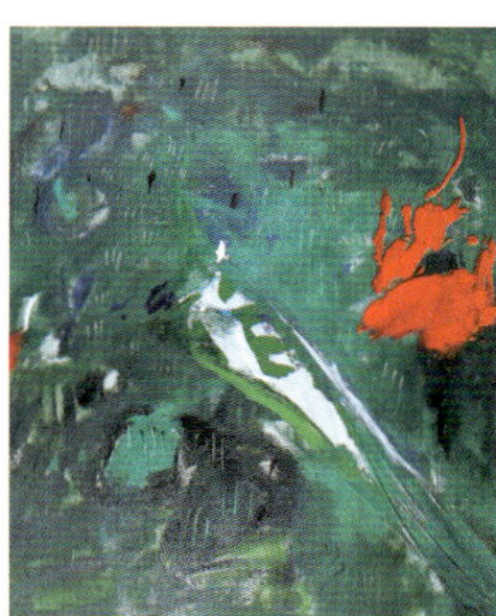
Black scratch III, page 75

ing down, facing away from you. I don t have any definite interpretation myself; the original idea was just to paint something and then scratch my fingers down it, almost like an animal, clawing at it. It is quite a definite idea, the scratching.

Black scratch II

Holed with green plastic. It gives the red a strange color, high gloss.

Yes, that was what I liked the plastic for. Again this was the same idea; these canvases are commercially made and they normally come in clear plastic. So as I was pulling the clear plastic off, I kept a couple of little sheets that had a lot of static in them, and they stuck. Electric. So they were naturally trying to stick to everything.

I started off doing a black canvas, but as I expected, I got a little bit bored. So to me those scratches seem to show desperation, like an animal. I don't know. Anyway, I got bored with just the black and introduced some other colors into the black: greens and blues and reds, just to make it non-black, just a dark mixture of color. Then the red got the plastic on it, and I liked the high gloss on it, like a very high varnish.

The canvas looks enclosed, or covered by a sheet; it looks like another material. Like islands within the picture that have another surface, the sheet makes drainage, little traces.

Strange little things, yes. It is like a natural thing that happened, really, as if the plastic blew up against it and I decided to include it. But I like the gloss, the gloss on the red; and the blue I just tried painting over, which lost a lot of the gloss.

I think in some pictures you are looking for random things to give them a structure in the picture.

And this white piece here is actually a branch, a mesquite branch, a piece of wood I found, and I liked its *Y* shape. It is in a couple of the other pictures.

And why did you tear the picture?

It was an accident, the hole was an accident, and at first I was disappointed. I thought I had ruined the canvas. It was just an accident. Someone moving the blank canvas made a hole in it, but I liked it. I know people like Fontana make holes, but I didn't want to copy him. But with the plastic over it, it was quite nice because it isn't actually a hole anymore: the hole is behind the plastic. It was quite nice, a window-through-to-another-world kind of thing. So that was another *Black scratch*.

Black scratch III

With green plastic. It is painted green. It's nice to feel. See me, feel me . . .

It is tactile.

This left-hand corner, I like the combination: the green is changing here; the blue, it's flowing.

This big fella to the right-hand corner there. The red was from the previous picture, the attraction of this varnish, this high-gloss thing. As you look at the picture, as you walk past it, certain little bits just reflect. Like a mirror.

Splashing the color.

I took these pieces of paper, and they were static. It is very light stuff, and a few little bits hang off.

And again you remember why you scratched here, but you have a special concept, a reason for the scratching?

No, I just woke up with idea. This all came from the idea of the black canvas, and I had just seen three black scratches as an idea. I don't know why; it was just an image in my mind. It reminded me of prison. It reminded me of IRA prisoners. I had then seen these three scratches as an idea. You may have seen that Richard Hamilton has done a couple of pictures. The IRA prisoners used to paint with their own shit on the wall. They used to put it all over the wall as an act of rebellion. They used to say, "You can't keep us in prison, but if you do, we will just shit and put it all over the wall," as a rebellious act. And something in my mind connected with the scratches.

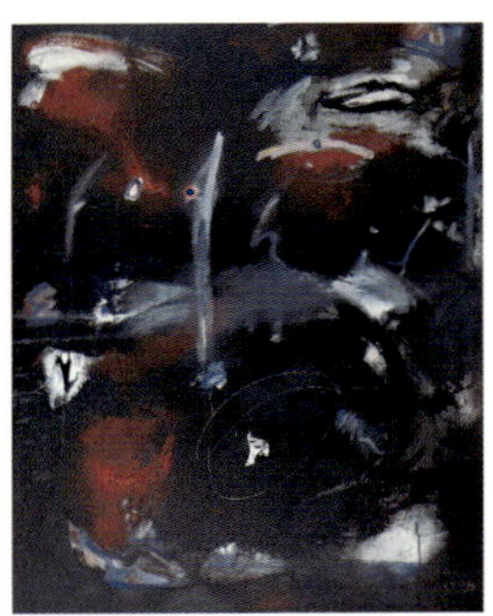

Black singer, page 95

Black singer

I had never done very dark canvases. If you look at my early canvases, there is not a lot of dark stuff, so I started to get the feeling that it would be nice to have the paint coming out of the black, like a night scene. So this started just to be a dark canvas, just to be black. The reds are mixed in the black, as you see. It is very dark brown in the left-hand corner, and the black is not one black but moves between different kinds. And, as usual, I was just enjoying the paint as it came on, and the intention was just to kill the canvas, the black canvas, but I started to see little things — like that *E* shape there. And I realize that you cannot actually see it; in fact, I am only just seeing it now, but I started to get letters in it — E, F, G, H, I, J, K. Almost M. There was no particular reason for that, except I started with the E and decided to carry it through as a little thing but to not make it too obvious. In fact, I have only just noticed it again. I don't think you notice it immediately. It's a bit like the alphabet going across there, the words and civilization and writing and so on, but the blackness itself is less civilized; it is more cosmic. So finally as I was finishing it, it looked like a big face. It started to look like eyes, and I started to put a big face in it. So I scratched the lip and had it then as a black singer. It really then turned out to be a big portrait of a blues singer.

And at the bottom of the picture there are three holes looking through into the world.

Yes, it looks like a sea view almost. These things just happened, and there is another one here underneath the I, J. That looks like the sky or something. And if ever the paint happens to form into a surprise shape — for example, that is a wet area that has just done a nice thing that looks like it's rounded, and it has got itself a nice little edge. I didn't do that; that would have done itself. If ever that happens, I then just stop and get off that area because there is something magical I am trying to keep, just as you say, to see through. . . . You can read it quite a few ways. I first of all saw that E, and I realized that it has a string of letters. It is like in the lyrics from "Across the Universe" — John's lyrics — "words are flying out like endless rain into a paper cup" — across the universe. Some image very similar to that: words spilling out. It has a little bit of that feeling to me, like letters dancing across the universe.

Unfinished symphony

This relates to the couple of other pictures where I use musical things. There is one called *C minor* and one called *Key of F,* and it was an idea I had to take something I knew very well in music, a chord, and try and paint the feeling it gave me. So *C minor* might be a rather lonely-looking picture because it can be a bit of a sad chord. This came on from those ideas, but this was then to try and paint a whole symphony. The whole thing rather than one chord; a musical explosion; an orchestra playing something. Abstract rather than specific. So for that I just applied a lot of paint and smudged it around and had a lot of fun with it.

This picture has so many different greens and different structure. It is like you had a lot of chaotic things and then you have parts that are calm, like a little concept.

Well, you know, one of my big inspirations is nature. I love nature and I love what it does. If you go down on the seashore and watch the water, see what it does to the sand, it bubbles up and goes back — what you could call chaos. And yet it's so beautiful, it leaves beautiful marks on the sand. I kind of trust to that, and that is a large part of painting abstracts — to try and think of myself as nature itself, without a mind, a sophisticated mind that knows how to play a piano or drive a car . . .

It is very spontaneous, I don't think there was a lot of thinking about that. But, you know, my composition generally is spontaneous. Some people I talk to will ask, "Do you do sketches

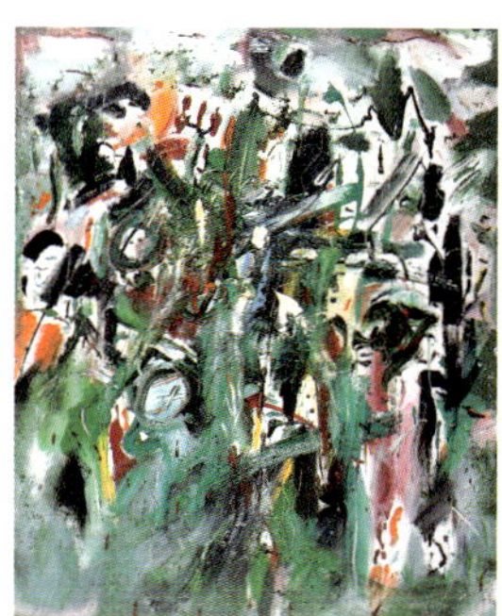

Unfinished symphony, page 77

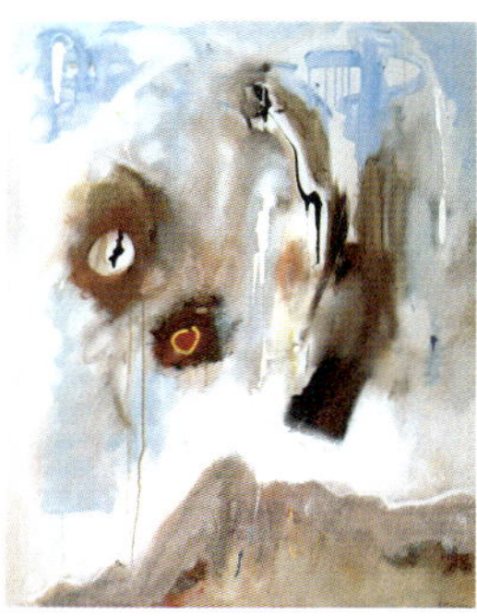

Pintos in the sky with desert poppy, page 2

beforehand?" And I will say, "No, it is alla prima." You know, I just love to play around with the paint and let the paint show me the way, and I sense they are not as impressed if they think I did it spontaneously. So I had thought once or twice of making sketches after I had done the painting. Do little sketches, show shapes, rub them out and change them, and say, "Oh yes, these are preparatory sketches."

I think most often, as we have said before, I enjoy shopping in art supply shops. There are certain stores that I like to go in. I don't like clothes shops so much, but I like hardware stores, looking at nails and hammers. I just like it. It smells nice.

I told you when I was a kid, in English schools there was always a cupboard where they kept the paper and the pencils and the supplies for the school, and the notebooks. And when they'd say, "McCartney, get the pencils out," or something, whenever I went in that cupboard, I had an overwhelming feeling of wanting to steal it all. I just wanted it. Plain paper. I just wanted it. Whereas if I was going into a kitchen and there were some chocolate biscuits, I might not be interested. But paper, plain blank paper, just the dreams it conjured up with me, and pencils, boxes of new pencils. I never did steal anything, but I still get that feeling if I go in a cupboard, like a school cupboard like that — I think I could steal things.

So what I was getting round to was that art supply shops remind me of the same thing; all these beautiful materials, and nobody has done anything with them yet.

Pintos in the sky with desert poppy

This picture has a lot of white in it. It isn't typical of your pictures to use so much white.

Or let the canvas come through, for the white. This is American; it was painted in America as well.

On holiday?

Yes, it is always holiday unless I am touring or something. It is nearly always holiday when I paint in America. So I feel free and in a good mood.

So the blue is the sky — just playing around with the sky — and Linda and I were both riding out in the desert and in the mountains quite a lot, and we rode pintos. *Pinto* means "paint" in Spanish. They are the ones with the big brown marks on their bodies, white and brown. So this was about the color of the pintos, that brown flying in the sky there, just above the mountains at the bottom. That is typical of the color of the horses, so it was nice, after having brushed the horse, having been there brushing its brown, to come in and paint a similar color, to play around and find a similar color, just because I had just seen it.

And the other thing that was striking on our rides round there . . . it was the time of year when you would see a poppy, the desert flower. And at a certain time of year in the desert, it blooms, and you will see these. Normally it is greens and browns, and then you will see, occasionally, a shock of red like someone has spilled some paint.

There is an organic accent in the picture here.

Yes, like a highlight. And then those mountains, those were the kind of hills we were riding in. And from then on it's just enjoying the surface of the canvas, doing a bit of Blendini here and there, and then as you say, using the white freely to get some space.

I like this picture. You have droppings and brushstrokes; that is a very courageous part of painting because it has to work within a composition. And it works. This here, the sky, it is a contrast here. That is form and that is form, the white contrasts with the brown, and the white again. Everything you do refers to another thing you do, in this picture. This picture has a lot of emotion and motion.

Yes, like looking through clouds in the sky. . . . It also looks a bit like a dollar sign. It has a slight graphic look to it, that little bit. But it has no significance.

The idea for me is that I'm not supposed to

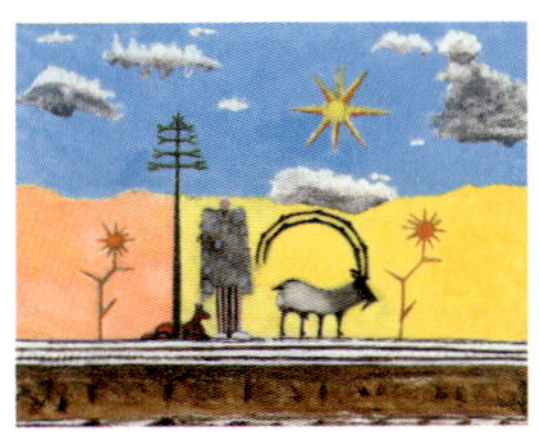

Egypt station, page 84

leave anything I don't like. That is how I like to paint when there is something happening. Like the surface of that white there; the rough surface of that against the smooth surface looks like water swelling, or air. It looks like a texture, and this has got the same kind of texture but it is more blended.

You are a very experienced painter because I can feel how you are painting. You paint this, you have it on the brush, and then you do this accent. It is like a net over this; everything makes a cross-reference to another thing.

I think that with all the stuff we are talking about, I can tell a lot of stories about what it is and what I think it is, but I think in the end it is really down to just having some paints, and being allowed to put them on this rather splendid white canvas is a luxury; at least, it seems a luxury to me. One good thing for me is that with painting, unlike music, I haven't yet been criticized for it. Until I have my first exhibition, it is a very private thing. So . . .

You have been criticized for your music but not for your painting.

When I do a piece of music, I am used to people saying, "Oh, I like it," or "I don't like it." I am used to somebody having an opinion on it, and it can somehow erode your pleasure in having done it. It is like giving birth to a baby, and then you have got to show it to everyone and sometimes you can be a bit jealous about that. You are proud to show it off but you lose a little innocence, a little something that was in your heart, and you have to give it to other people. It is life, you know. But for me it is so important to enjoy painting, and that is why I don't really do it unless I feel like it.

Egypt station

My original inspiration was similar to a picture we were talking about the other day, with Egyptian symbols and shapes from looking at a reference book on Egypt. I was interested in the way they drew sunflowers, and two appear on the left and on the right. It was a nice shape, so I took that and then I love the way they symbolize trees.

It is a special kind of tree. It is called a *Lebensbaum* in Germany, the tree of life.

It is a cedar tree, I think. I like the way they reduce the tree to just some very simple symbols. And as I say, I use this kind of idea later on in the Celtic pictures, where the trees are quickly drawn. This is the basic symbol I based that on. So I put the tree and the sunflowers in; and then the sun is another symbol that I took, and then the ibex, the animal there with the long horns. I loved its horns. I think it is called an ibex. It's an antelope, a gazelle, or something. This sitting dog was another Egyptian shape. So I seated them there, and why I called it *Egypt station* was because it looked like a station, like train lines at the bottom, and underneath that, the edge of the platform. In fact, that was taken from a piece of pottery.

The platform?

It looked like the platform of a train station. But this is just a bit of design on the rim of some pottery. That is what it is taken from. And then the landscape is the actual landscape of where I was. The sky and the clouds in the sky were the actual patterns: a very strange pattern of clouds, but they are very accurate, quite an accurate picture of how the clouds were that day, and so I just copied them. And then the man — originally done by James, my son. When he was very young, he would occasionally do little pencil drawings on canvases; he had done a little pencil drawing of this man, and I liked it so much that I filled it in. So he was actually James's, that guy, but I painted it in.

It looks like a coat covered with balloons.

Yes, it is an interesting coat, that, like a jacket with little striped trousers, pink hair. Again that was another thing that came from the music: you had to decide what your attitude to that was, whether you would say, "No, please, you must listen to the words I have written," or say, "No, I love the variation you have got." There was a famous Beatle line from "Strawberry Fields" that says, "Living is easy with eyes closed," which is one good statement, i.e., it isn't so easy when you open your eyes and stop ignoring things. But I have a friend who always thought that it was "Living is easy with nice clothes" — and we loved that! There is something wonderful about that! Well, I think that is just as good a statement, although it isn't the one that we started off with; it is a mutation.

Some people don't like that. They would see it as misinterpretation; I see it as more interpretation.

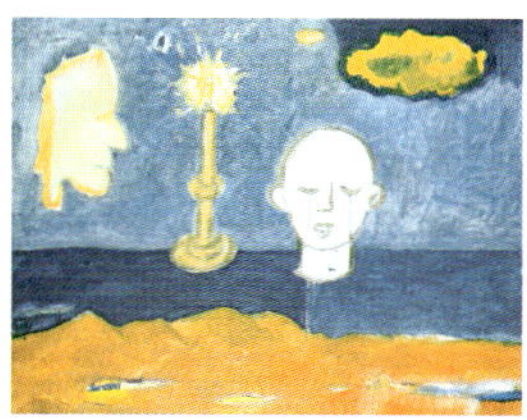

White dream, page 25

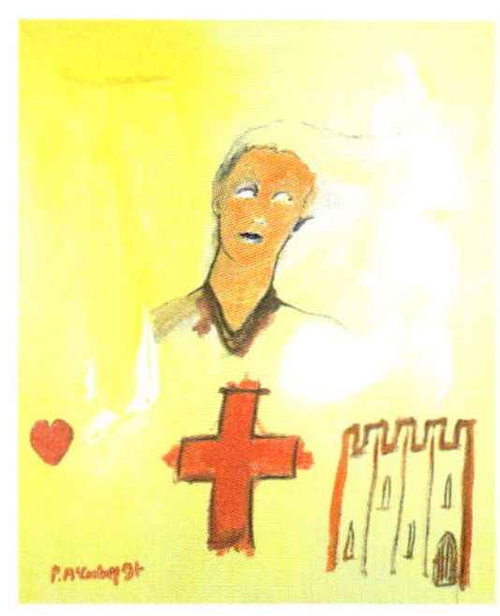

Linda yellow red cross, page 85

Linda yellow red cross

From 1991. She looks a little bit like a nurse.

I think that is probably because the red cross immediately makes you think medical, of nursing.

. . . medical and medieval.

I would say, you know, this is me enjoying experimenting with charcoal and pencil. I used to not use charcoal. I used to just sketch with paint and work it up with paint. Whenever I made a line in charcoal and put yellow on it, it would dirty the yellow, so it was a technical problem that I didn't enjoy having. So this is trying to deal with that originally. I have just sketched some items there that seemed to me to go together.

To me it is a very English picture because that red cross is also the cross of St. George. You know, Scotland has its design, its cross. Northern Ireland has a cross, and this is the English one, which is a red cross on a white background, so with that and the kind of castle keep, it seems to me to suggest a very English thing. But it also has the medical connotations and, as you said, medieval, old English. And then this red cross and the heart, also to do with medical. Maybe that makes Linda.

White dream

One of the things I love about painting, if I am in the mood, is creating an illusion. Just making a dream come to life. It is one thing to have images in your mind that flash through, like in dreams, a memory of something you thought of the other day, something that has been worrying you, an image made from a half glance in a shop window. So I enjoy occasionally doing this kind of surrealist thing, since you don't find white faces like this floating above coastal landscapes. The face itself was sketched, not painted. You can see I have used a gray, very wet, a rough gray color with a lot of turps in it, just to map out the shape of the head.

There is a rhythm to the painting in the sky, the brushstrokes. Instead of just filling it in as one big plain color I have left brushstrokes visible so there is movement in there. Then the candle around it appears to give off some kind of light that lights the face to the left, which is like Indian Joe or somebody. It is like a carved head of an Indian. For me there is no particular meaning in these objects, but of course, once you have placed them next to each other like this, the viewer makes a meaning for it. I have called it *White dream* because of the white face, because it is dreamy, and because it is a little bit of a joke on a wet dream. White dream, wet dream. So that is the joke of the title.

It will be interesting to see what interpretations other people would put on this. The candle, you can see, has some kind of religious meaning. It looks like a church candle; it looks gold and substantial, and the teary face could be sadness, mystical, Indian. I don't interpret my dreams, they just happen. I recognize their existence; I don't know what they are for, but they are for something.

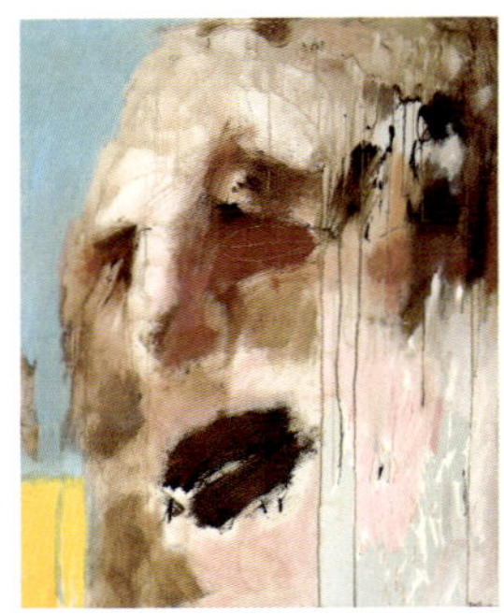

Big mountain face, page 63

Big mountain face

I think of it as *Big mountain face* because to me it looks like the side of a mountain, somewhere you could climb up if you had the right gear. So it is a big monumental face. The whole of the canvas is taken up by this face.

I like this brown; it is burnt umber and siennas.

I like these earth colors. I like what happens when you water them down a bit, the nice earth colors. I know I have said it before, but soil and the earth are very important to me. Living on a farm, a love of nature as a kid, so it should be important. It is all over the whole surface of our planet, which makes it pretty important, really. So these colors attract me.

And this picture is very courageous because it looks dark, muddy, as if you went over the picture with your footprints.

Yes, roughed it up a bit. It was very free. Those for me are the best times of painting, and it isn't always possible to be free. I think there are so many constraints on us in life, like maybe with your mood; you will just come with a tight mood to a canvas. But this is one that I enjoyed, being very loose and very free and just letting it take me somewhere. And it took me to this great big face. Which is very loosely painted; the mouth is two big brushstrokes. And all this in the right-hand corner, the browns.

It is the McCartney style, it is drainage. I think we talked about this picture being like the face in the mountain.

Yes, like in Mount Rushmore, the monumental faces of the American presidents. It's as if someone has carved this great big face on the side of the mountain.

For me it is a very fast picture. That is a fantastic thing with pictures: because they hang on the wall, you can see the process and how color came and flew out, and it is like a collection of different moods.

It was painted out West, in America, and it was painted very quickly. It's a very fast picture with a lot of liquid, a lot of fluid in it, which caused all the draining in it. Being a farmer, I am interested in drainage.

Do you work in the fields sometimes?

Yes, you have got to be careful with drainage in fields, or you get flooded areas. As I say, when I moved to live on a farm, I really got to appreciate how water drains, how a stream ends up.

One thing I have learned, not just about painting, but in life in general, is that the more precise you try to be about a thing, somehow the less you achieve. You can get too wooden. It can all get very tight, and you can lose the spirit of the thing. I have learned that. Just for instance, the eye on that boxer: to just put three lines like that will actually do a better job than really figuratively working that in and doing the eyelashes and putting a little eyeball in. Somehow these very casual quick little lines indicate a much more precise effect. They get a much more precise effect than spending four hours and getting a really precision-drawn thing. Somehow they seem to awaken echoes, those little half-glimpsed moments.

And then maybe by random it becomes meaning, like the little brown things there, like drips or something.

And all the drainage here, all the dripping here. If he is a boxer, then this is all the sweat and the effort. If he isn't a boxer, then it is a big mountain face and that is water draining as it would, down the mountain face.

You remember that is a human face but you remember the earth and water, so it is a very elemental picture.

It is one of my favorites. It just seemed to work. The left eye as we look at the picture, on the left-hand side, that line is just enough.

I enjoy applying paint to canvas, so as those little bits round the side are still canvas, I can still keep applying paint! You know, we used to have a guy who drove us and he loved the open road like I love canvas, and he used to say, "Oh, I love it, still two hundred miles to go." He wasn't one of those people who wanted to be home quickly. He loved it when there were still two hundred miles left. For me I can equate that to the canvas. I love it when there is still a little bit of canvas left to play with.

Paul – Long Island
brushstroke
East Hampton, 1990

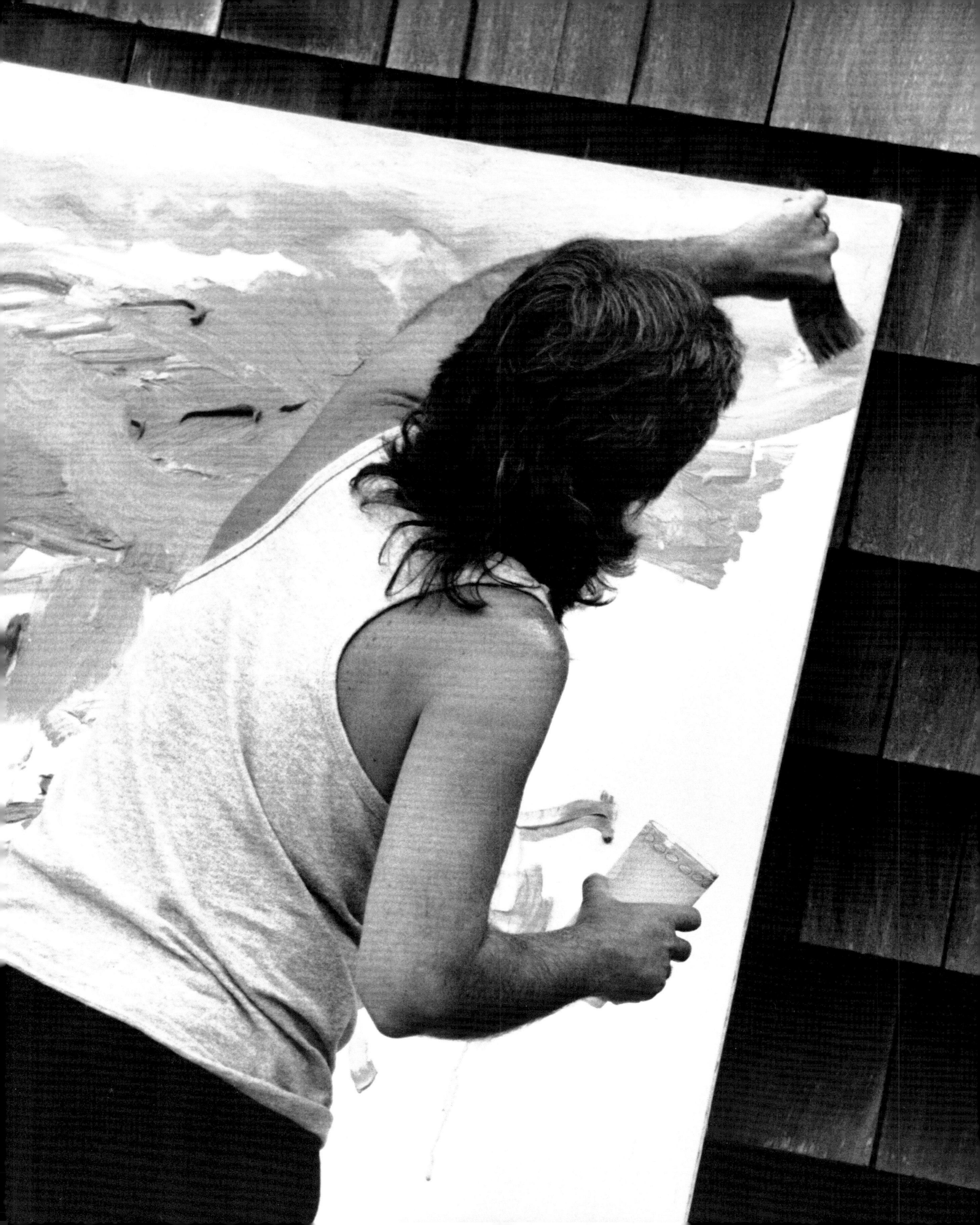

PAINTINGS

Big mountain face, 1991

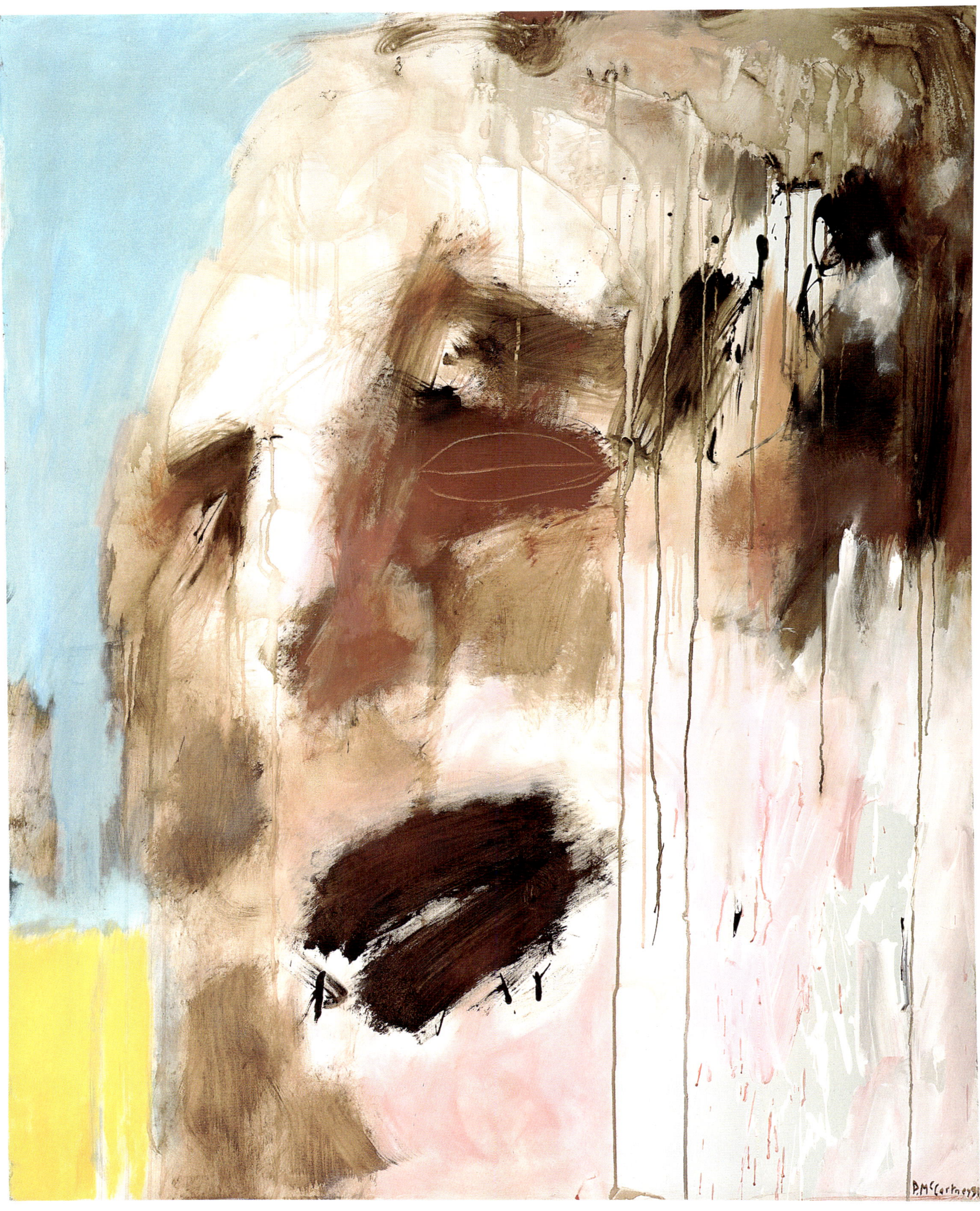

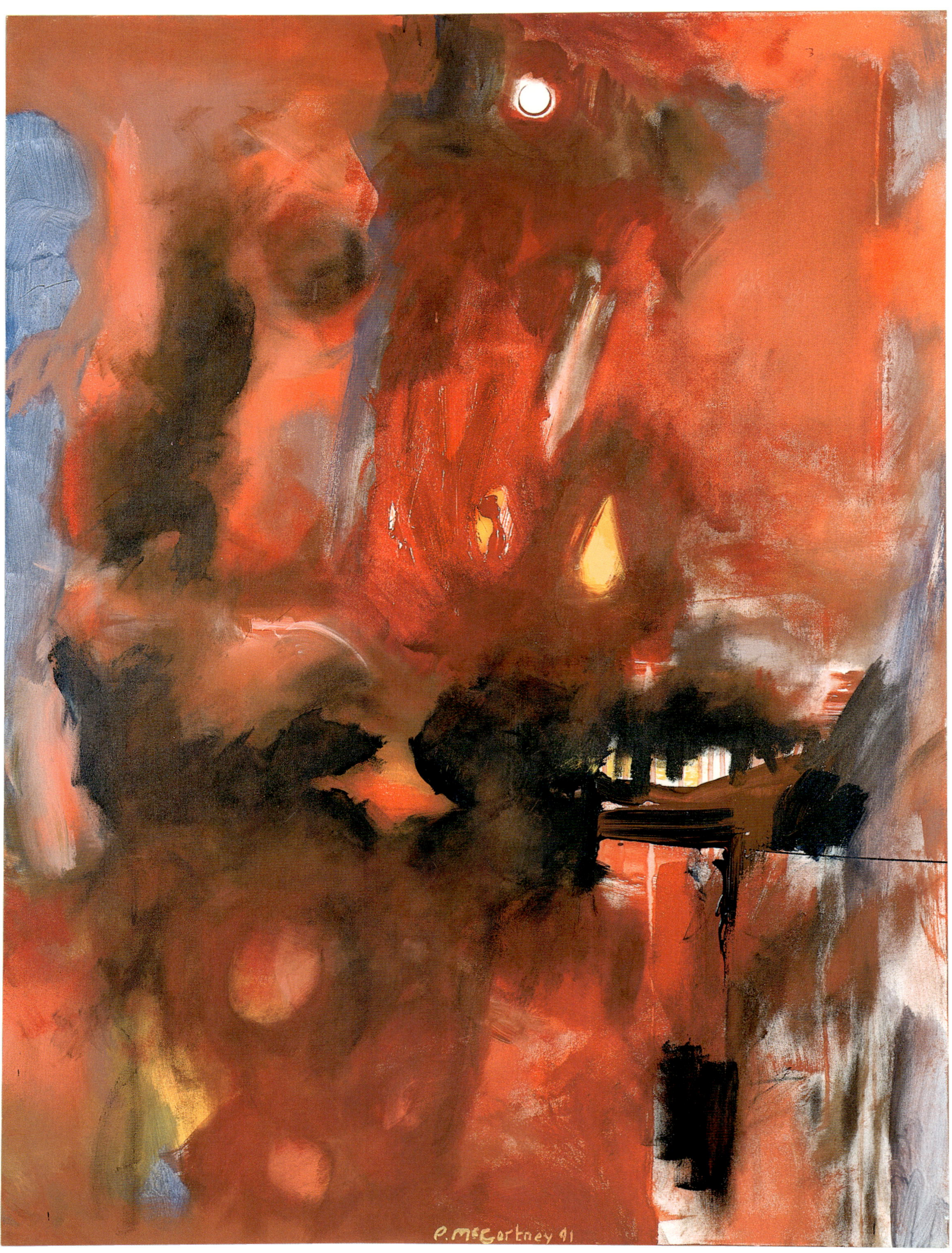
P. McCartney 91

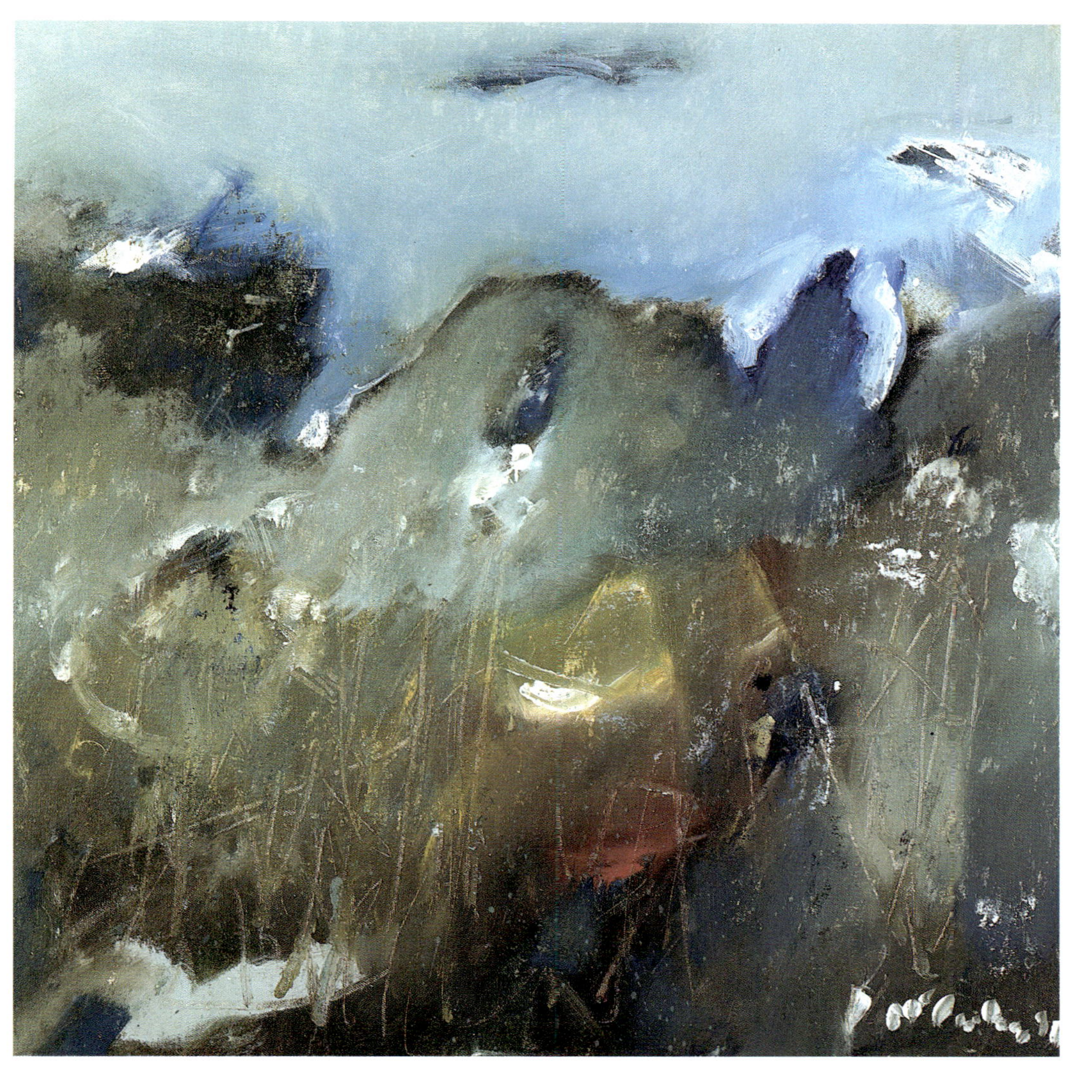

Mountain landscape, 1991

<

Red abstract white moon, 1991

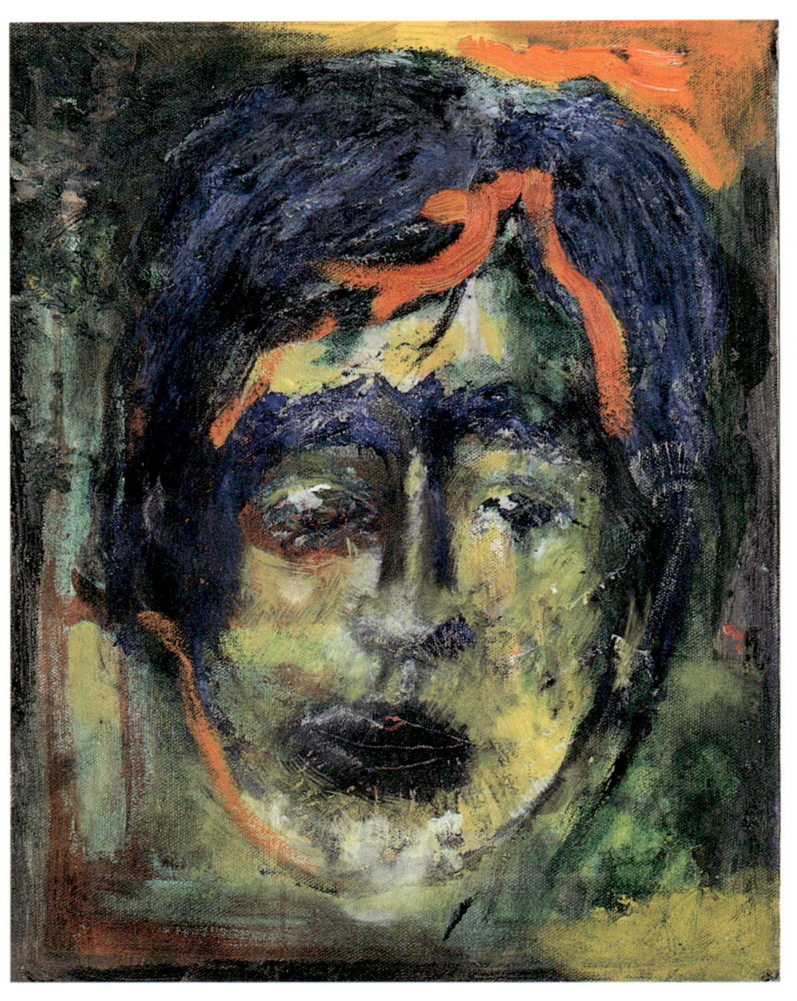

Is this a self-portrait?, 1988

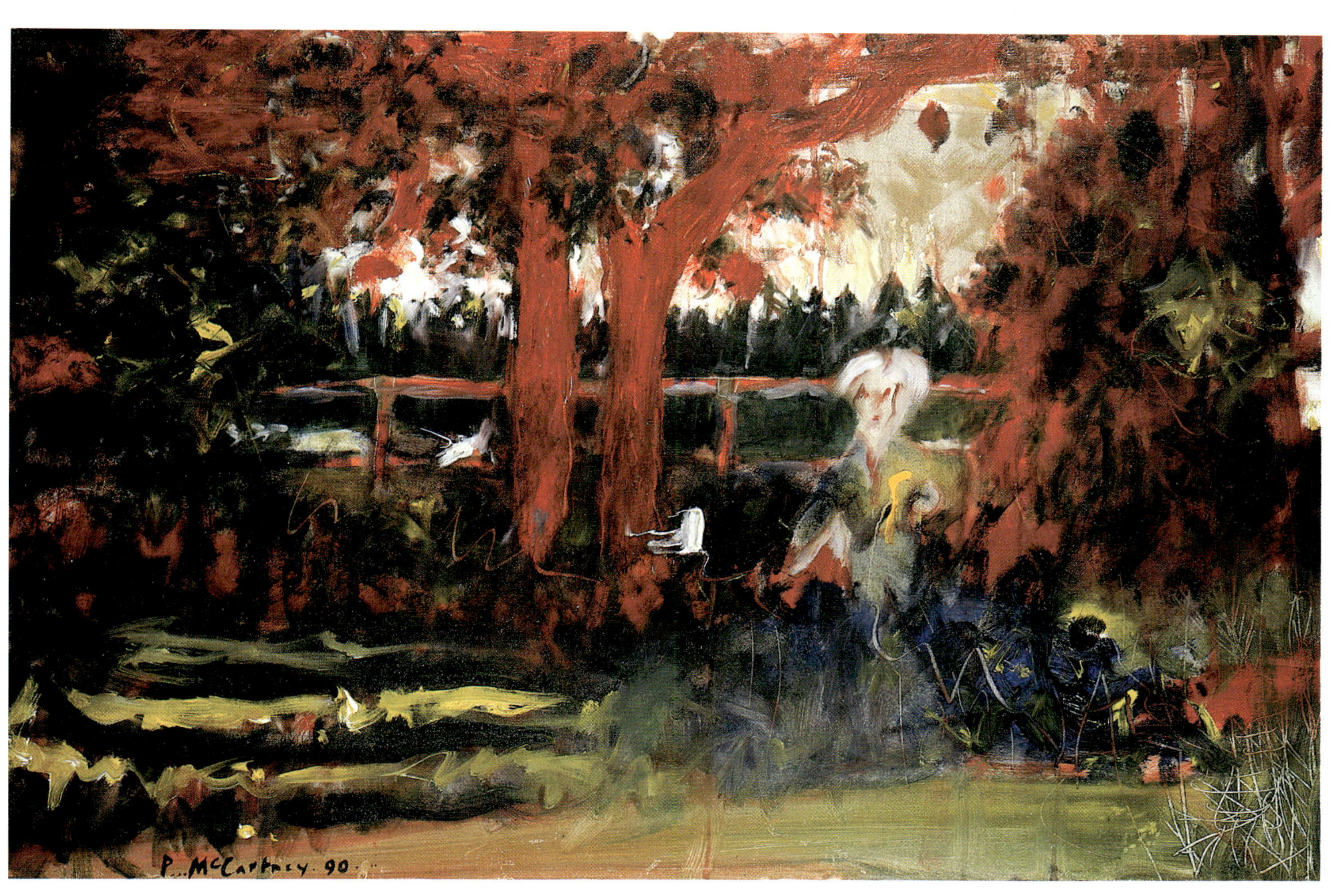

Andy in the garden, 1990

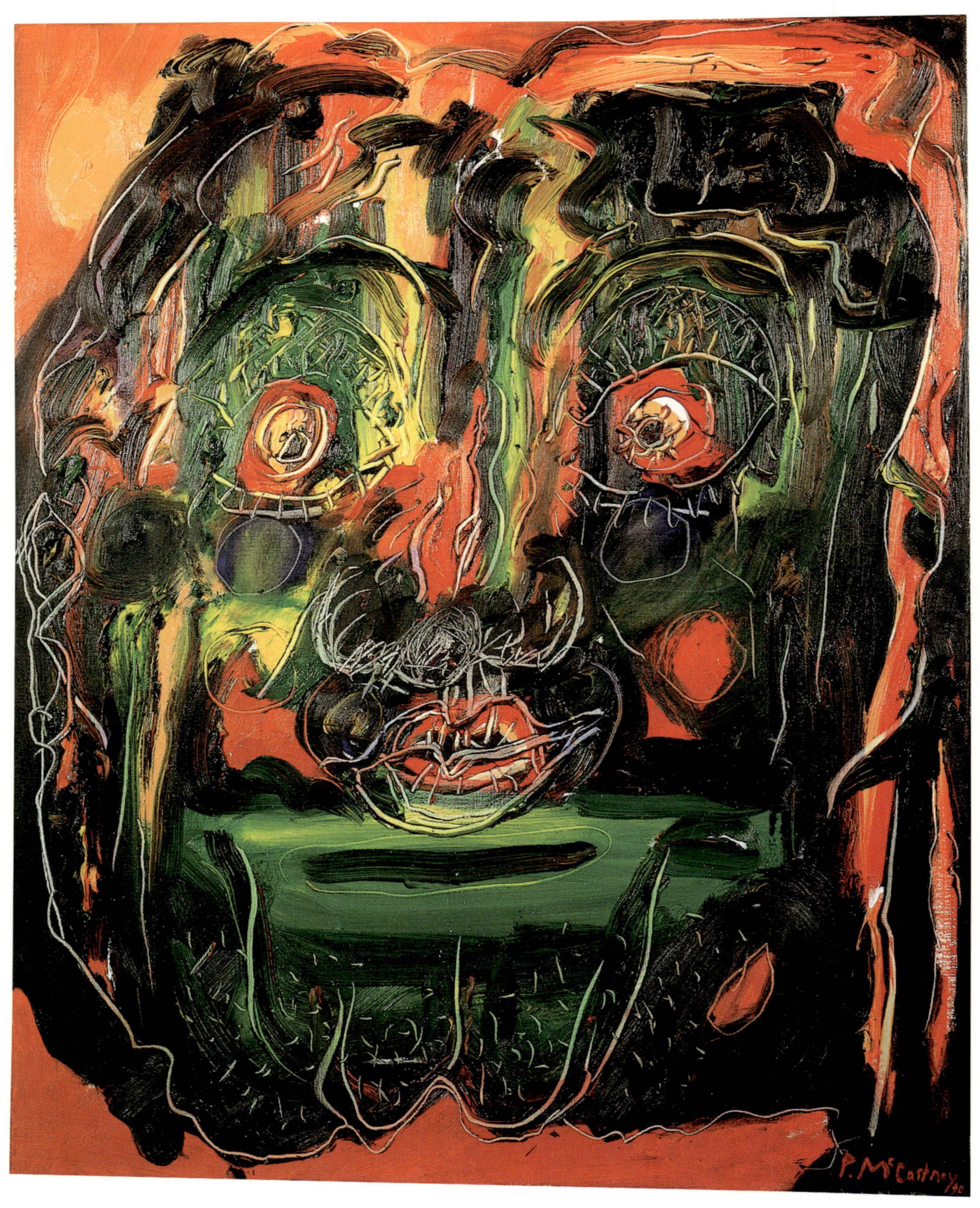

Sea god, 1990

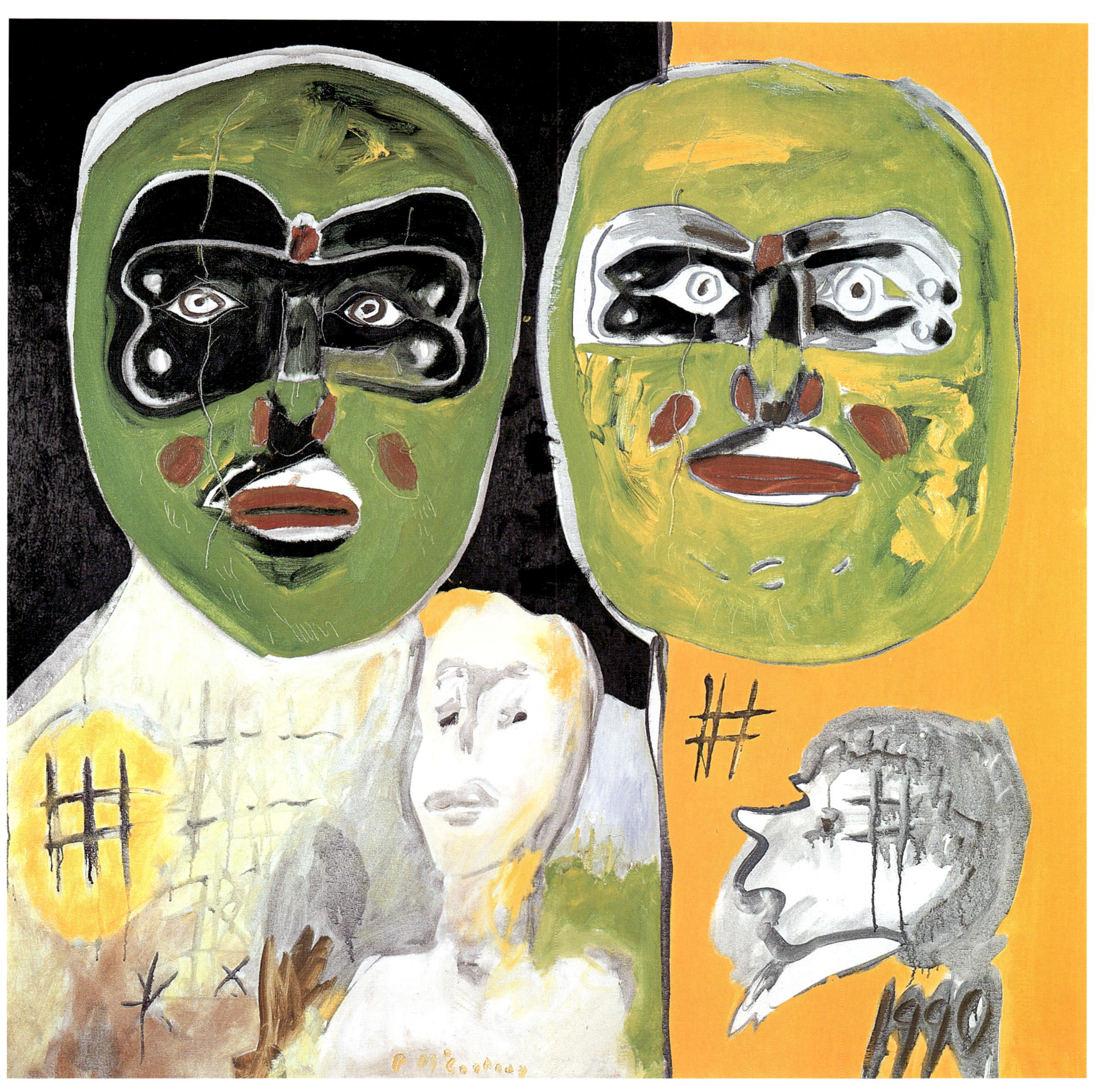

Twin freaks, 1990

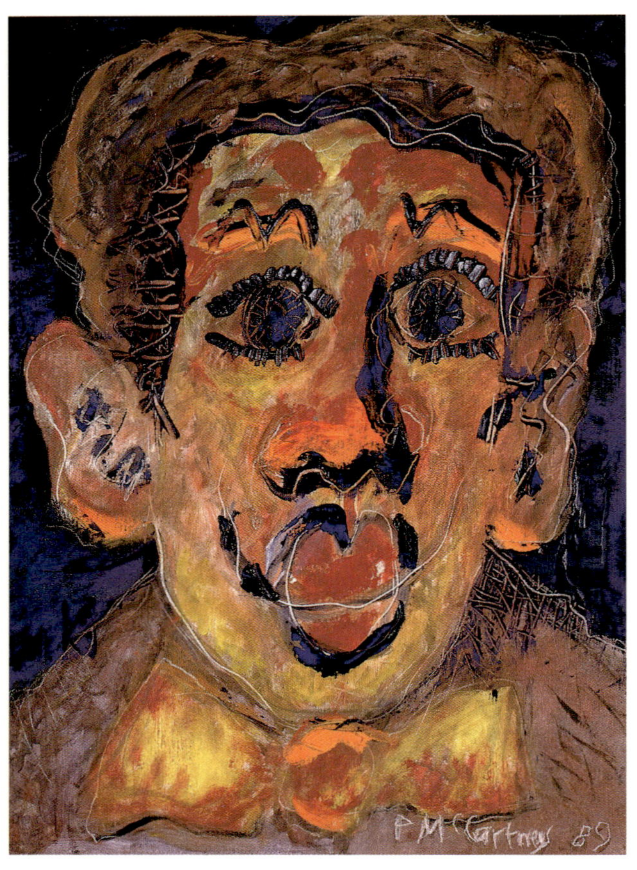

Yellow bow tie, 1989

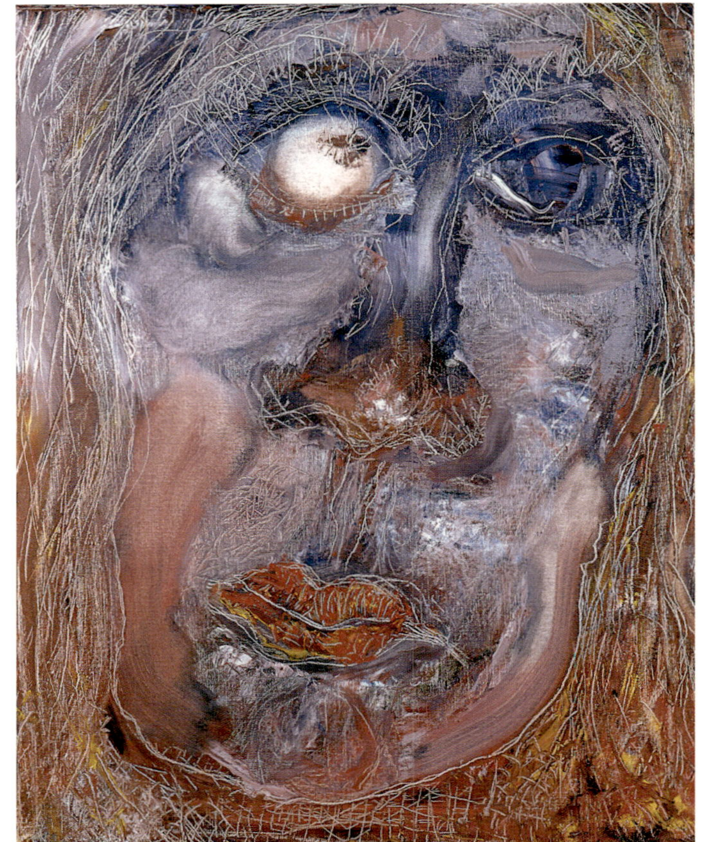

Scratch man, 1989

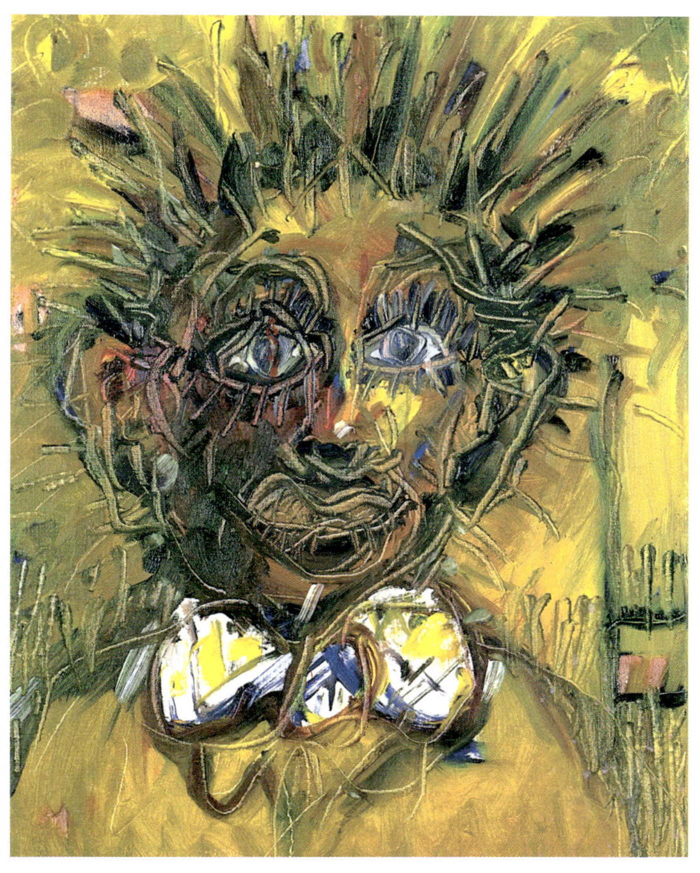

Shock head, 1989

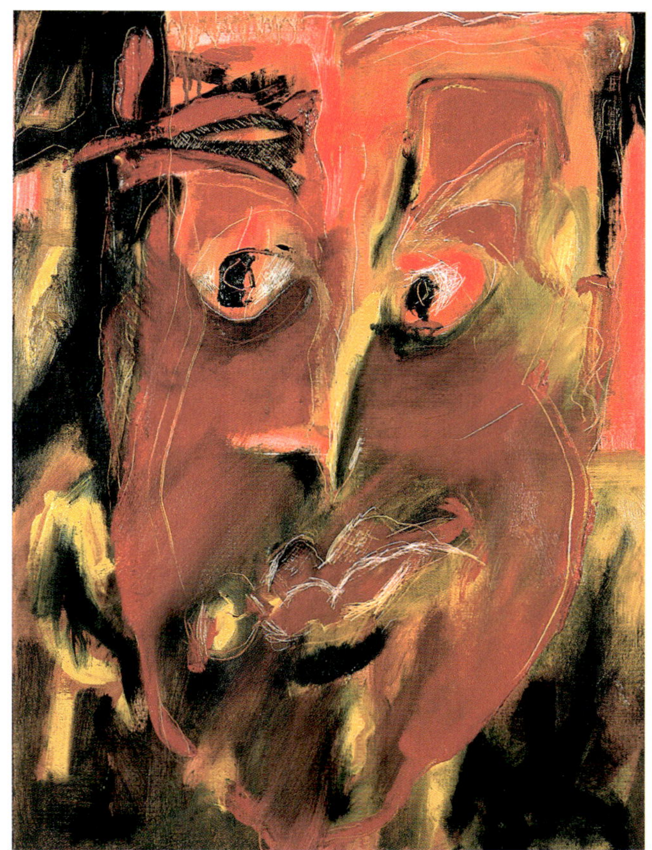

Red yellow face, 1989

Black scratch I, 1994

OVERLEAF:

Black scratch II, 1994 (left)

Black scratch III, 1994 (right)

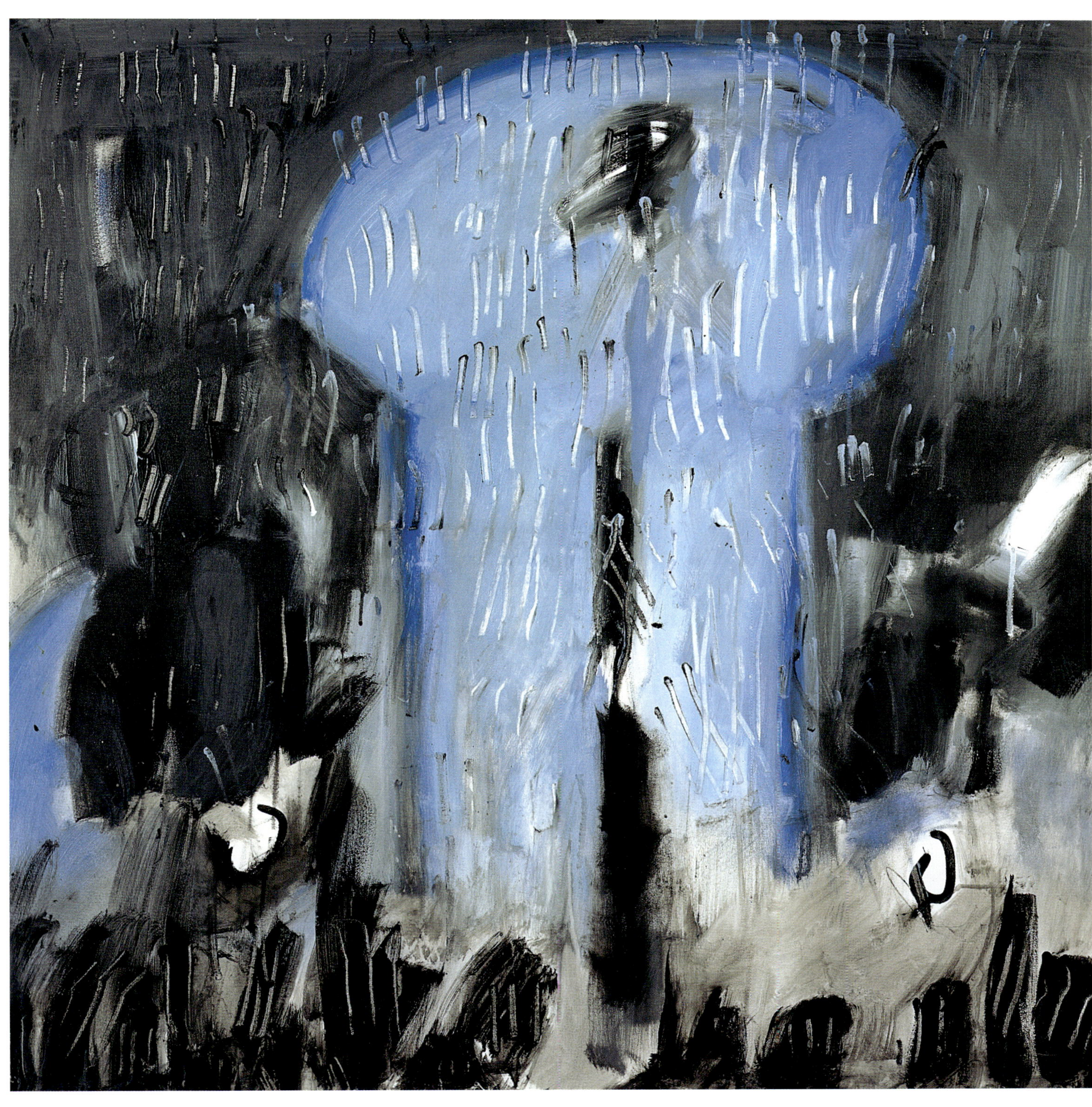

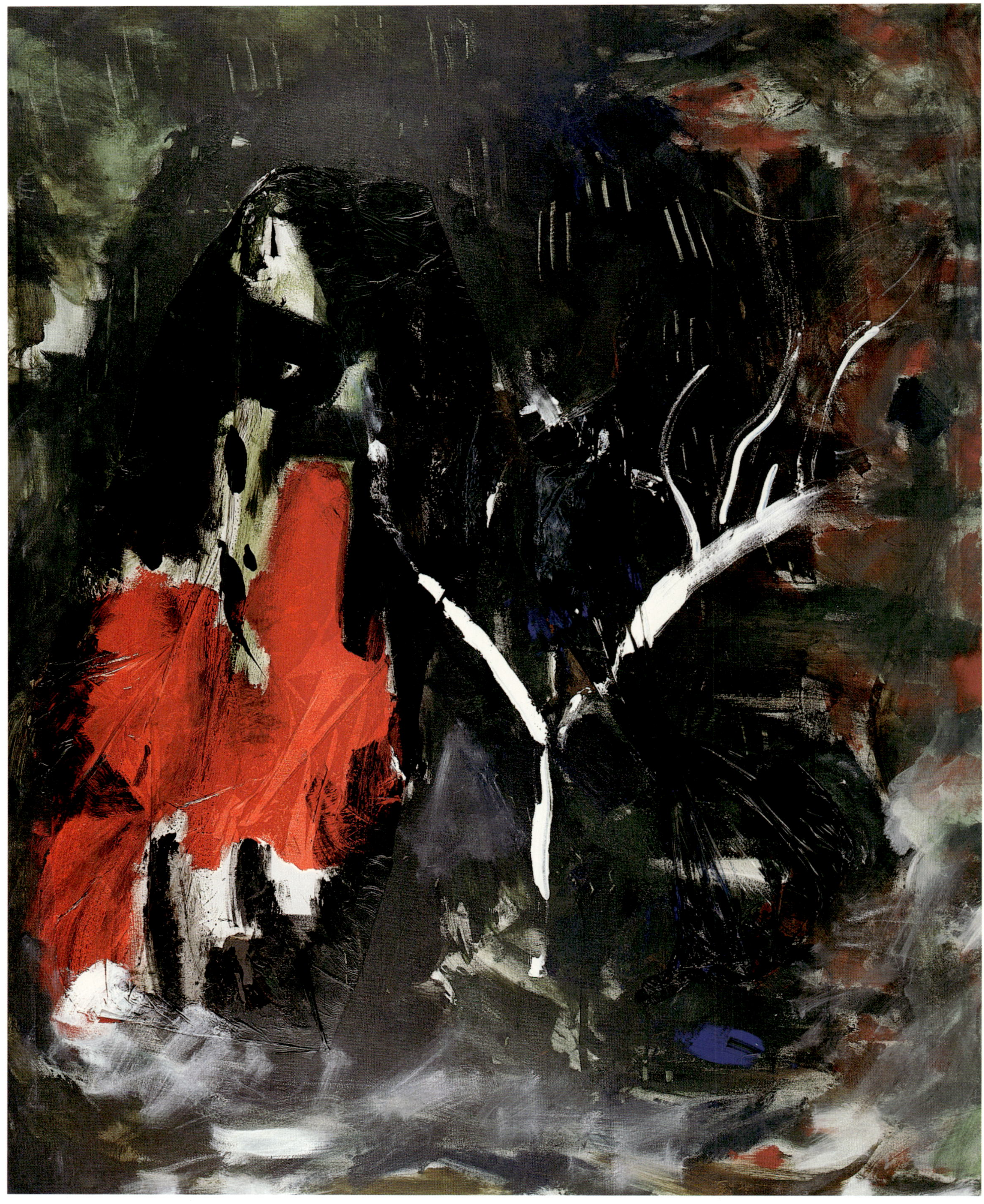

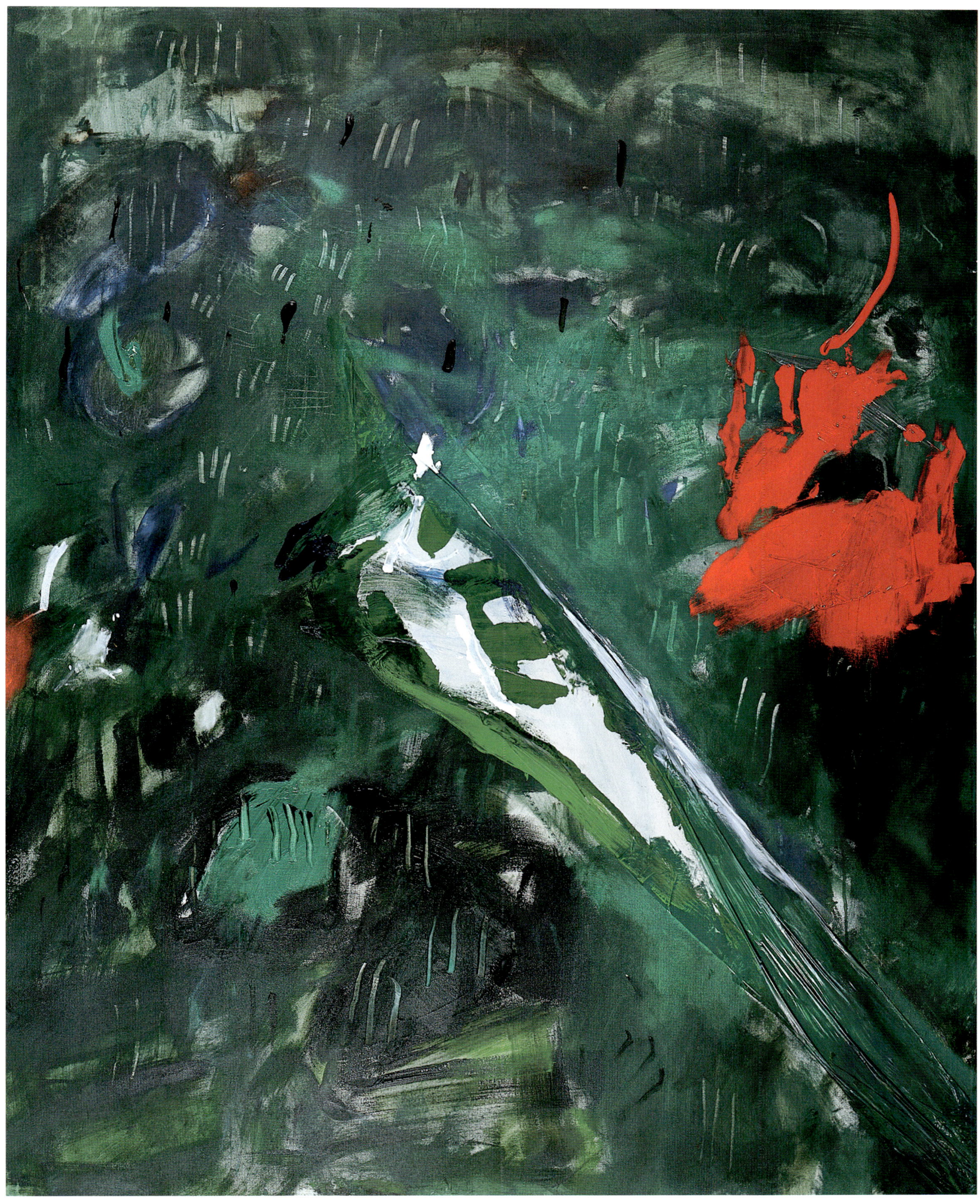

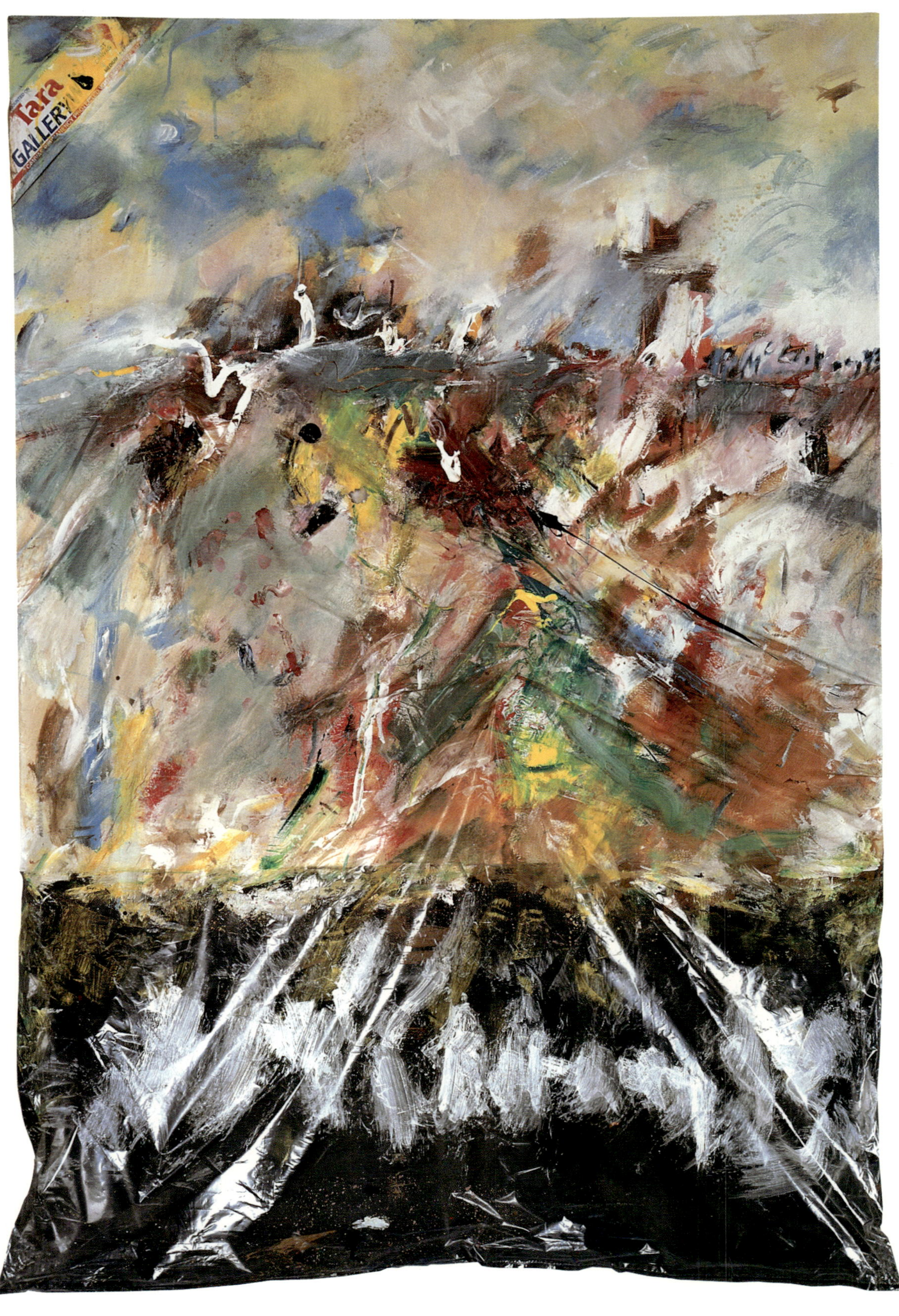

Tara's plastic skirt, 1992

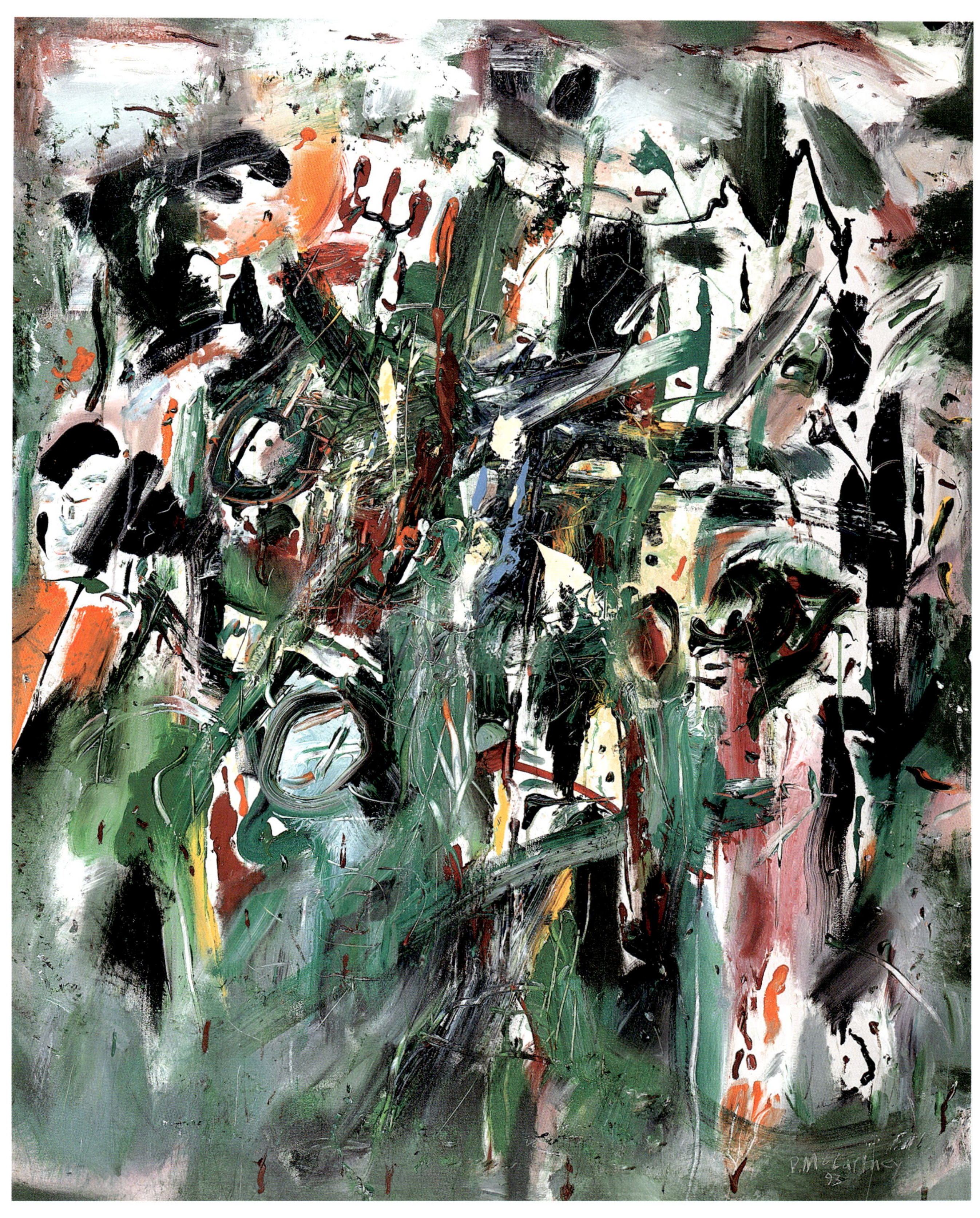

Unfinished symphony, 1993

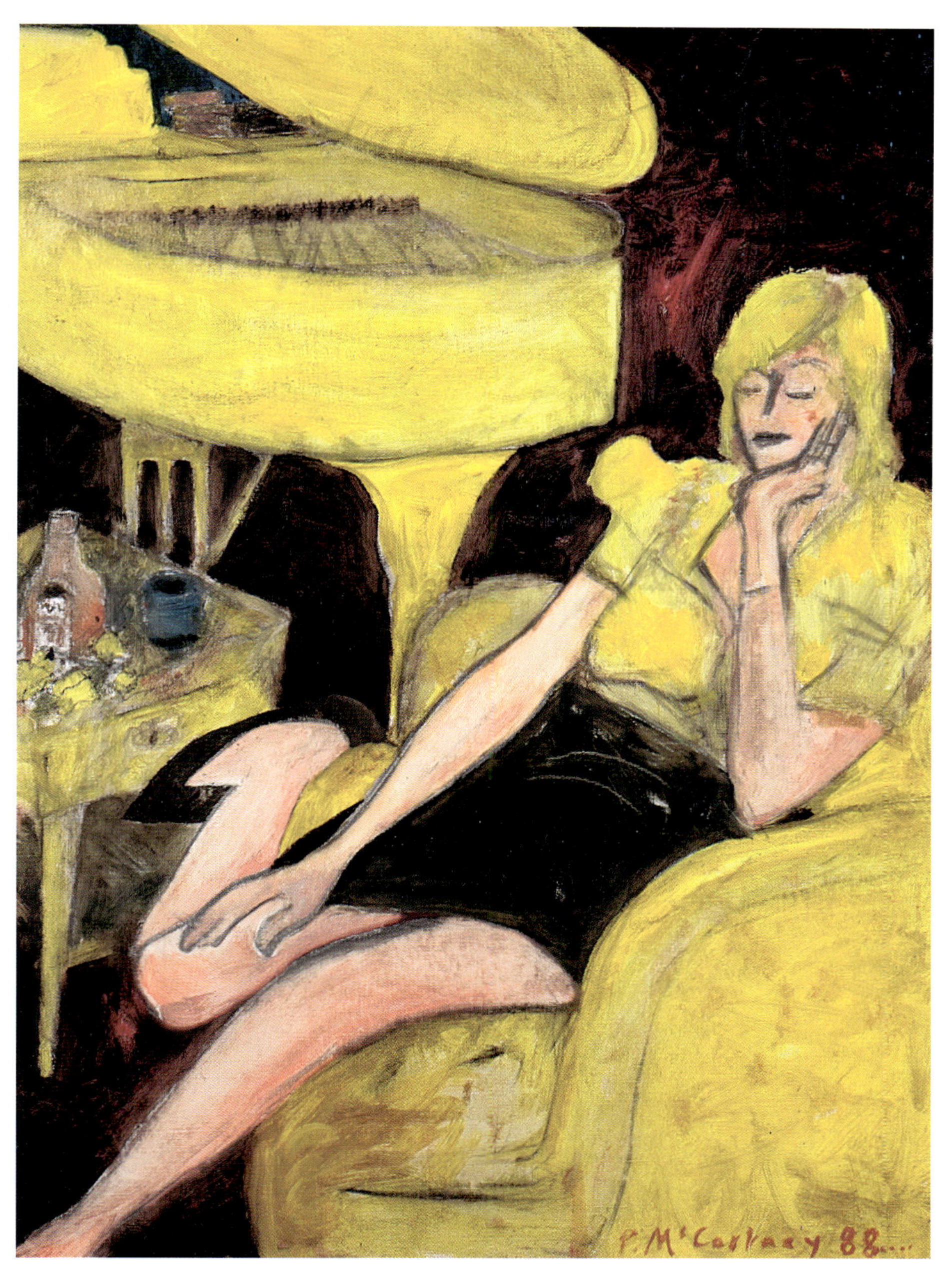

Yellow Linda with piano, 1988

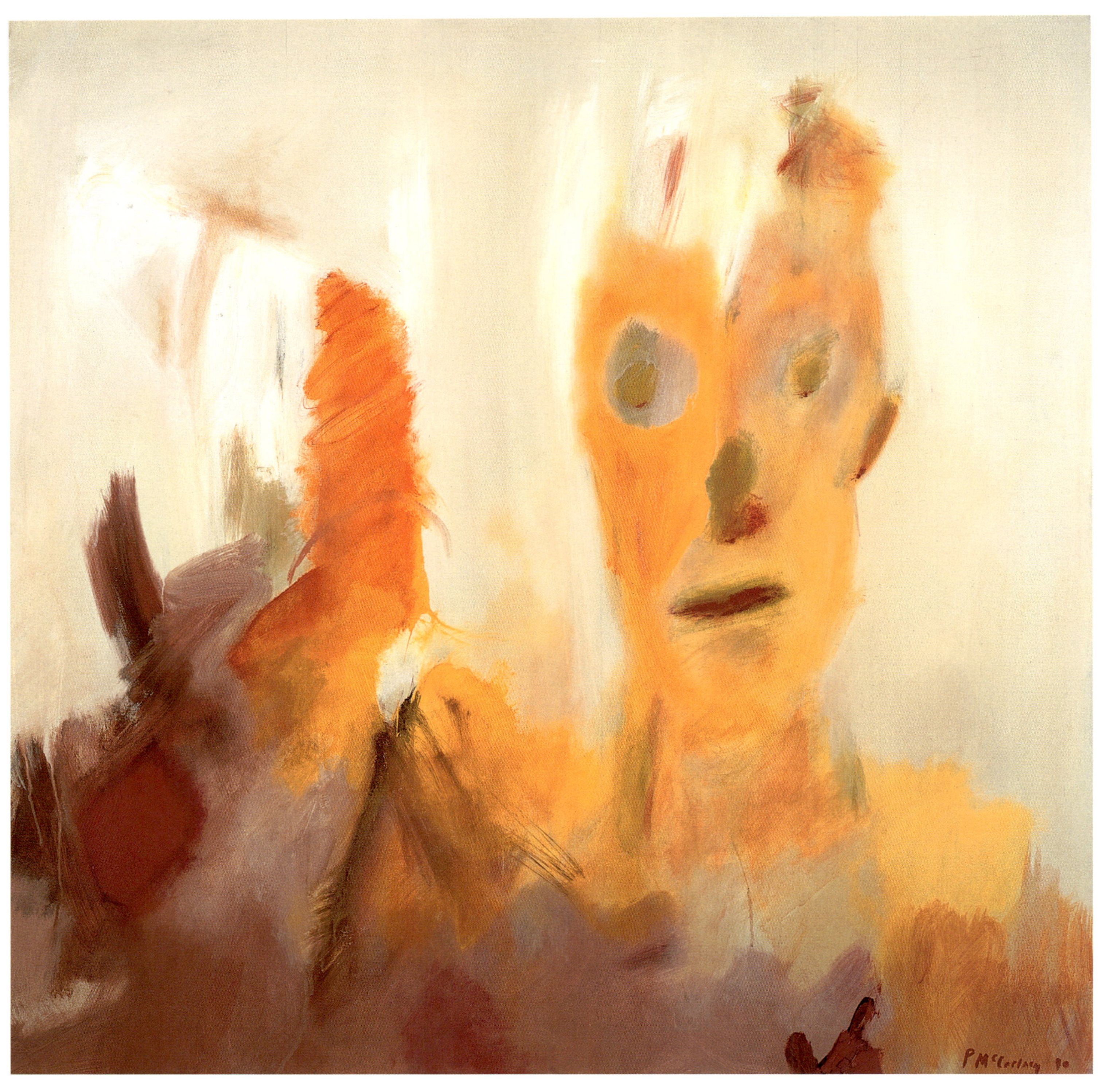

Large yellow face, 1990

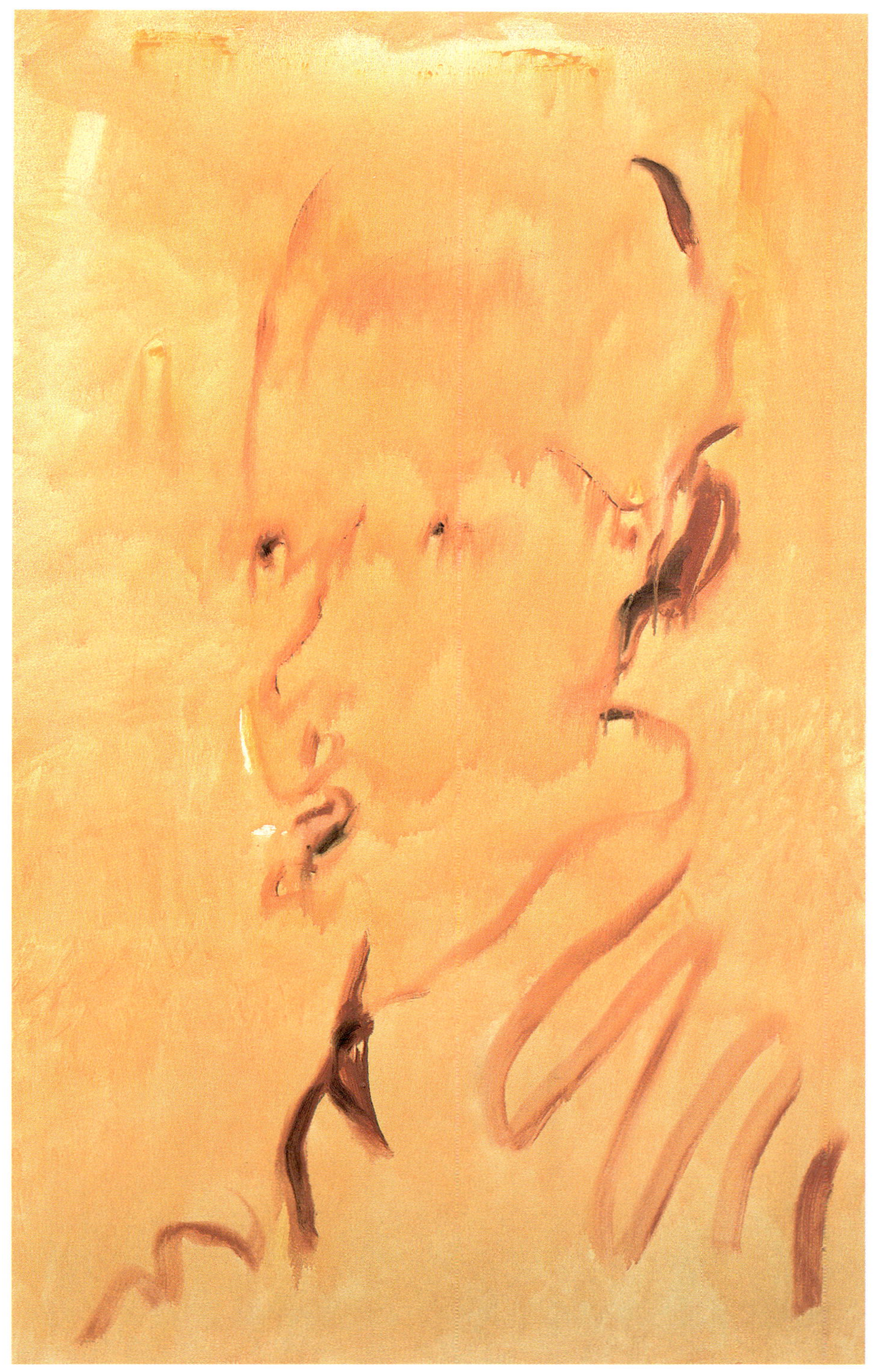

Chinaman, 1990

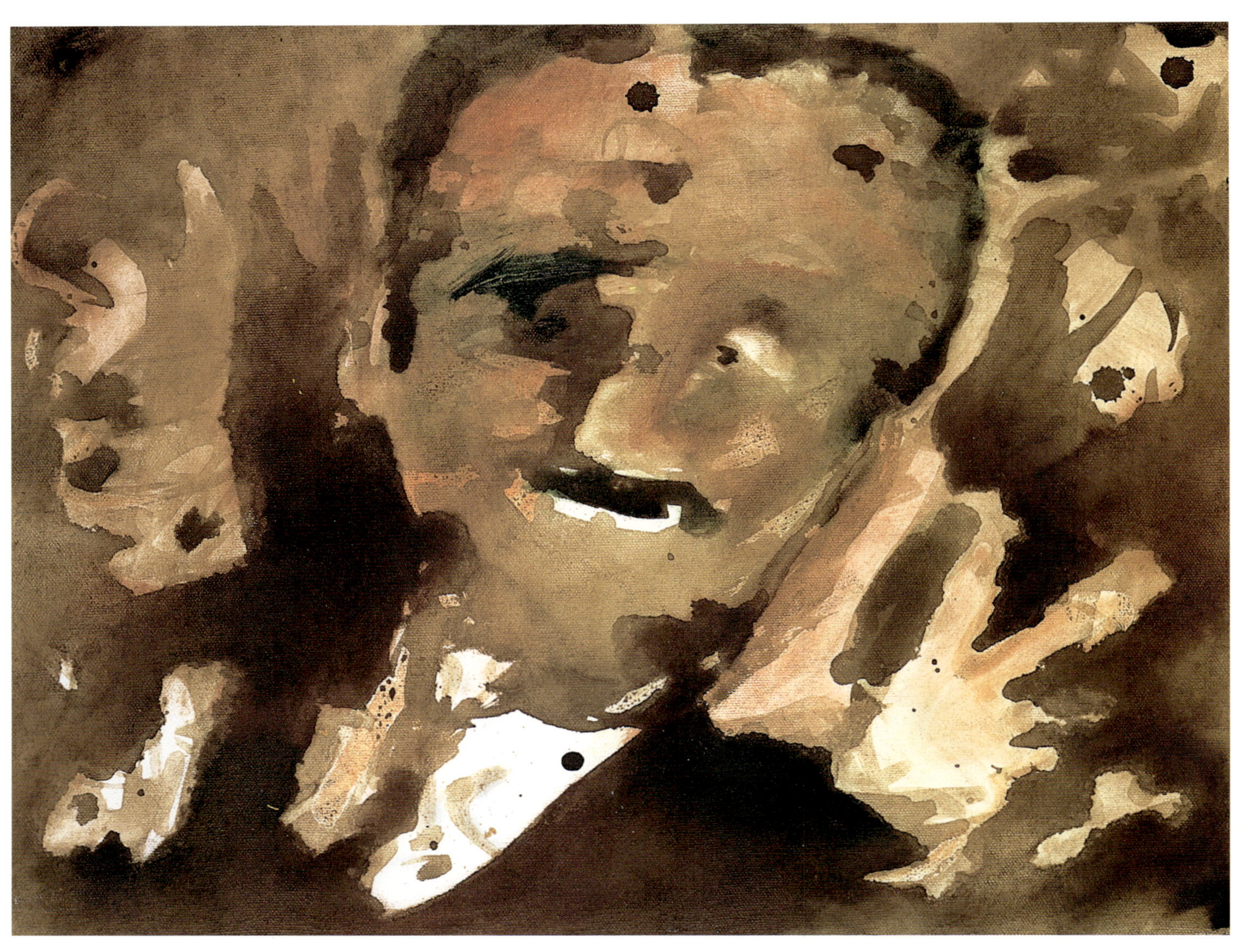

Oak apple twenties man, 1988

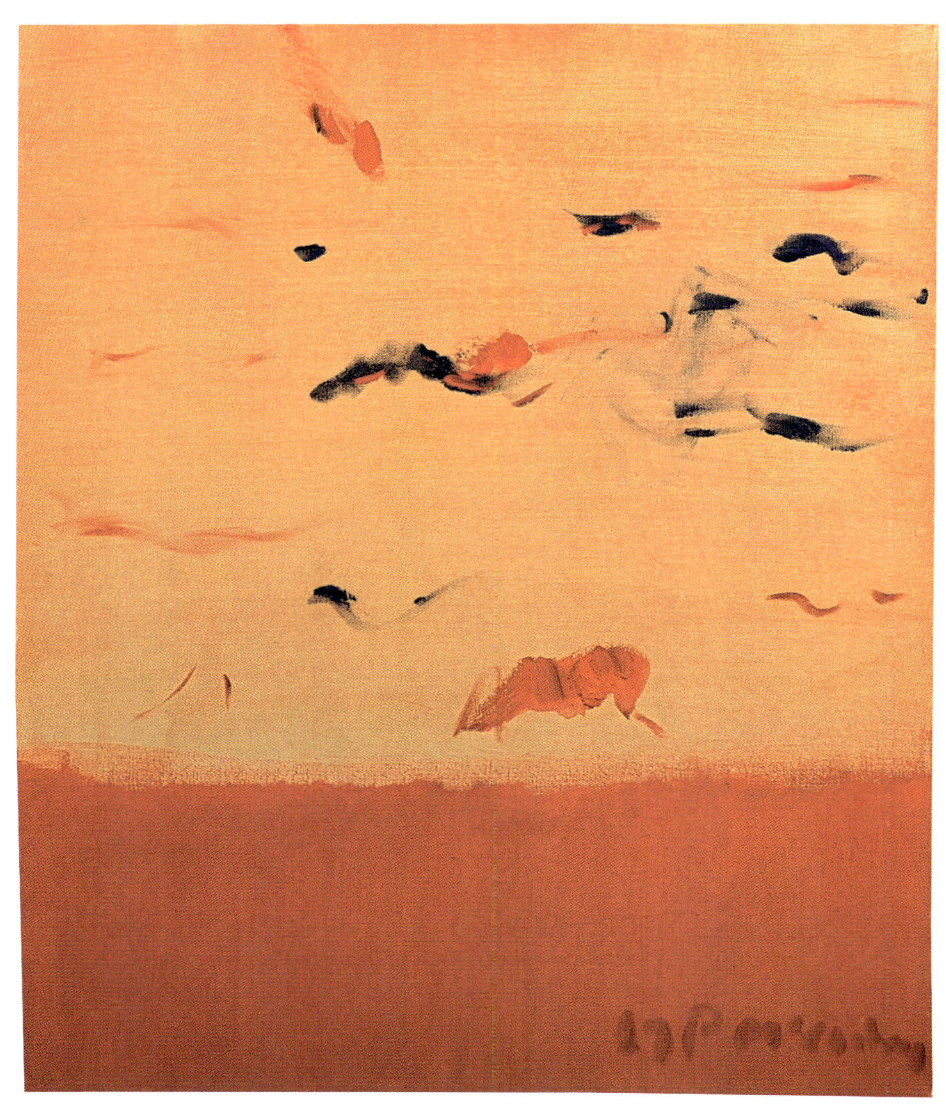

Prehistoric antelope, 1989

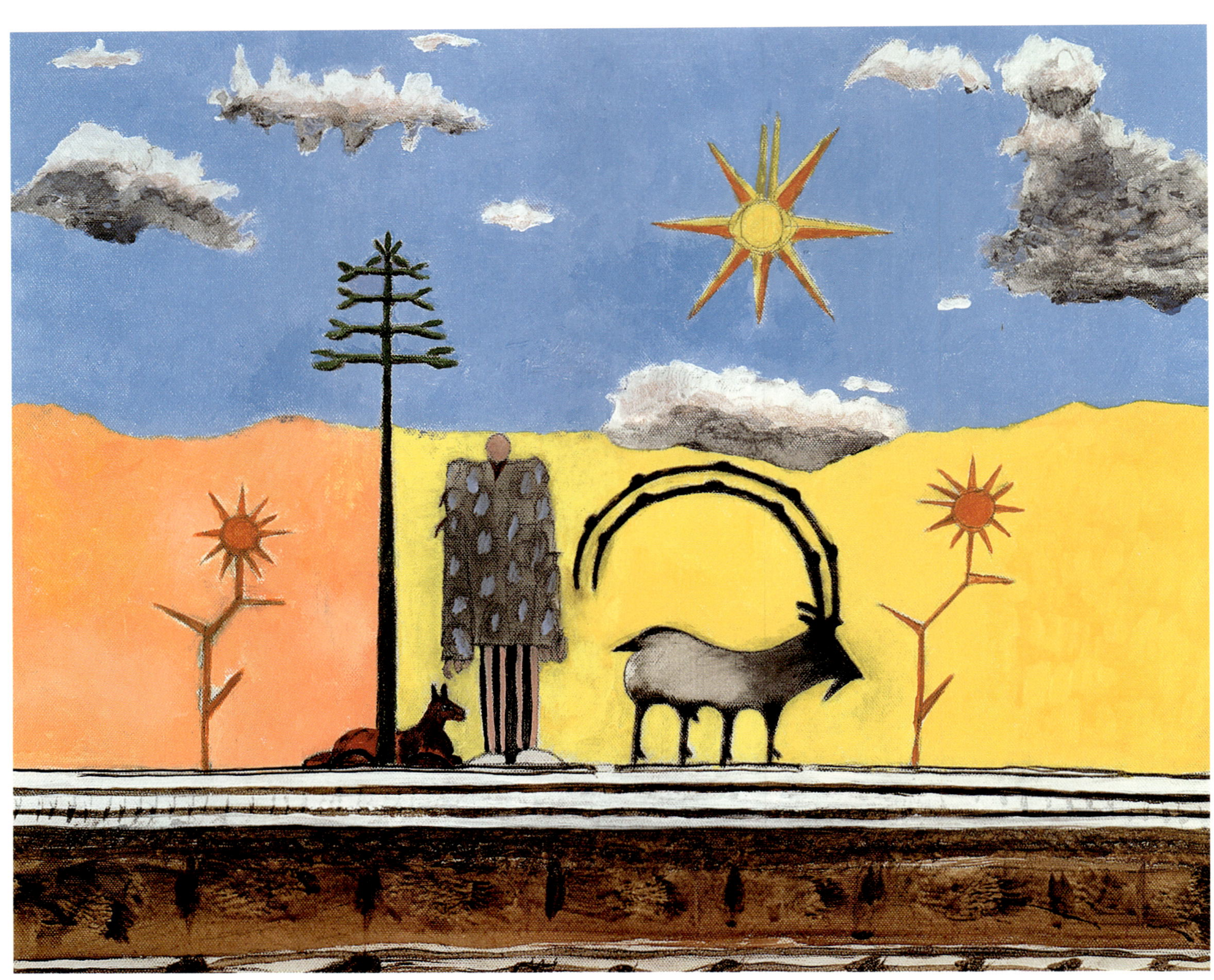

Egypt station, 1988

>

Linda yellow red cross, 1991

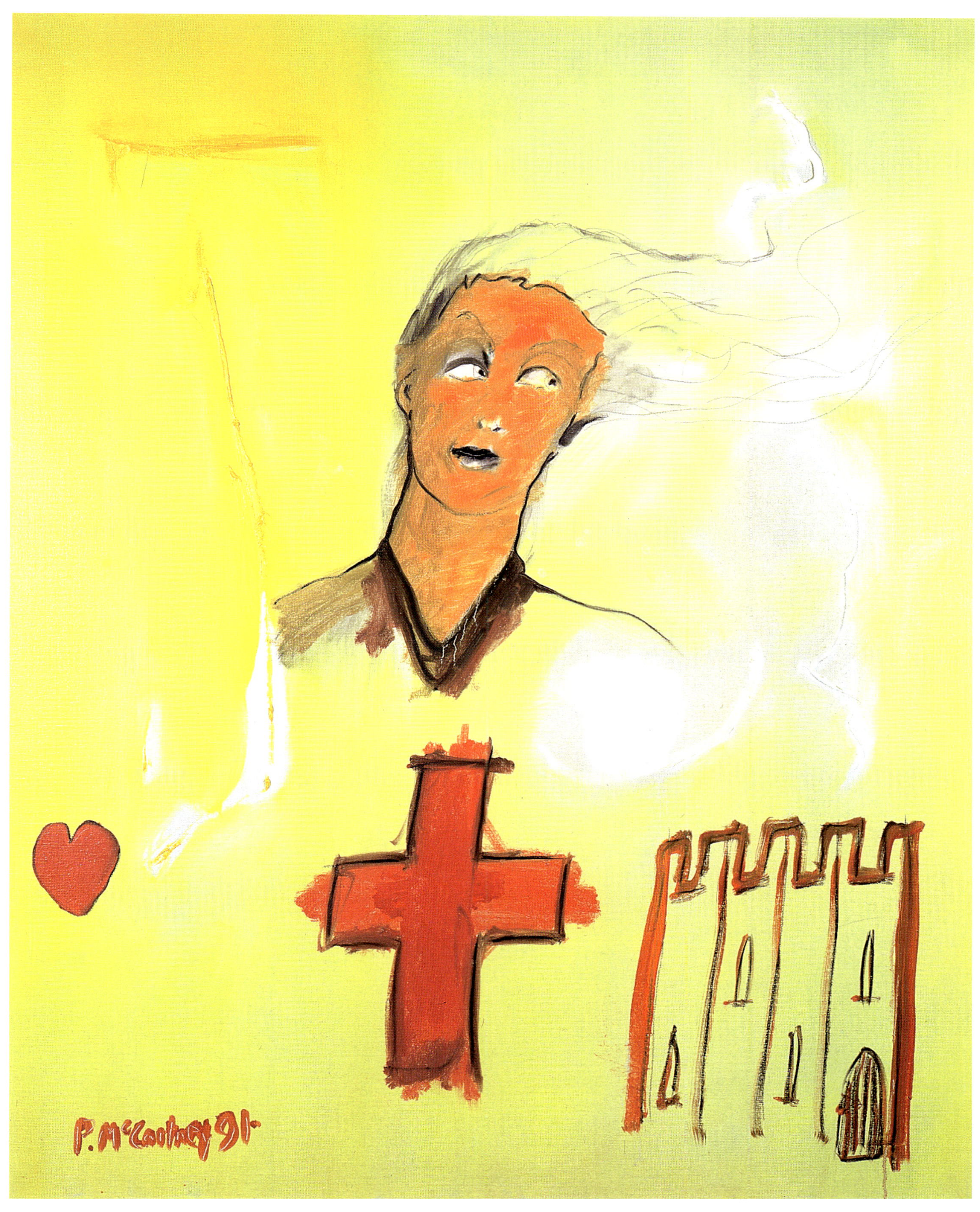
P. McCartney 91

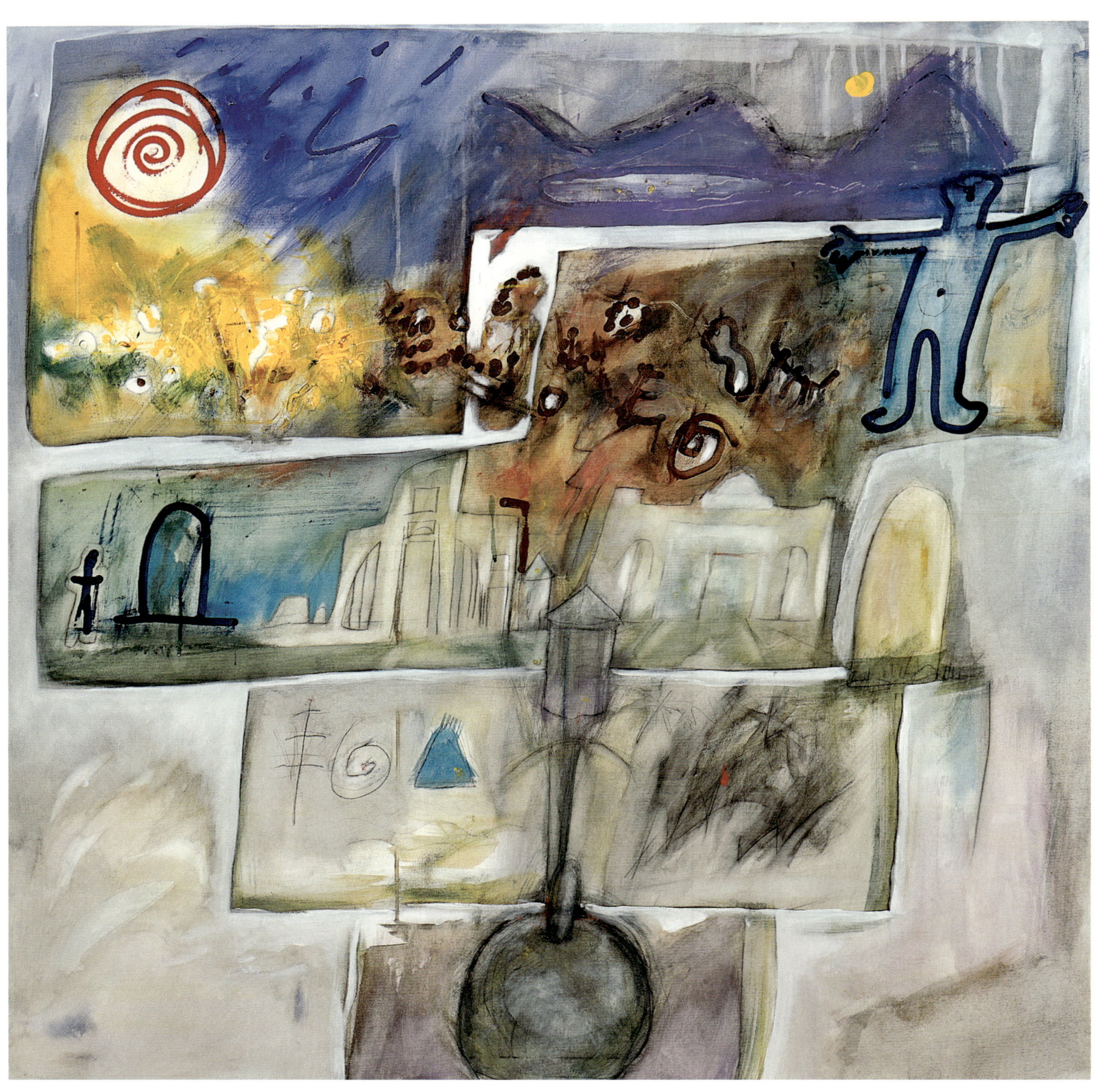

Standing Stone story, 1994

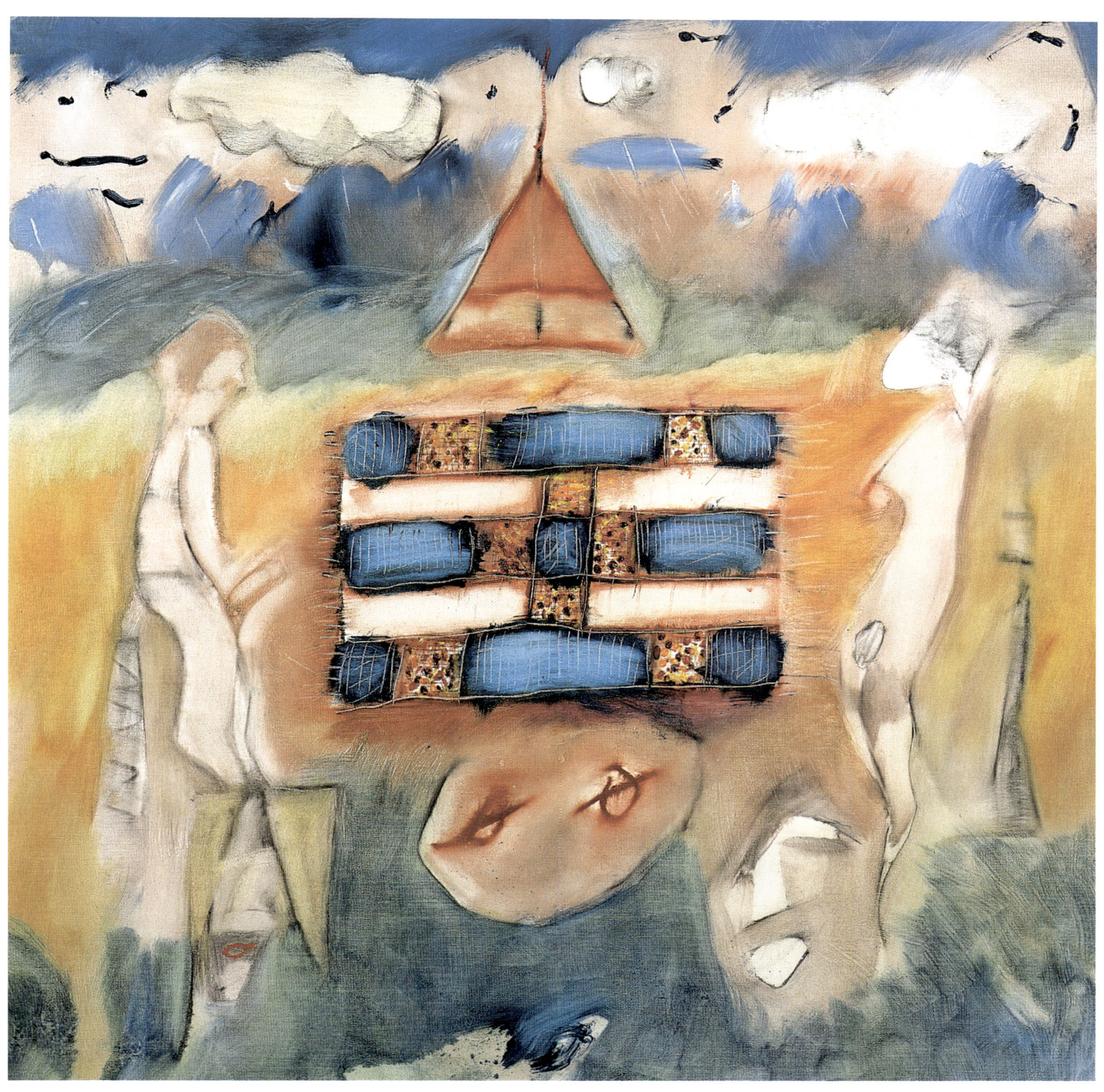

Chief rug, 1994

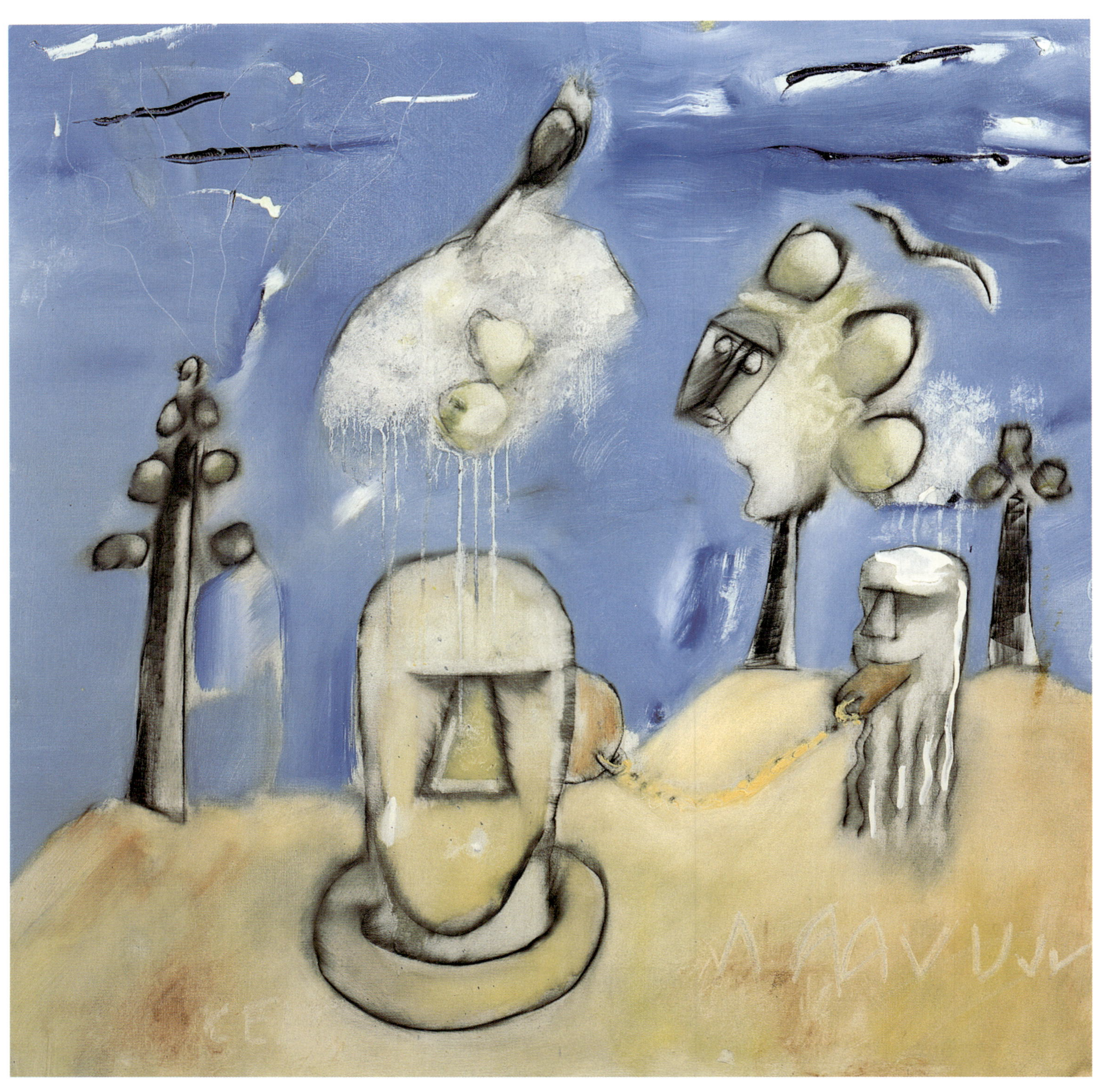

Celtic eloquence, 1994

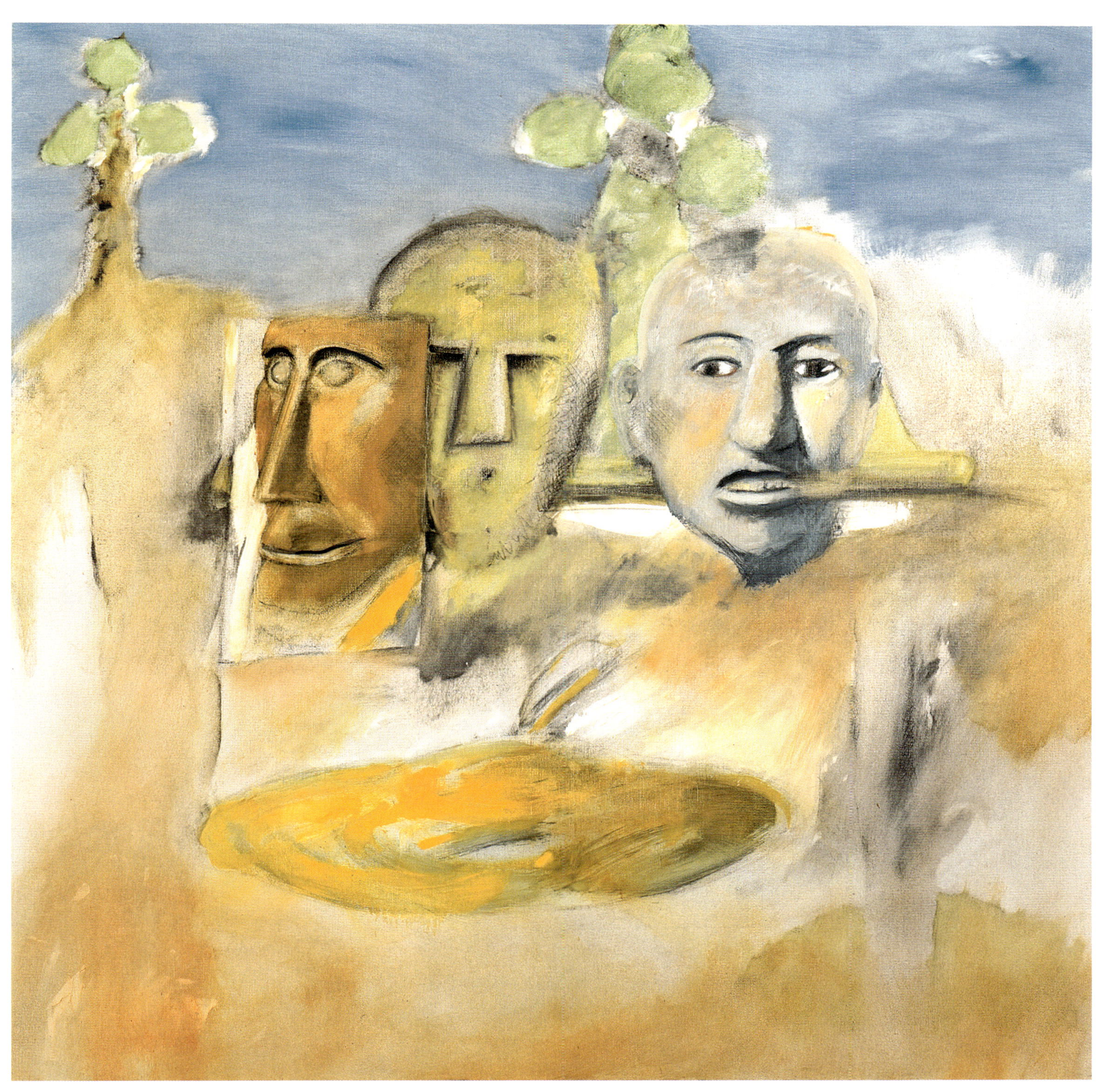

Ancient connections, 1994

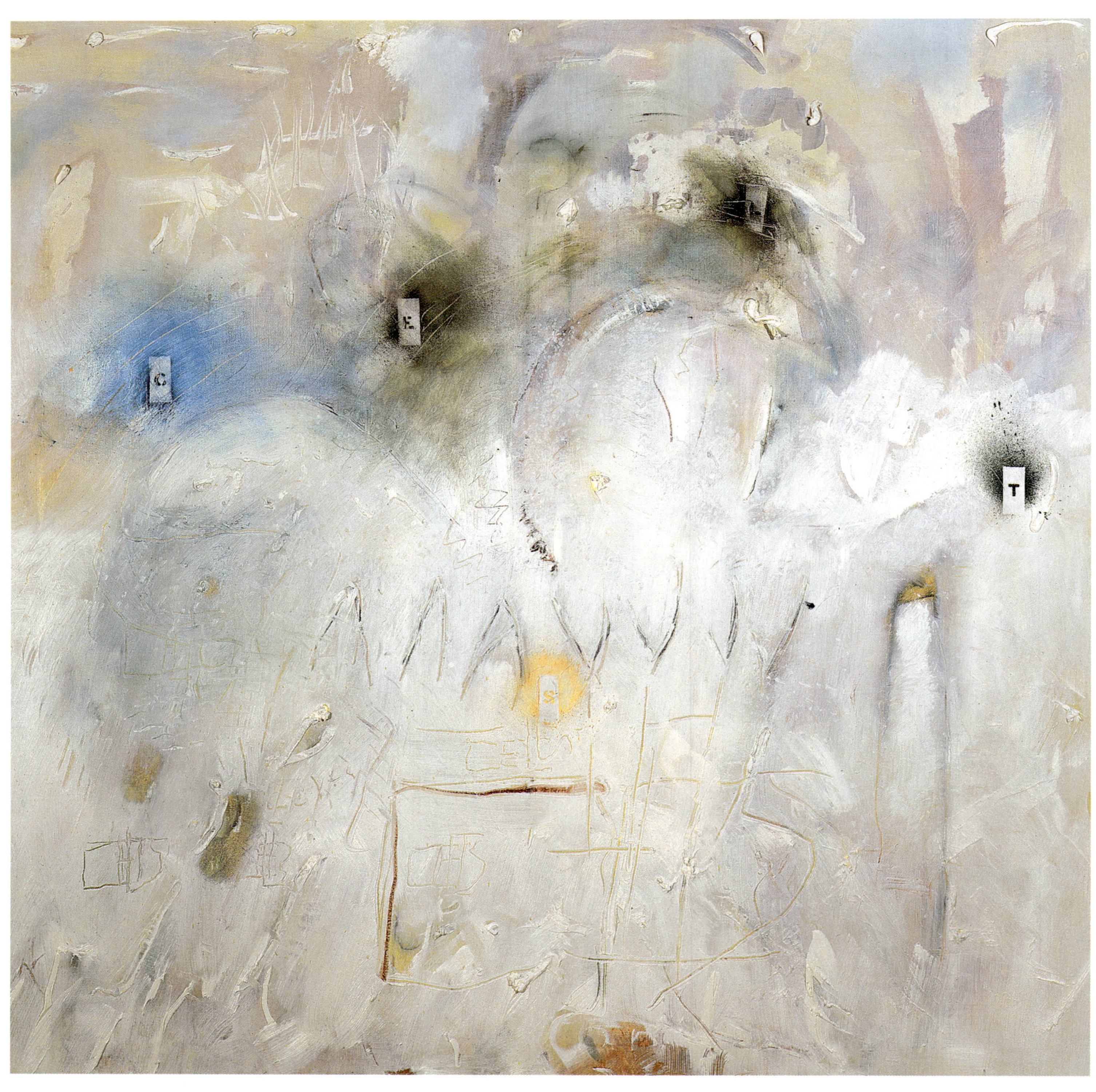

White Celts, 1994

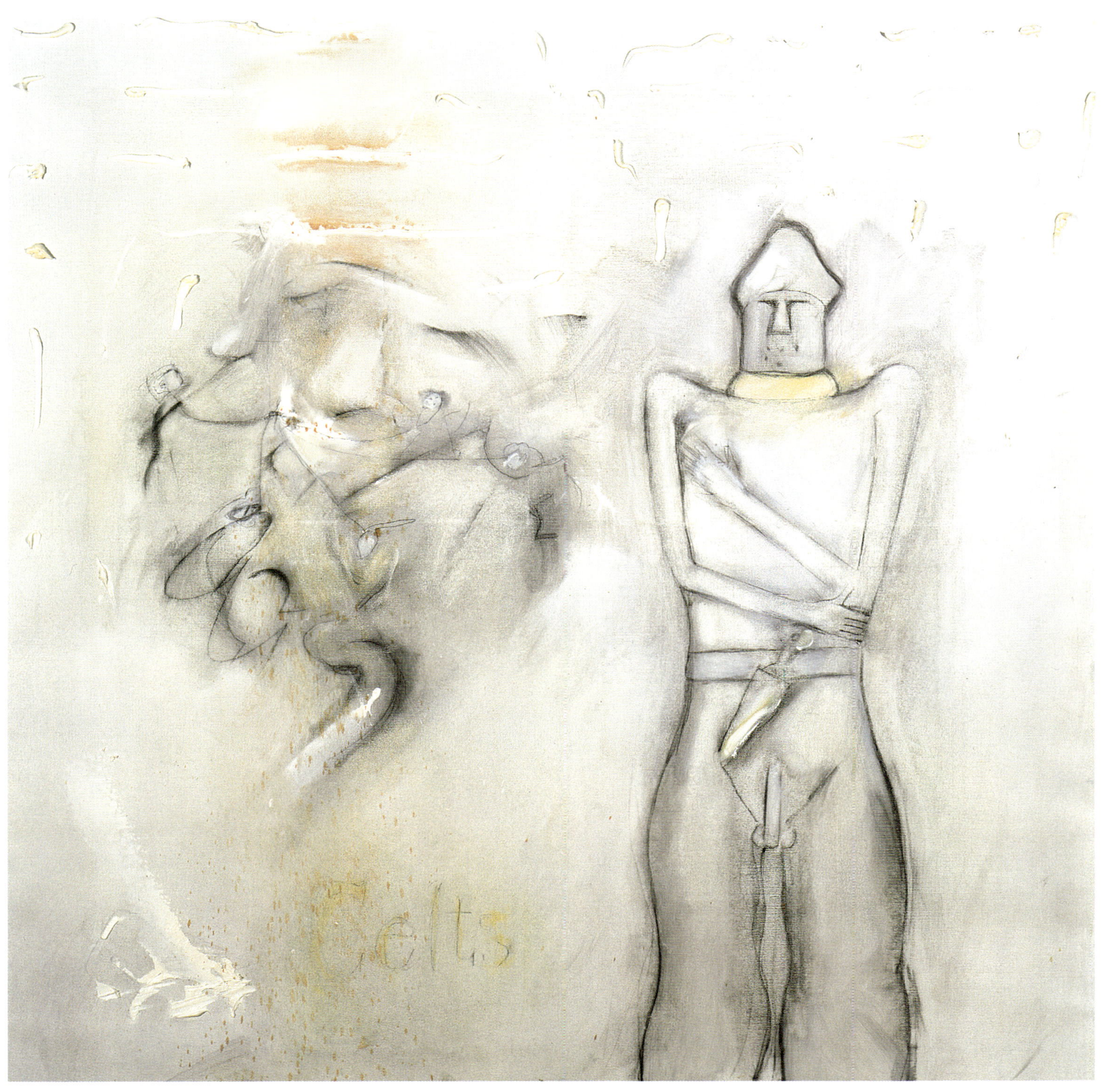

Celts, 1994

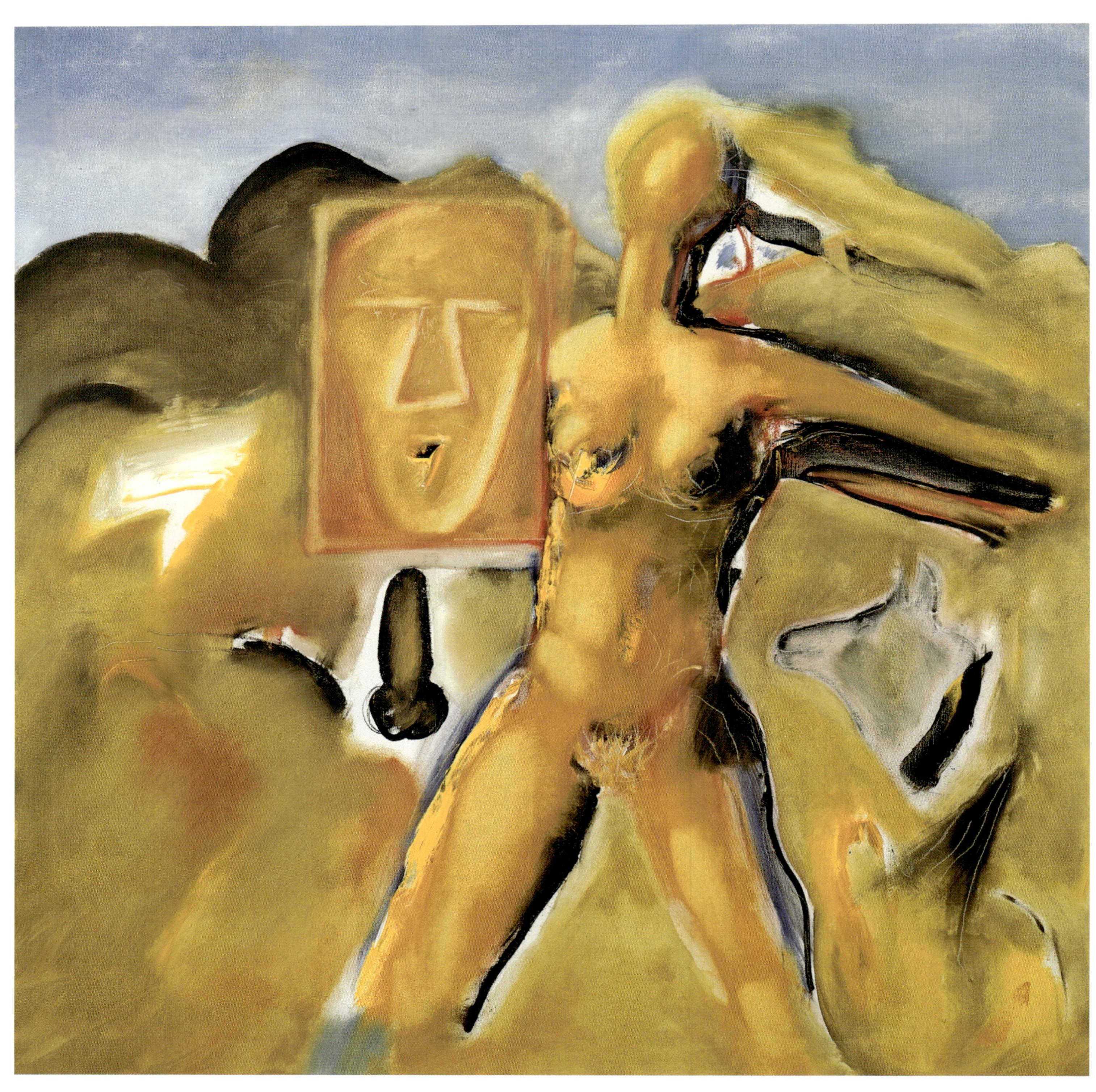

Celtic fertility, 1994

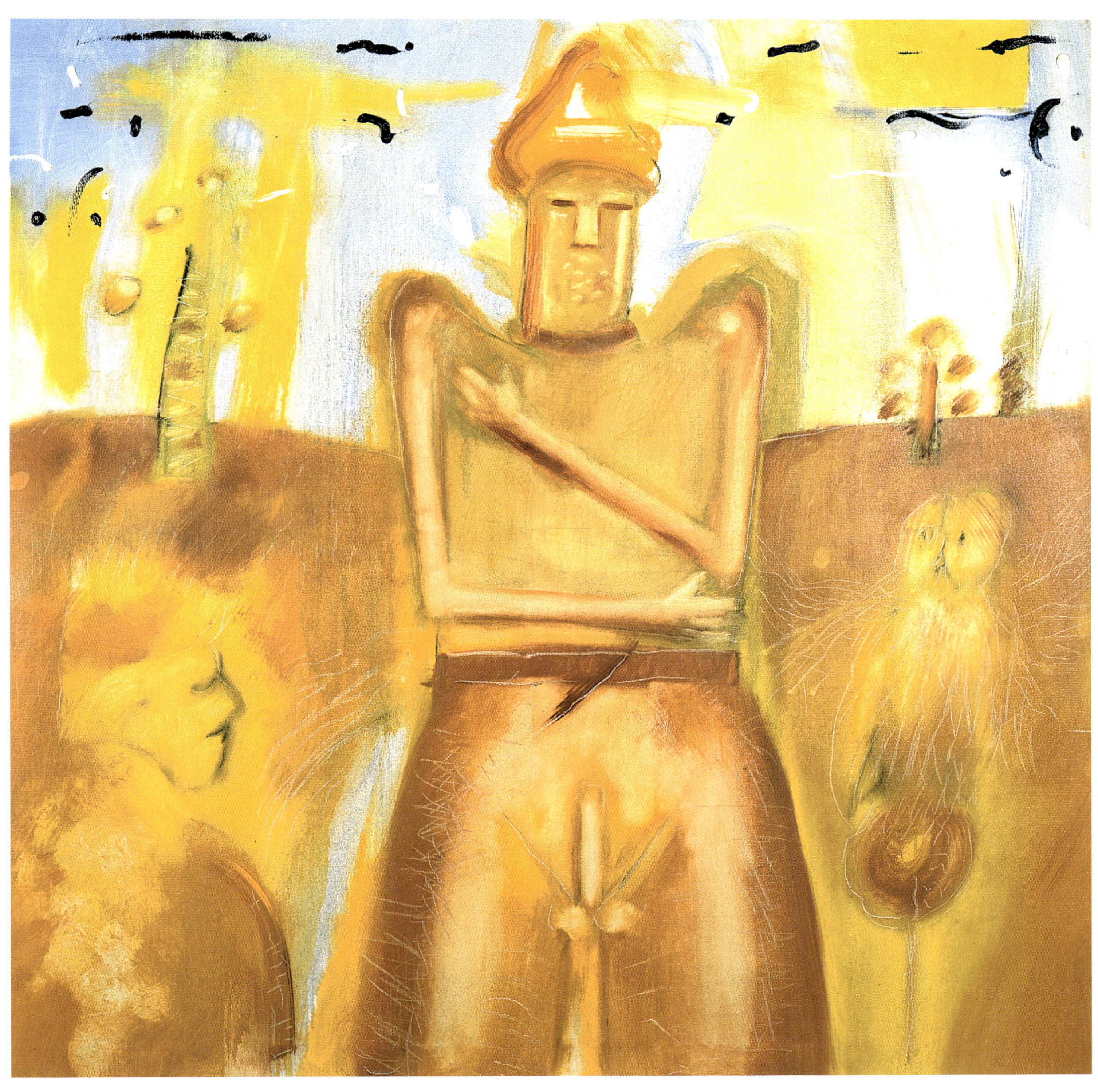

Yellow Celt, 1994

Black singer, 1991

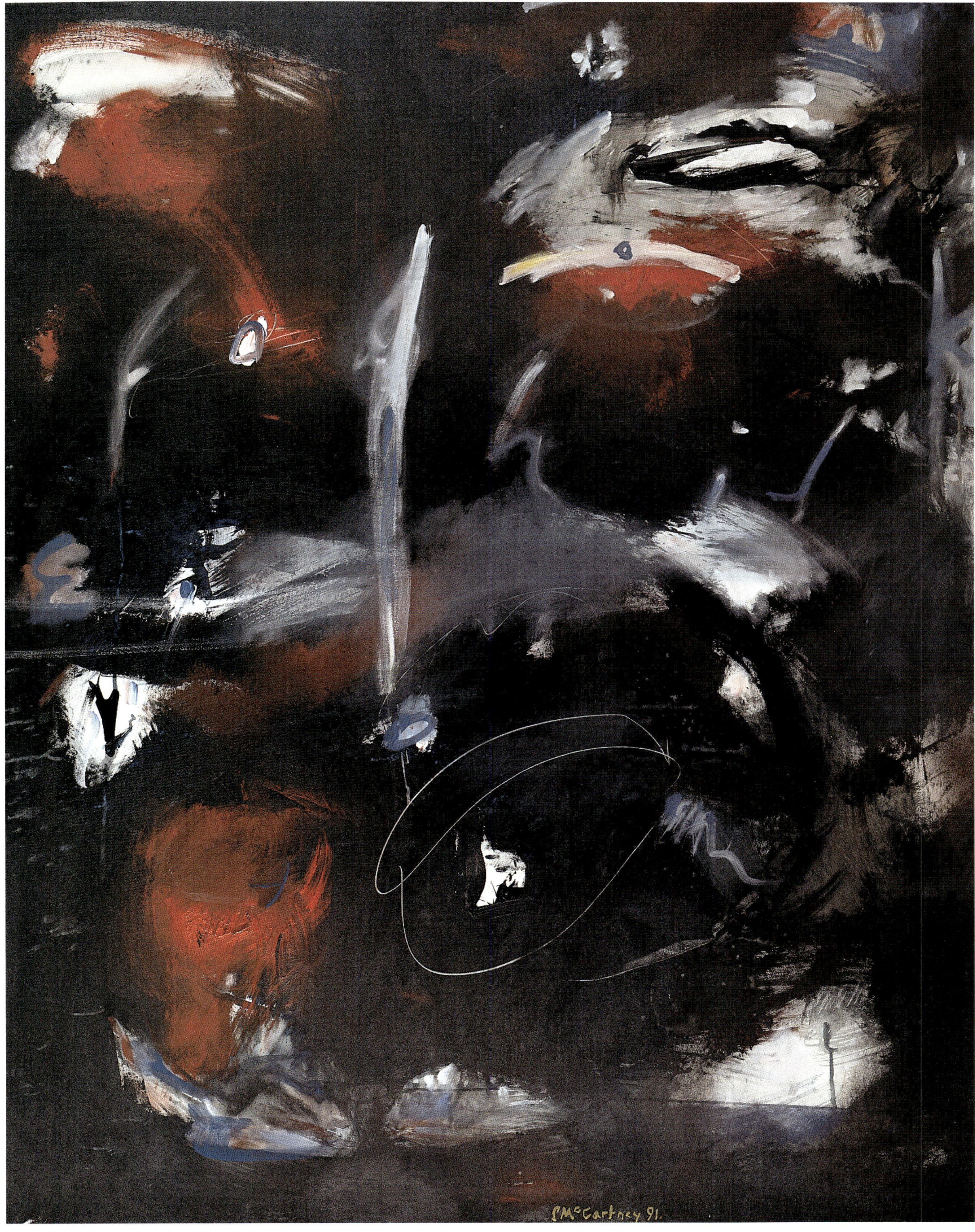

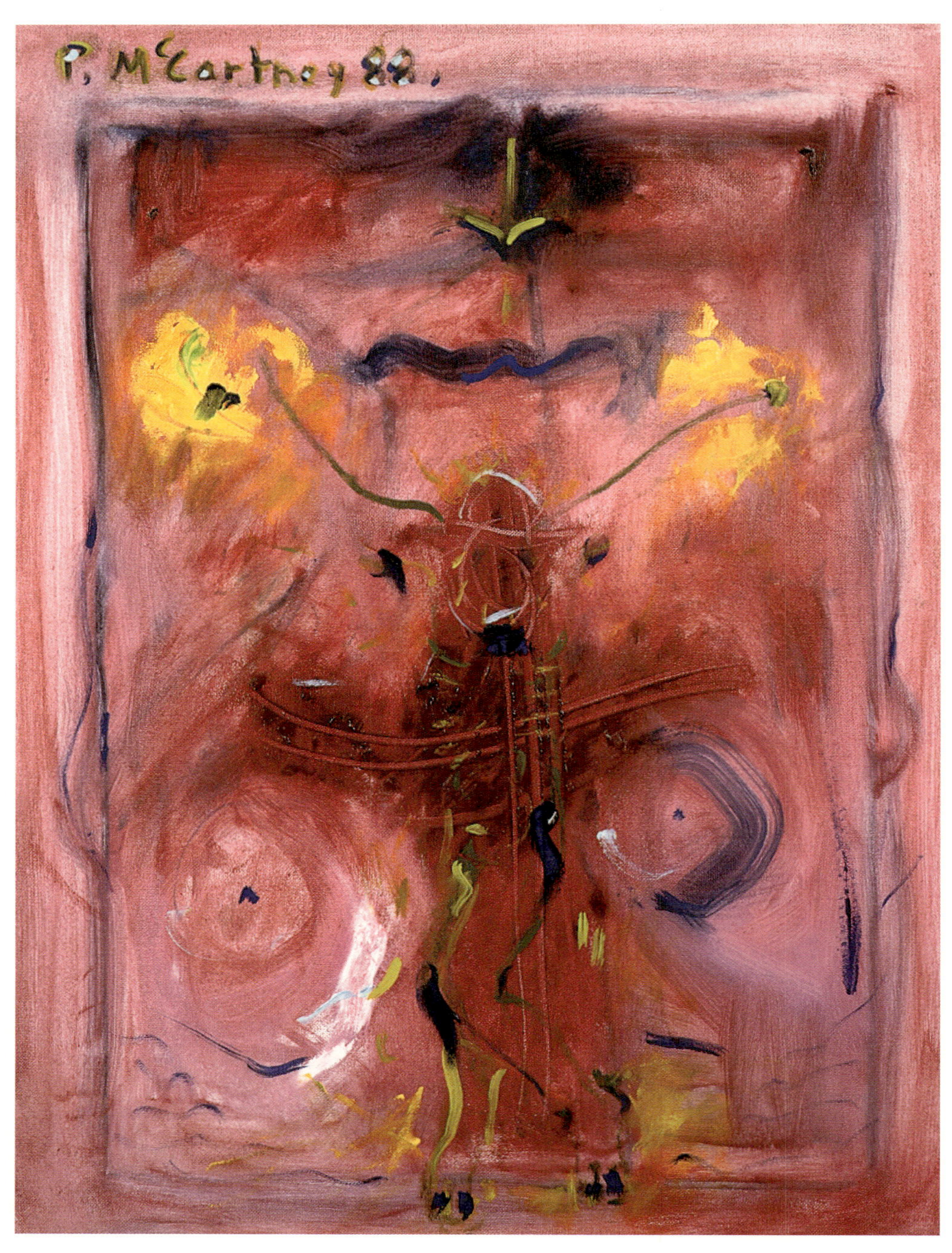

Upturned critic framed, 1988

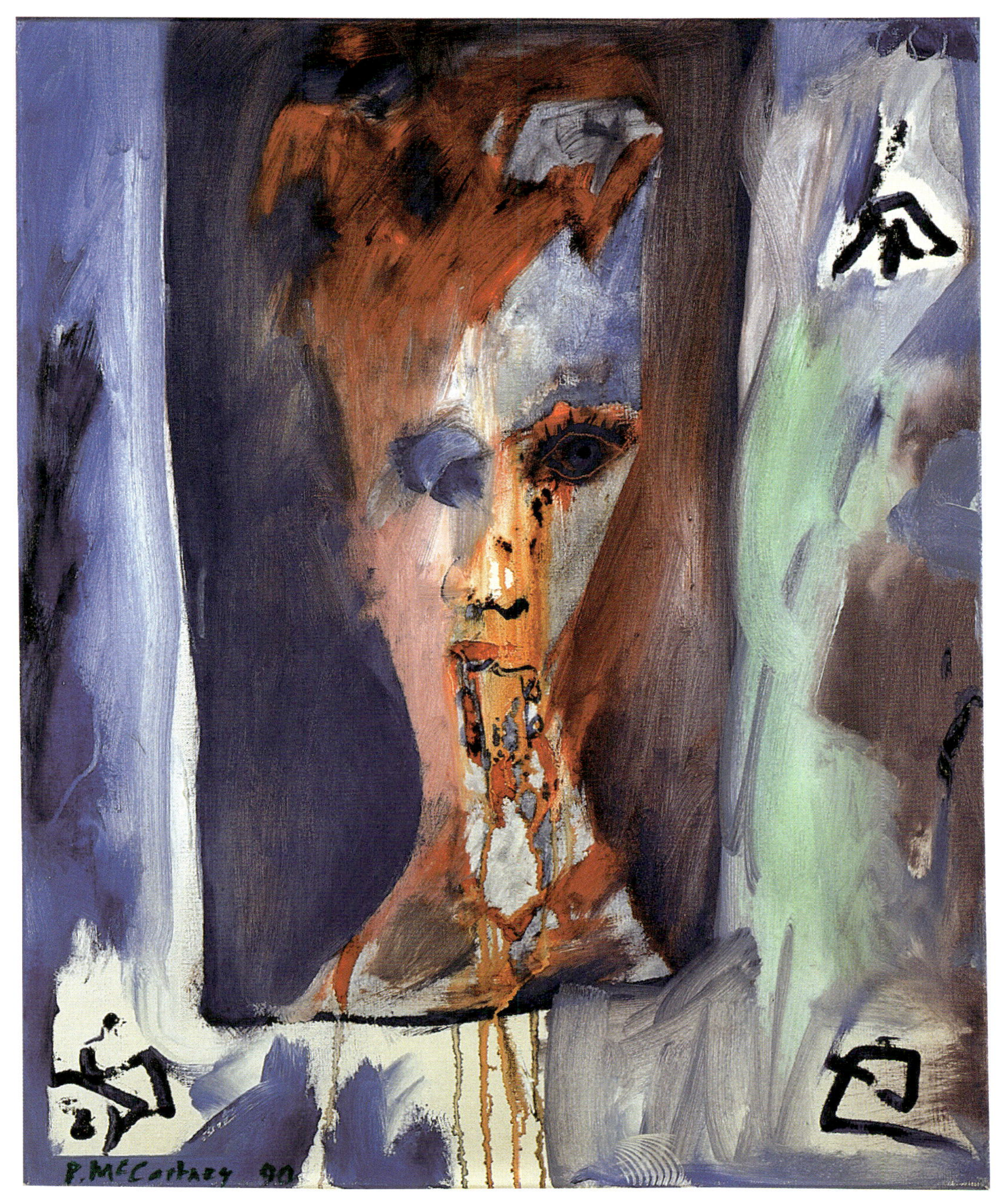

Bowie spewing, 1990

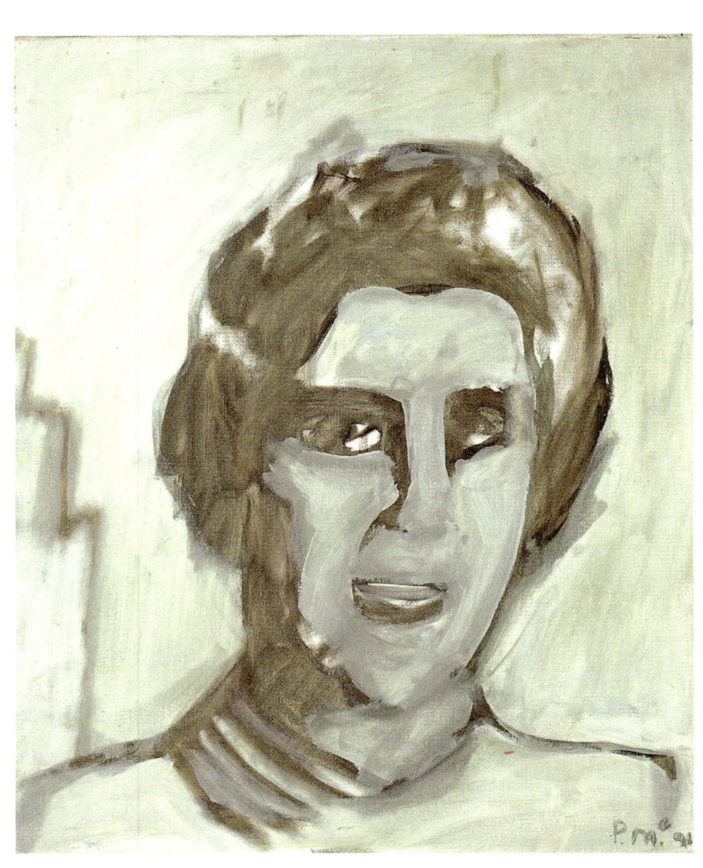

The Queen after her first cigarette, 1991

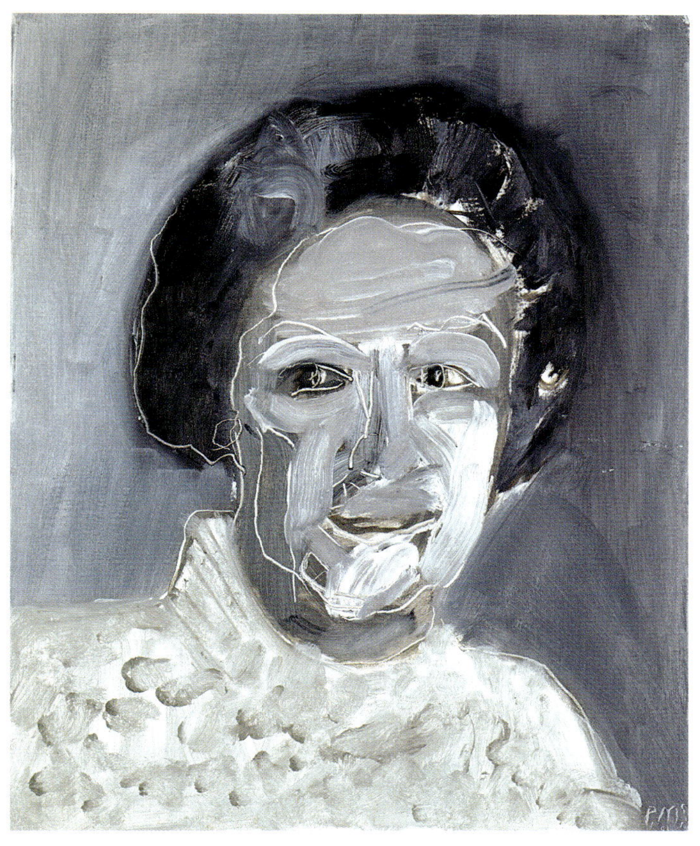

The Queen getting a joke, 1991

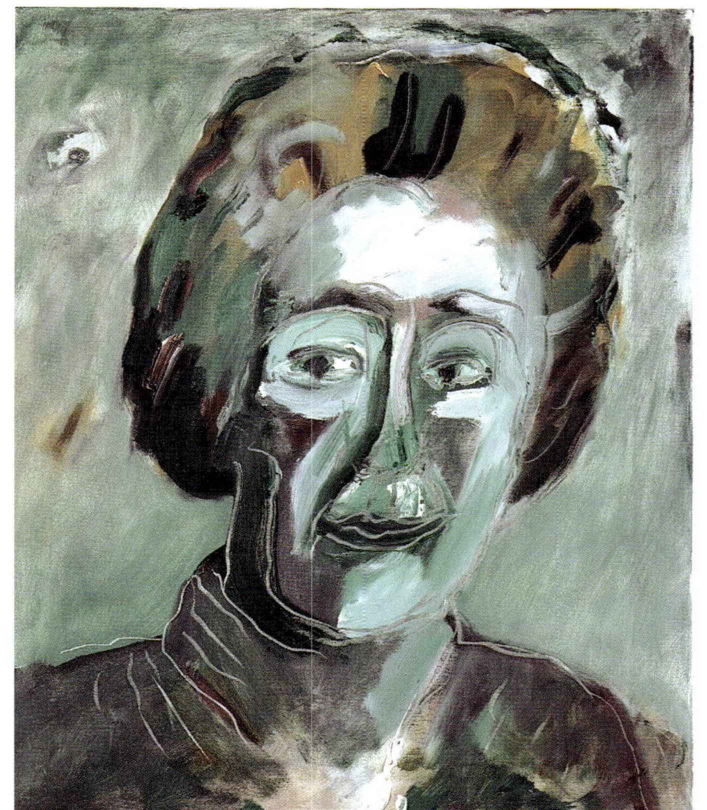

A greener Queen, 1991

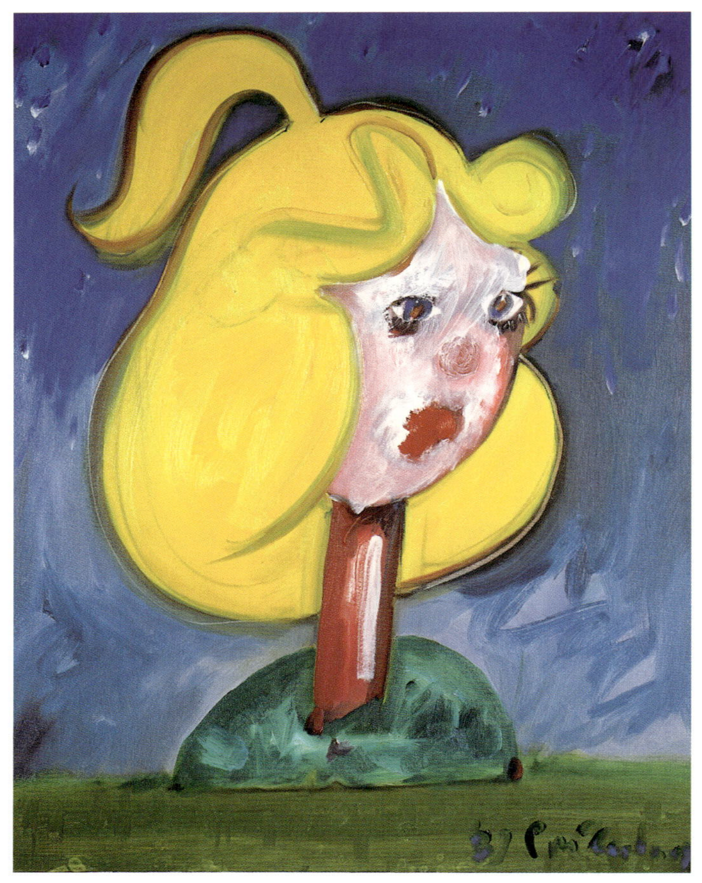

Patti Boyd, 1989

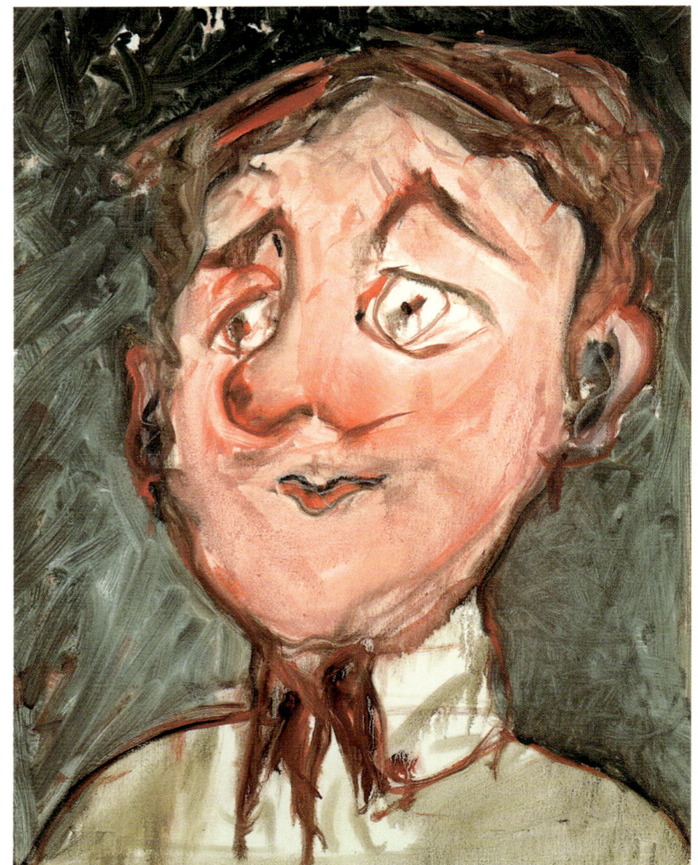

Mr. Kipps, 1988

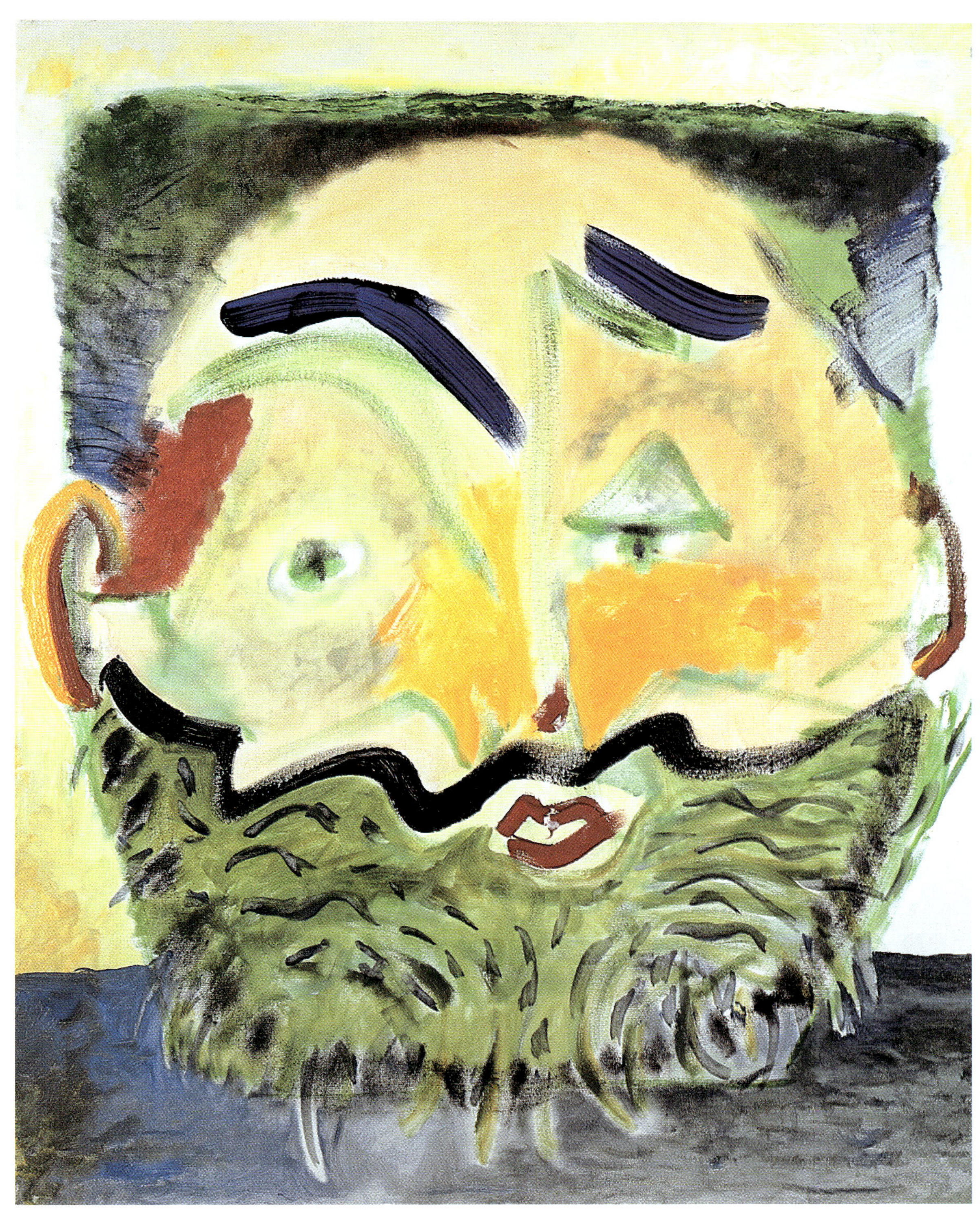

Man o' the sea, 1988

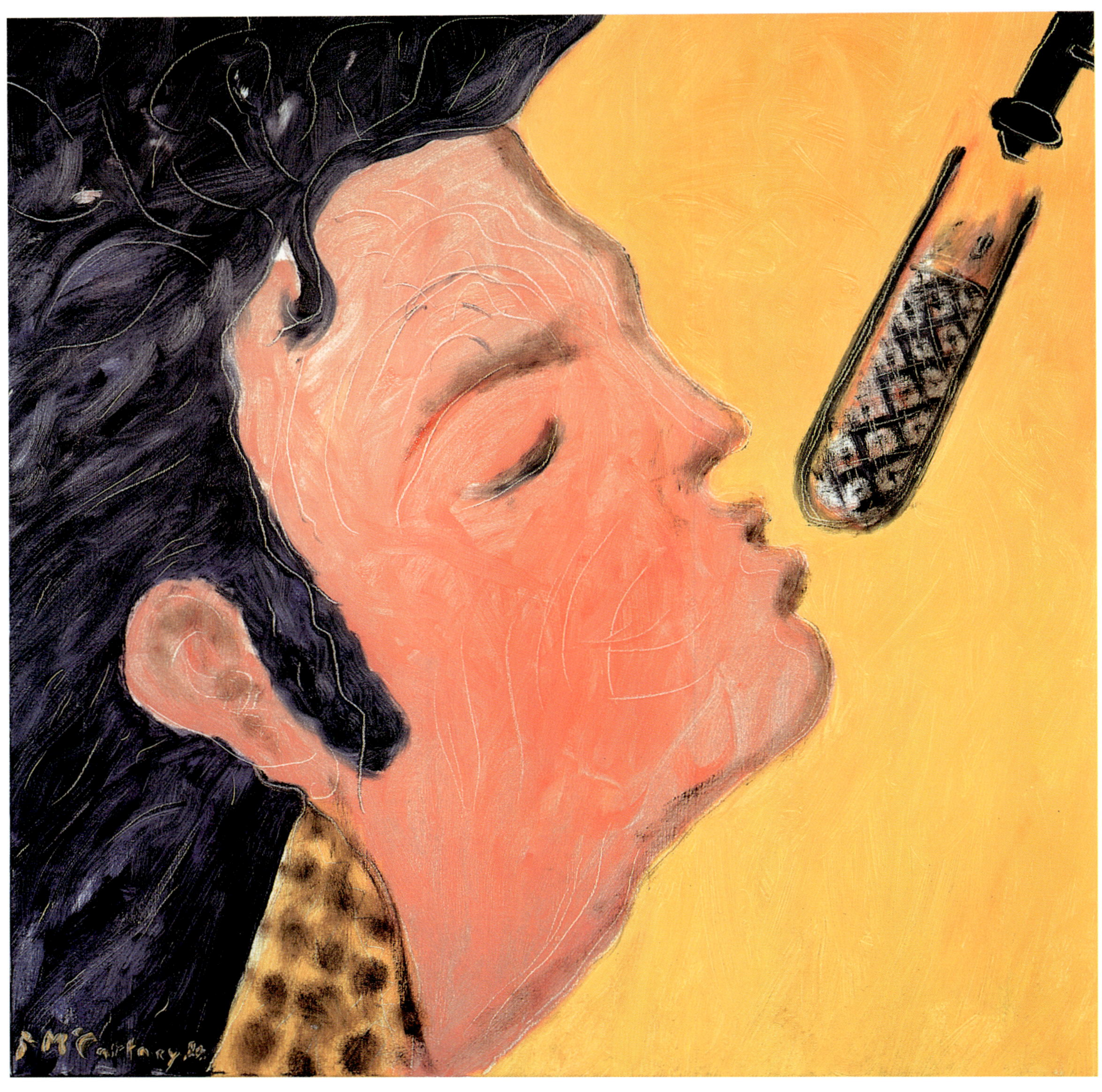

Elvish me, 1989

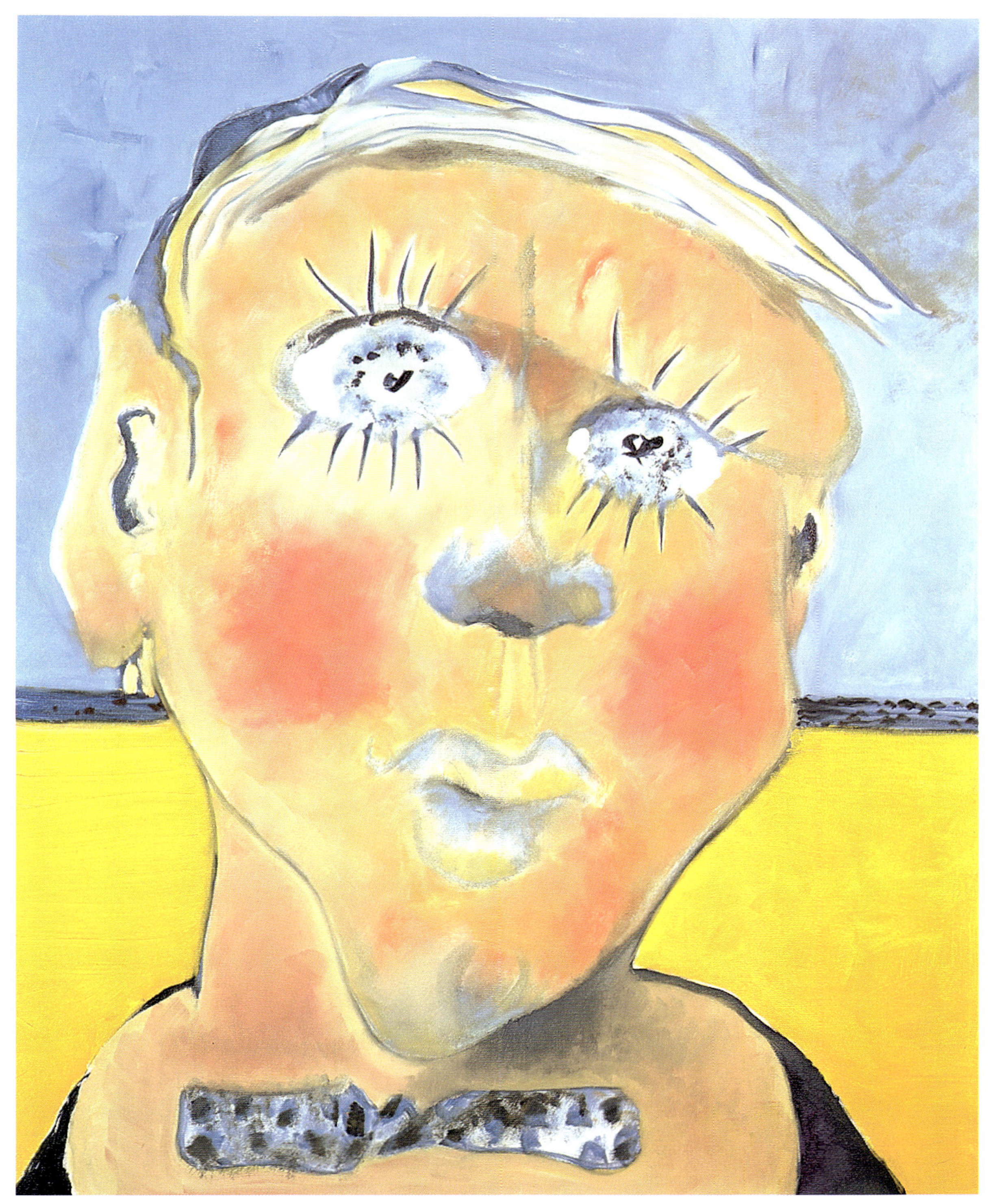

Beach boy, 1988

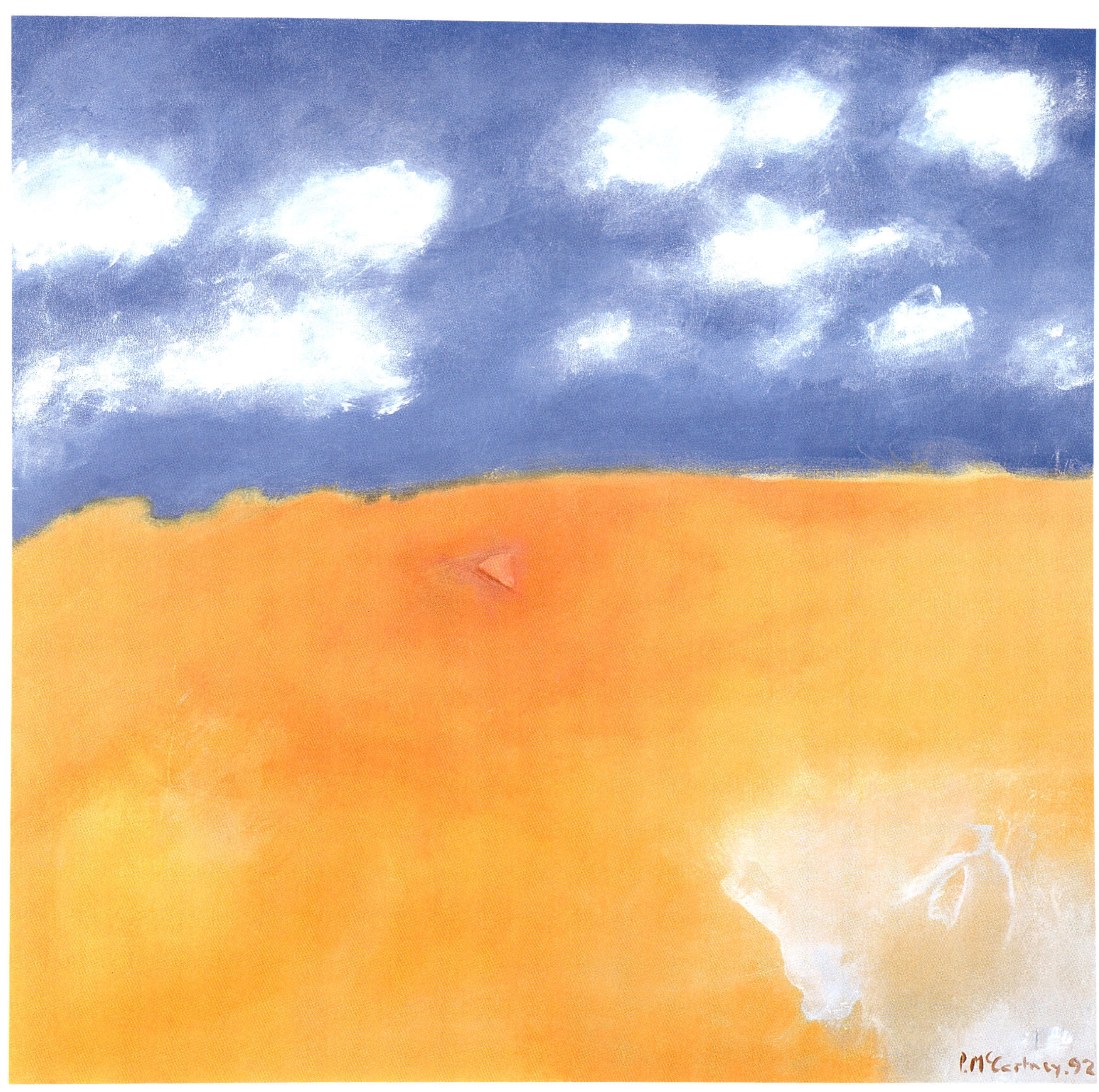

Red triangle sand, 1992

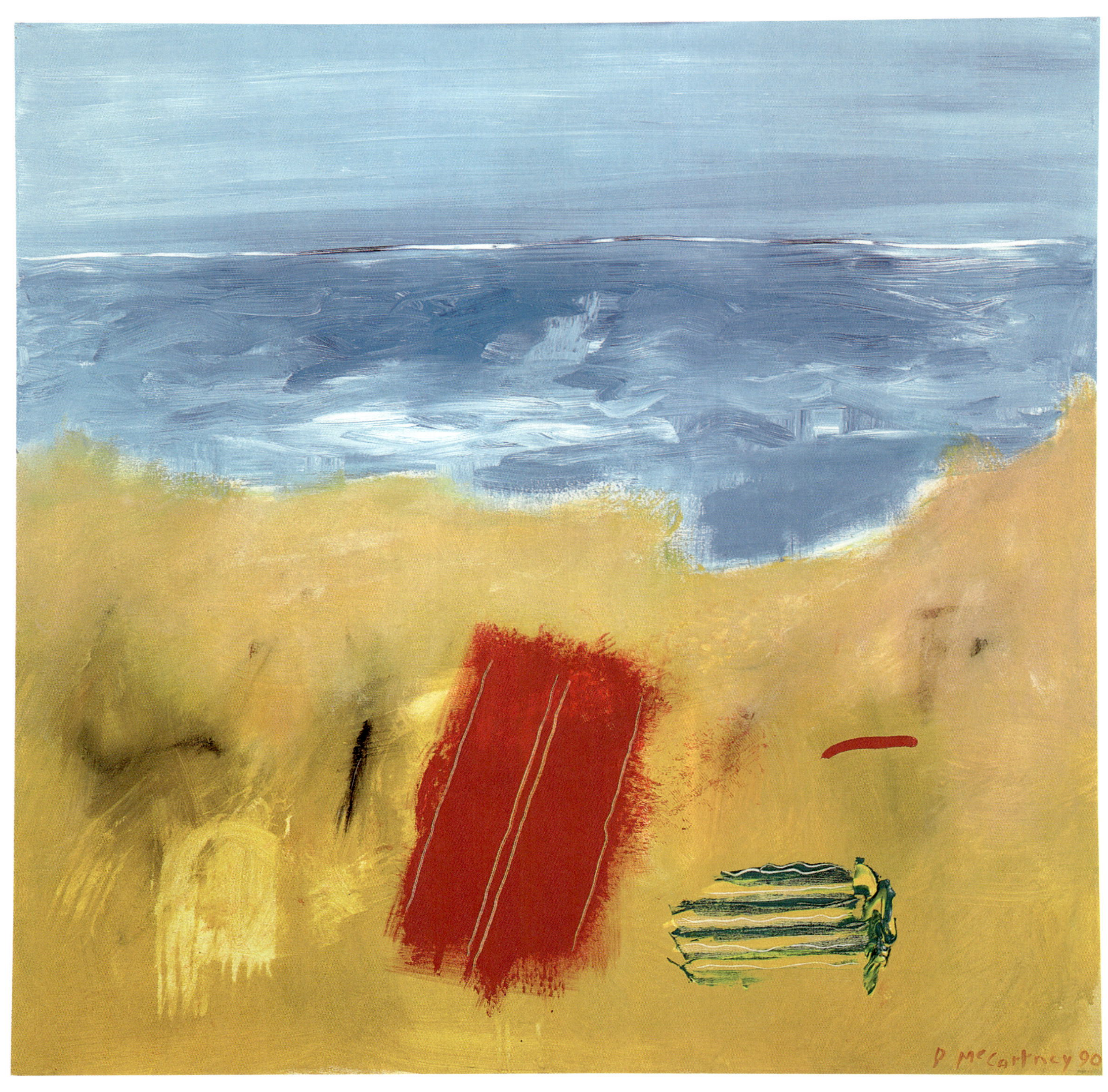

Beach towels, 1990

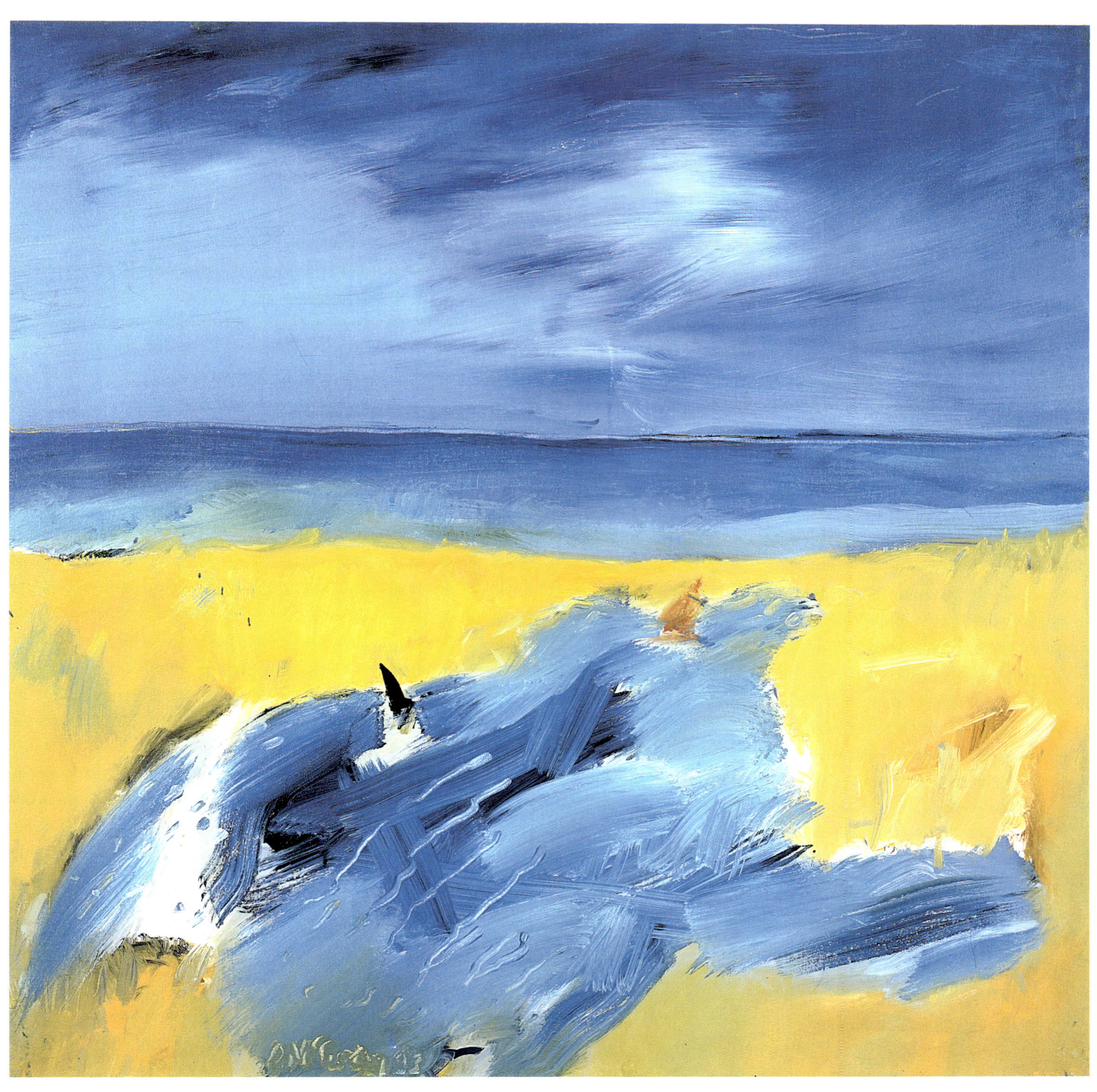

Shark on Georgica, 1993

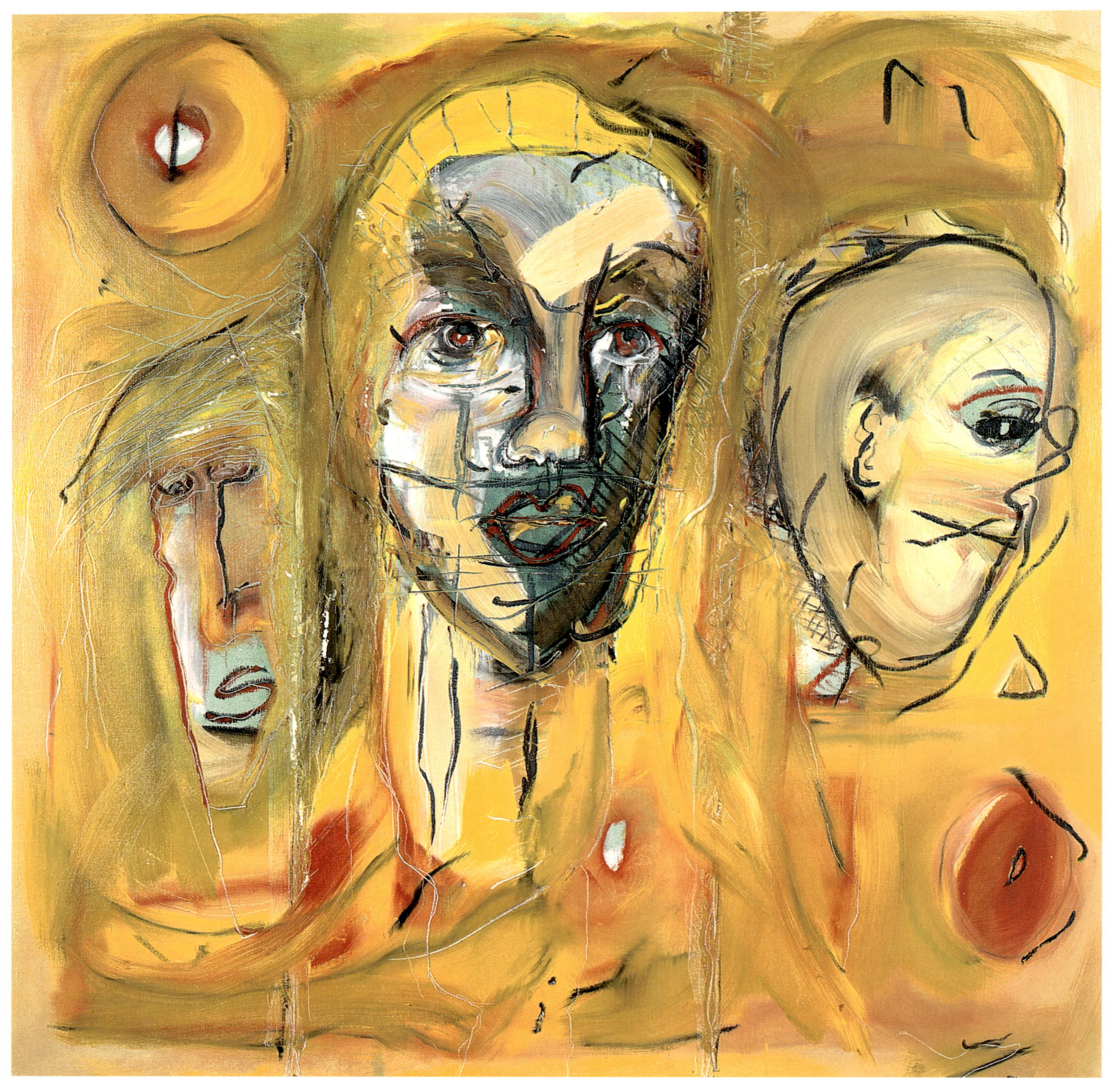

Unspoken words, 1994

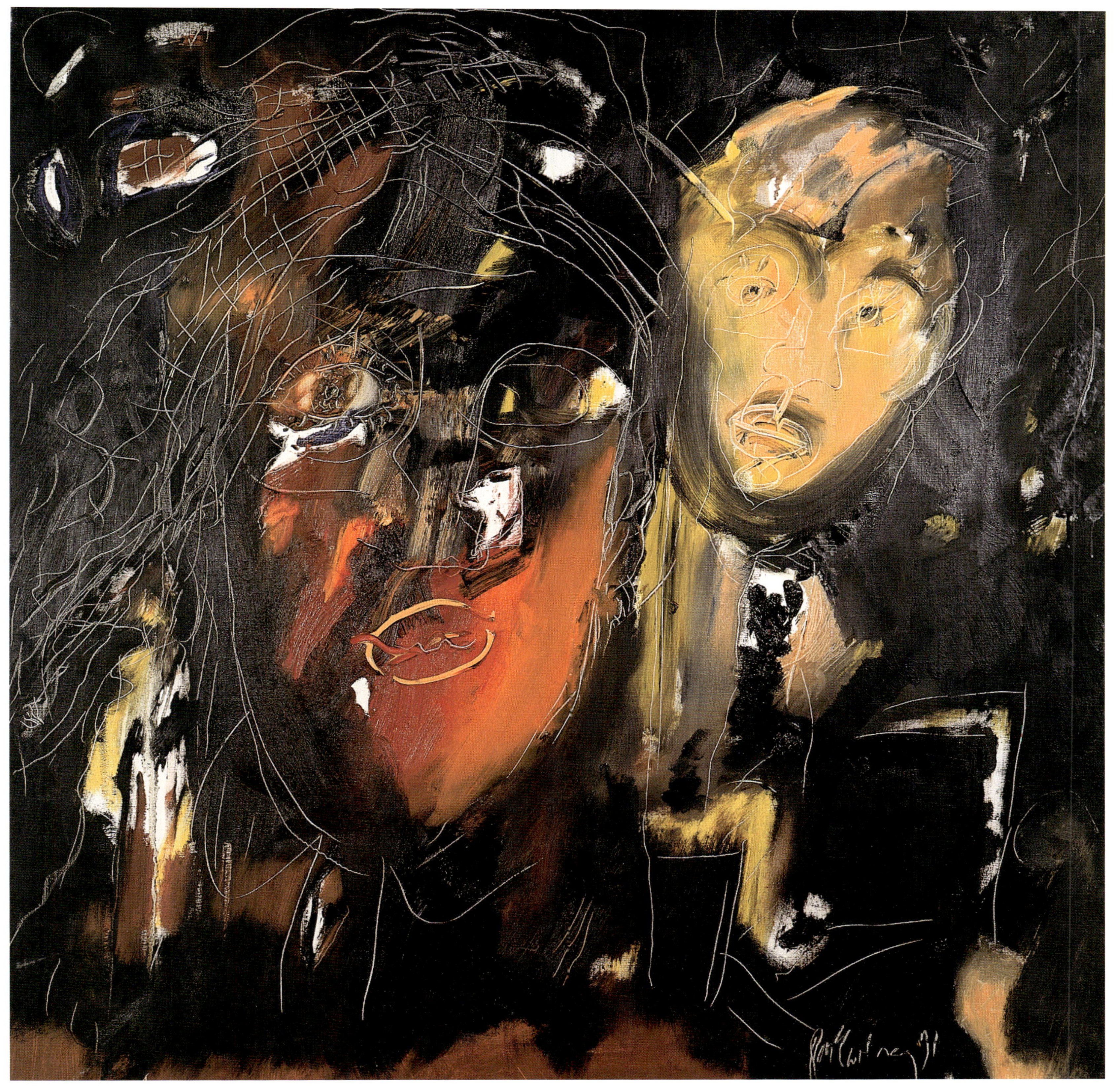

Dark faces, 1991

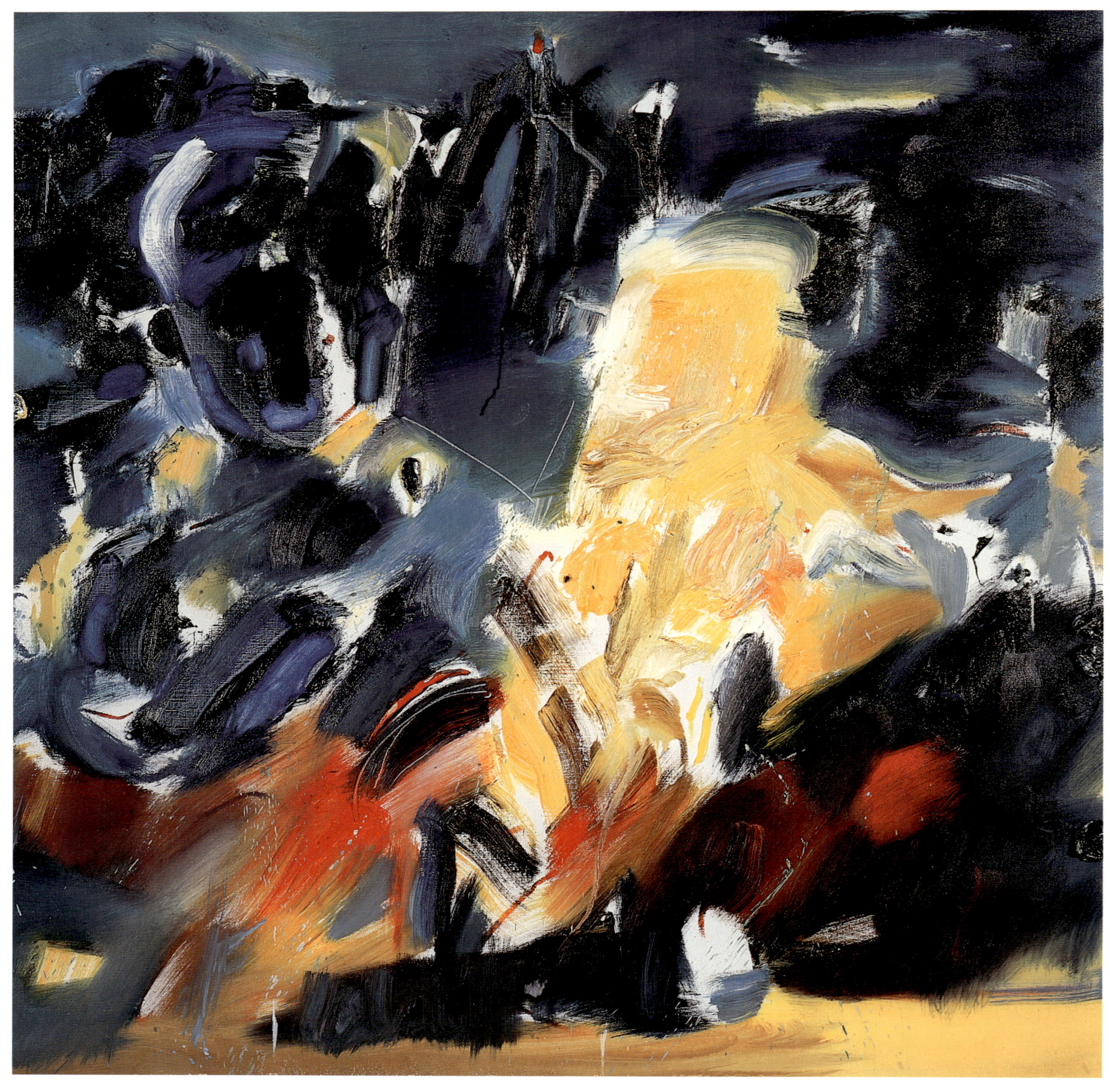

Robot and star, 1995

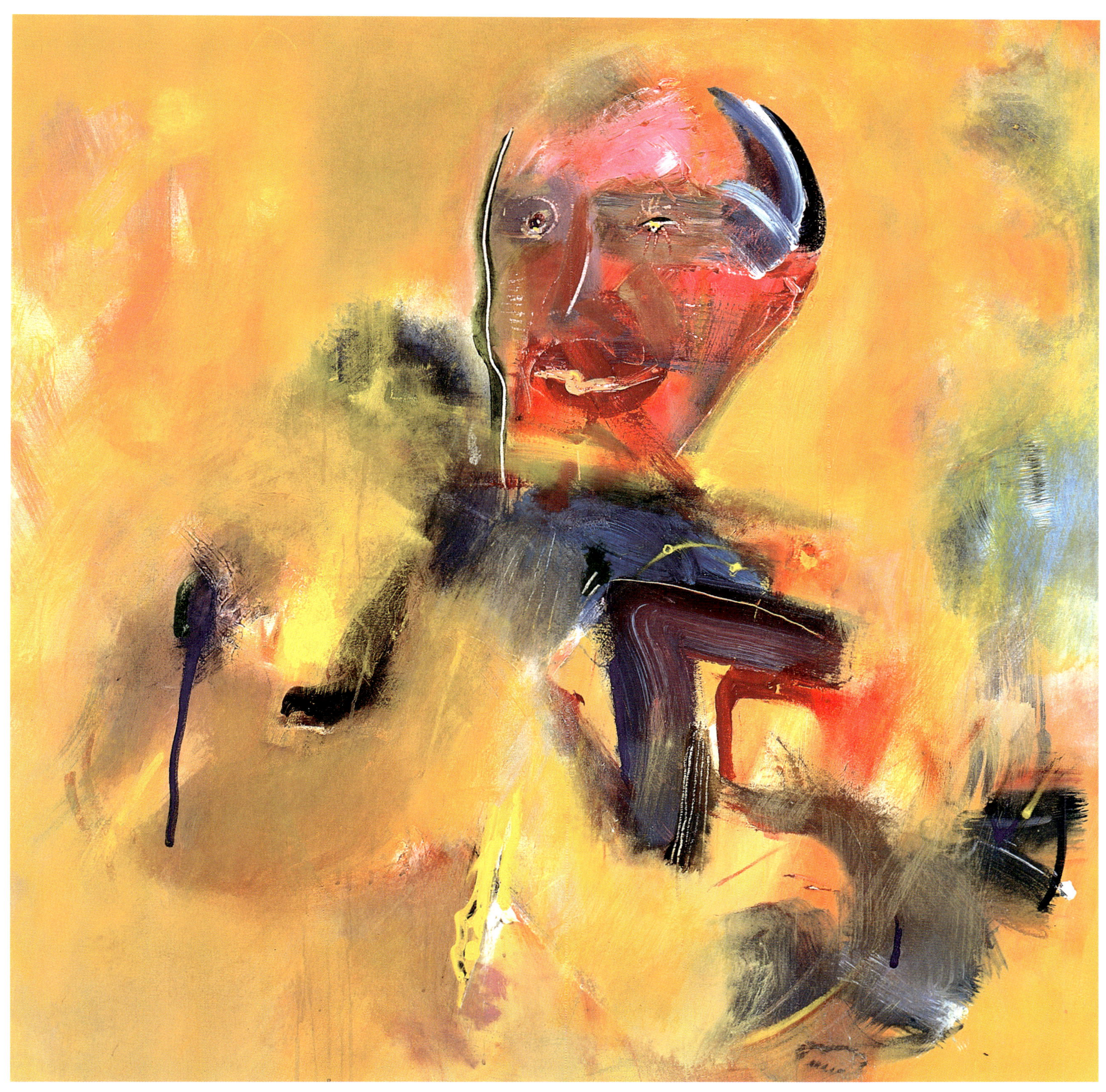

Abstract coloured twenties man, 1989

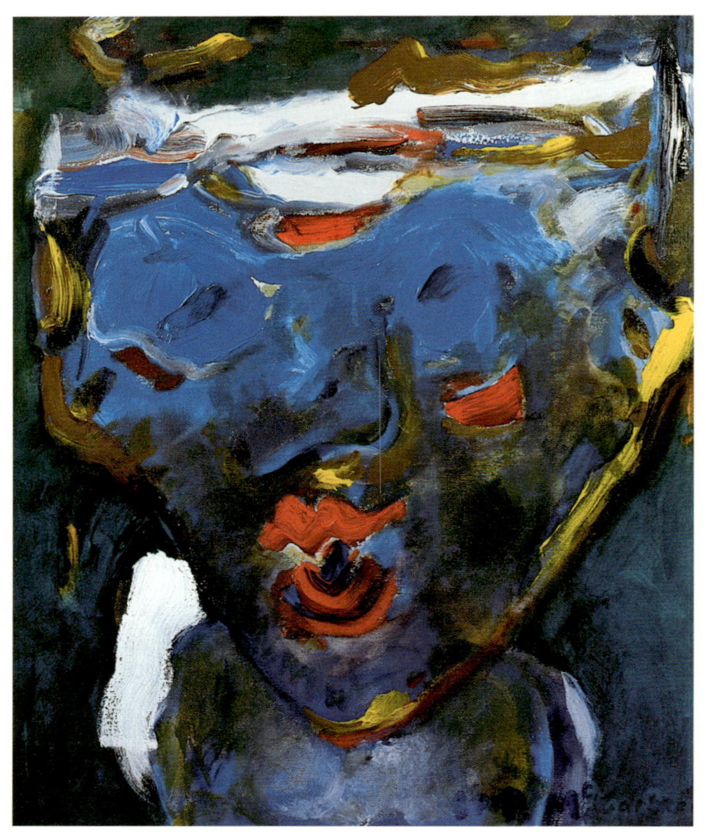

Blue mask, 1989

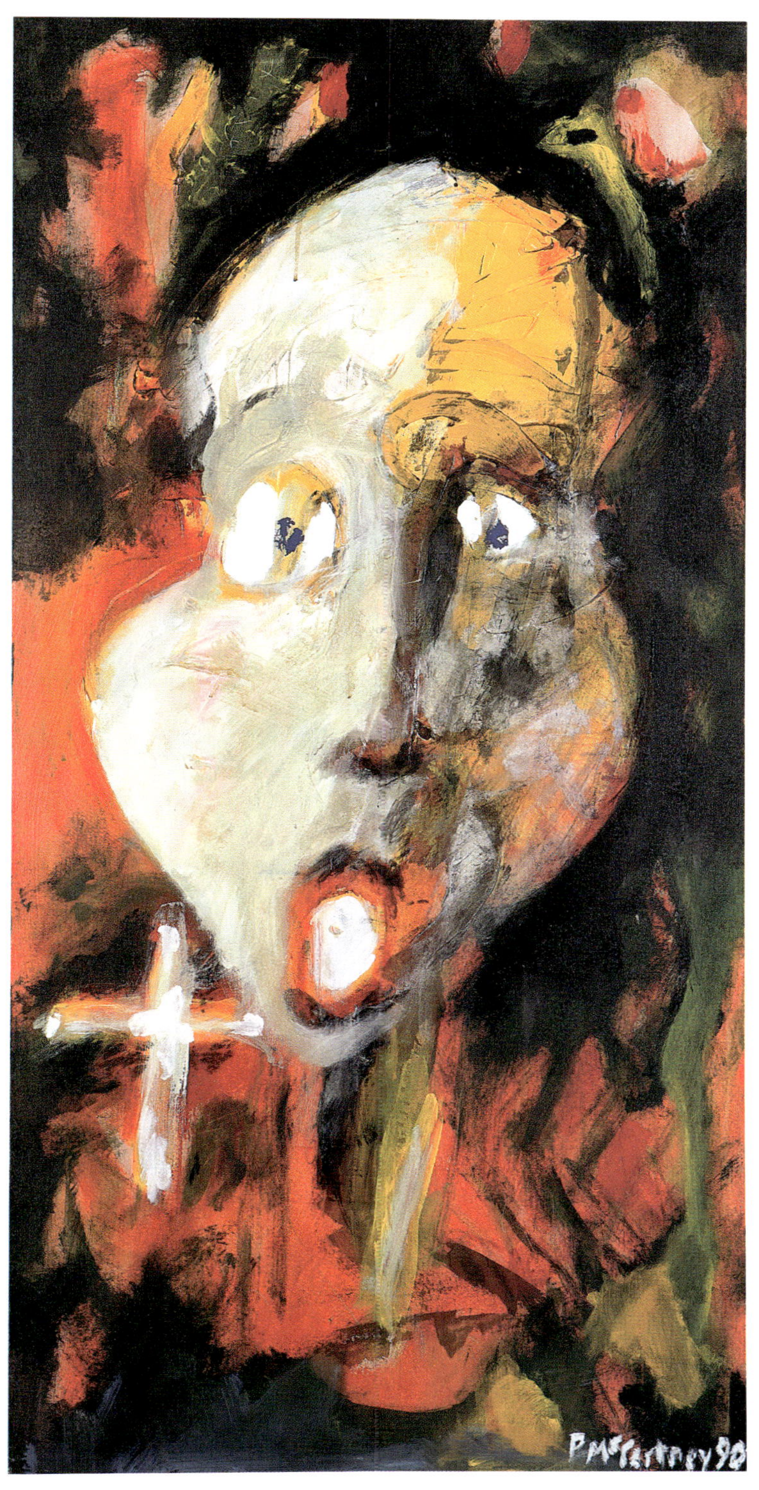

White cross face, 1990

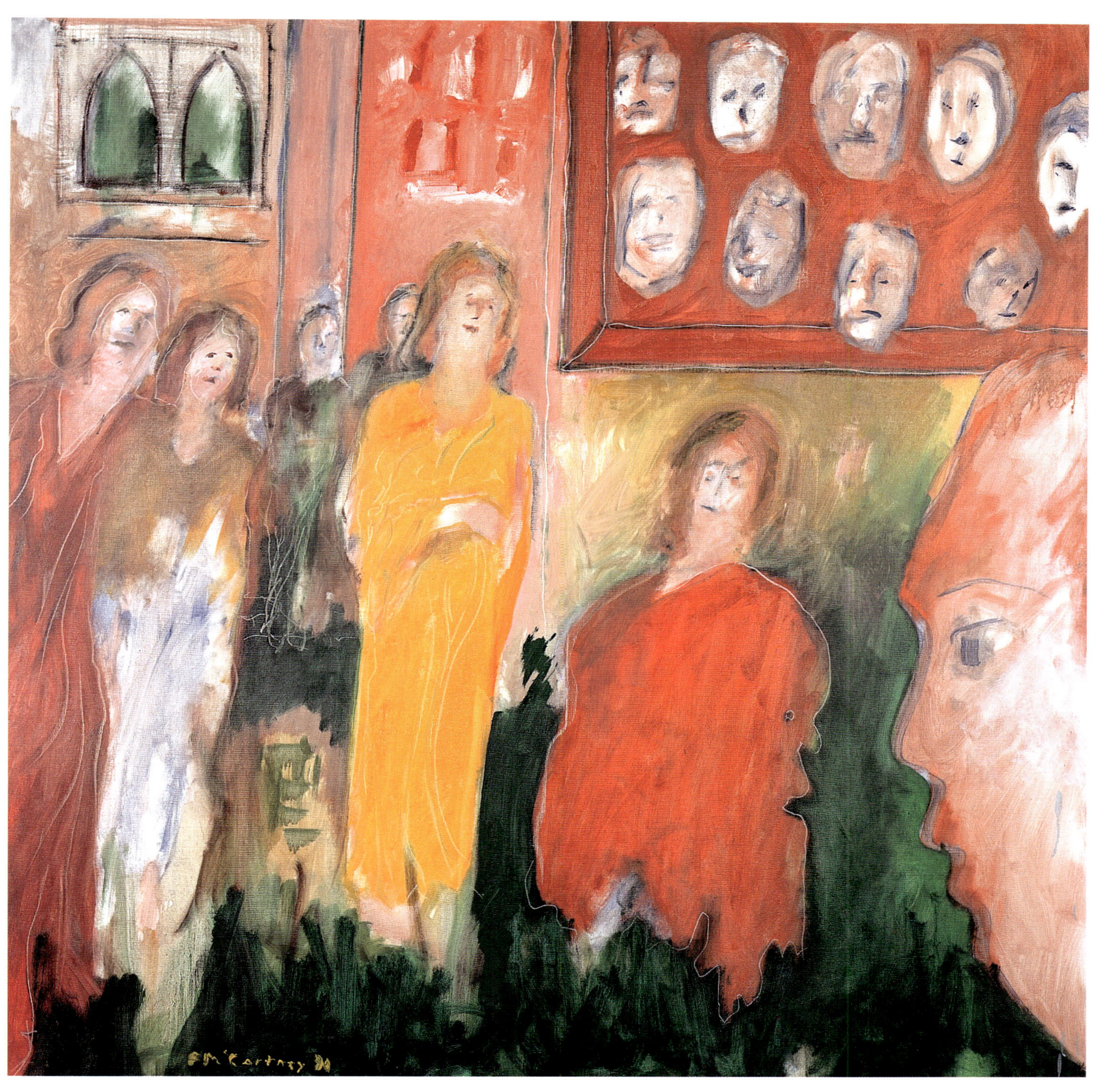

John's room, 1990

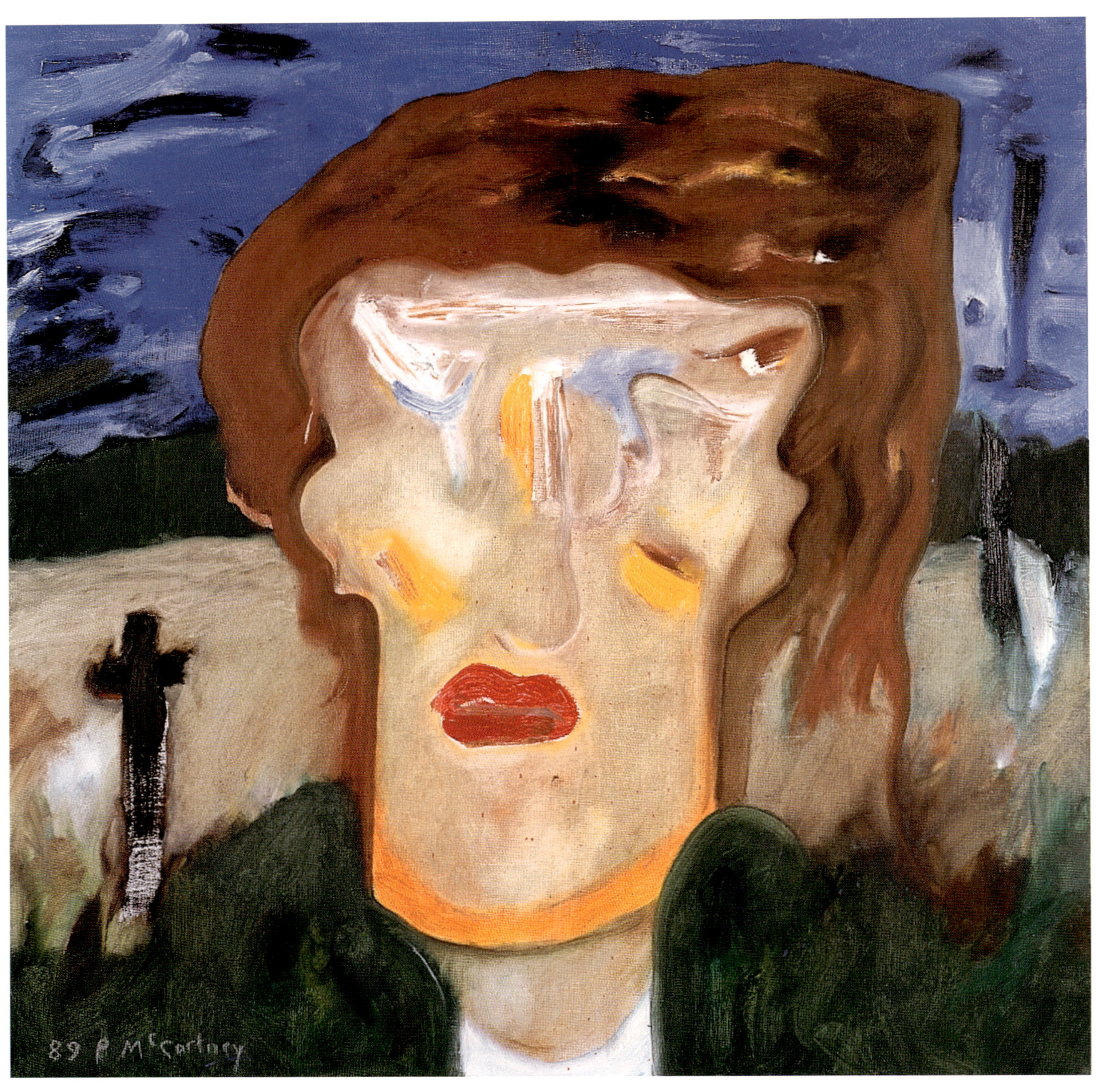

Green jacket with cross on shoulder, 1989

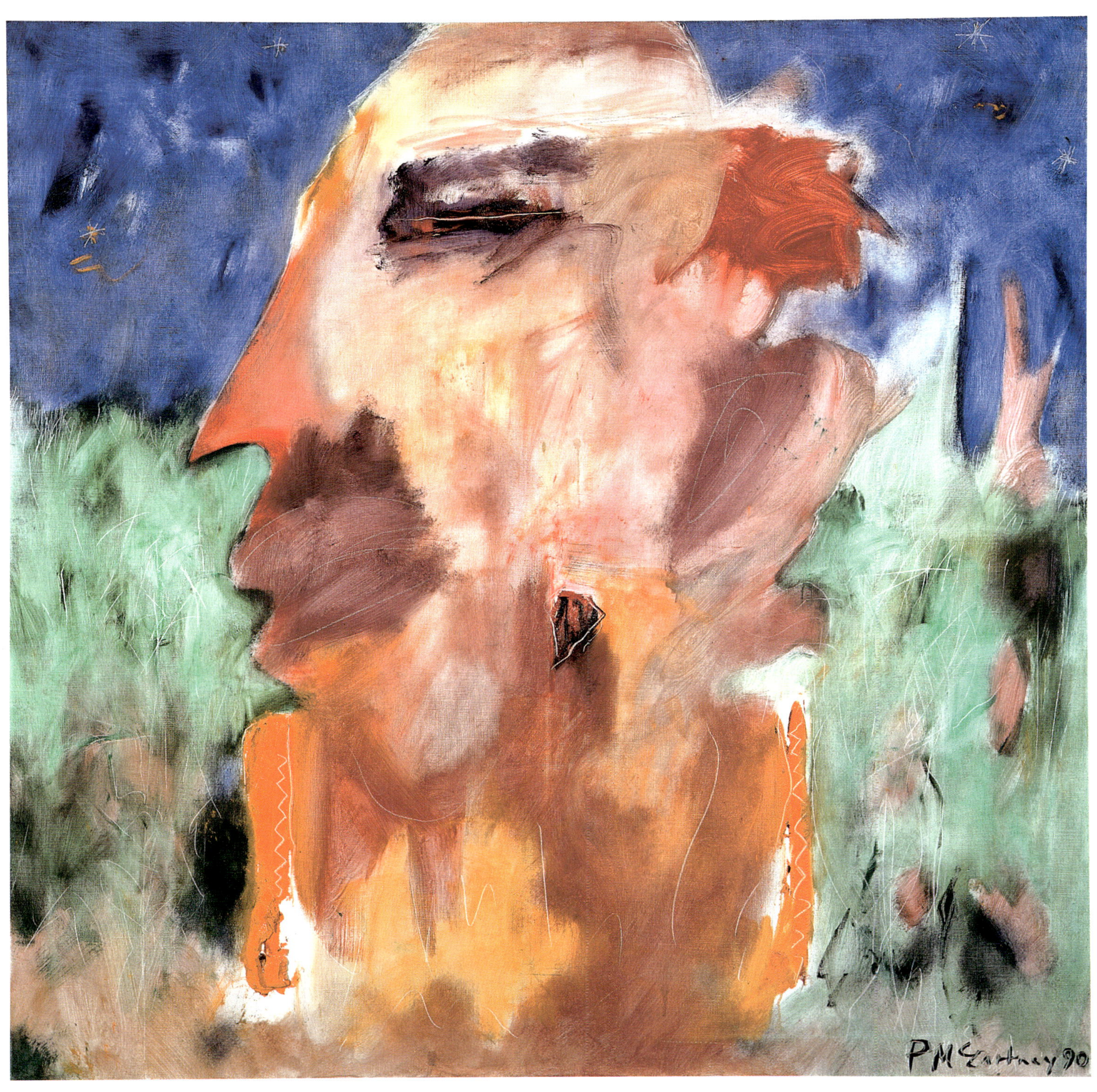

Bald head, 1990

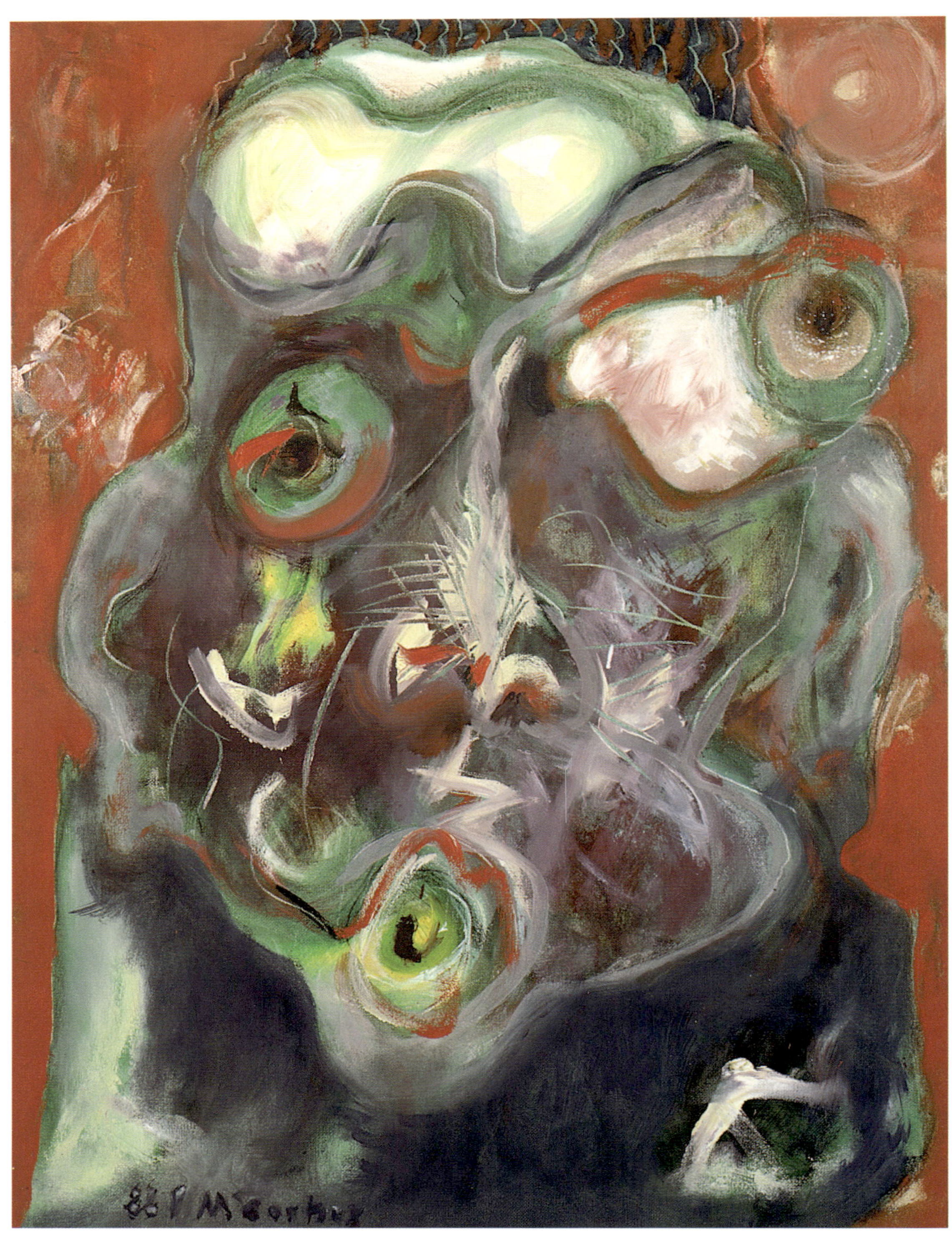

Insect face, 1989

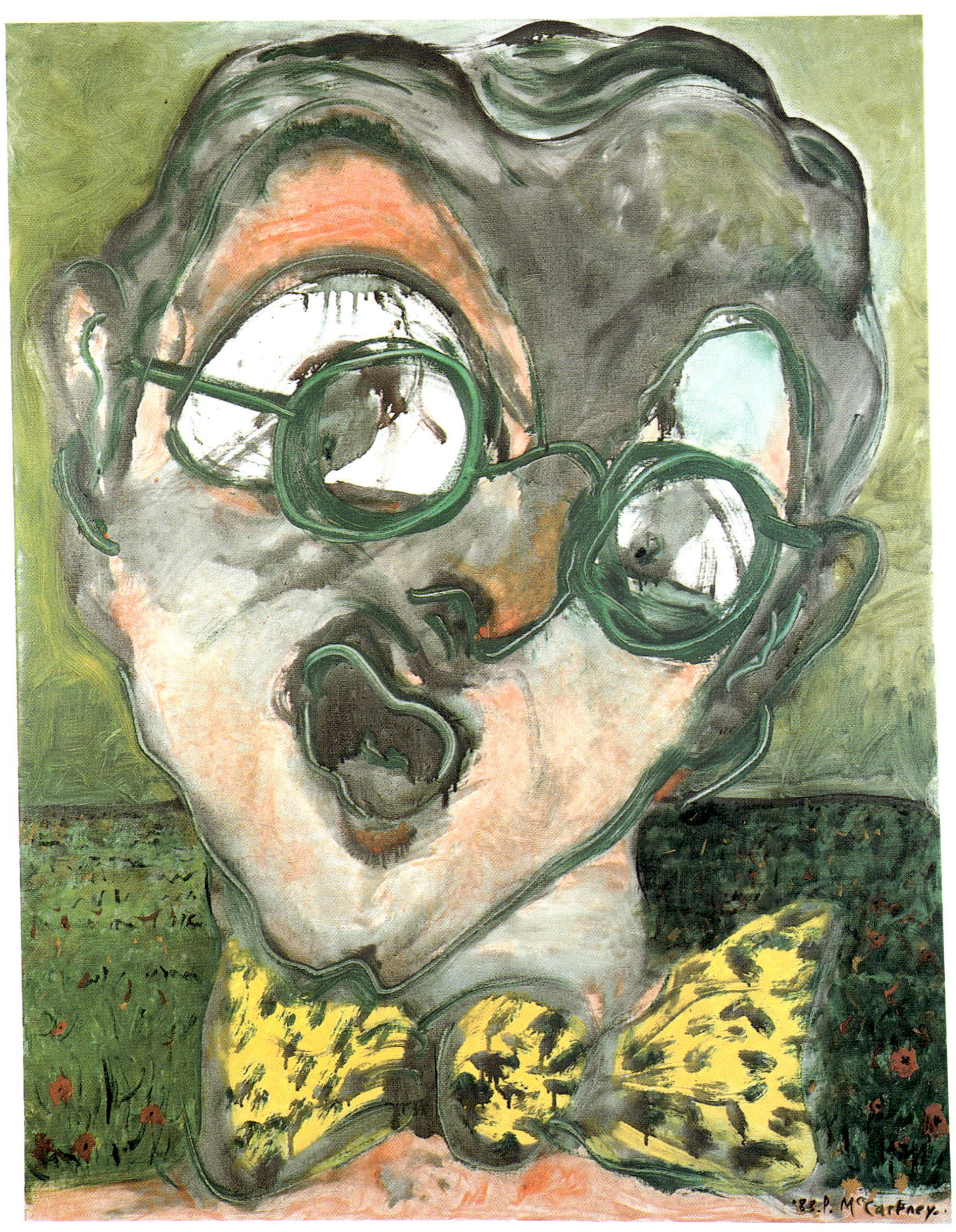

Green head, 1988

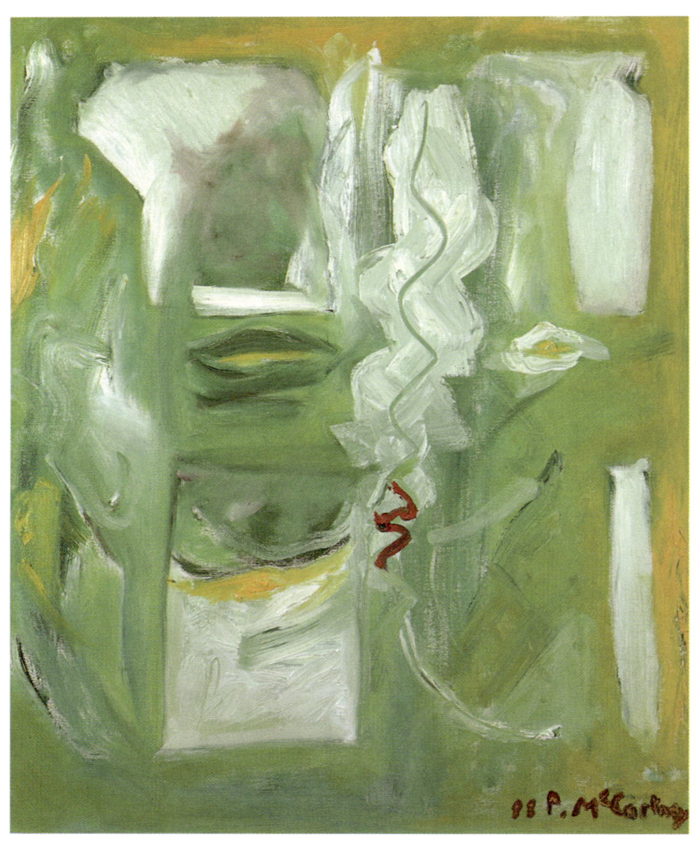

Green kiss, 1988

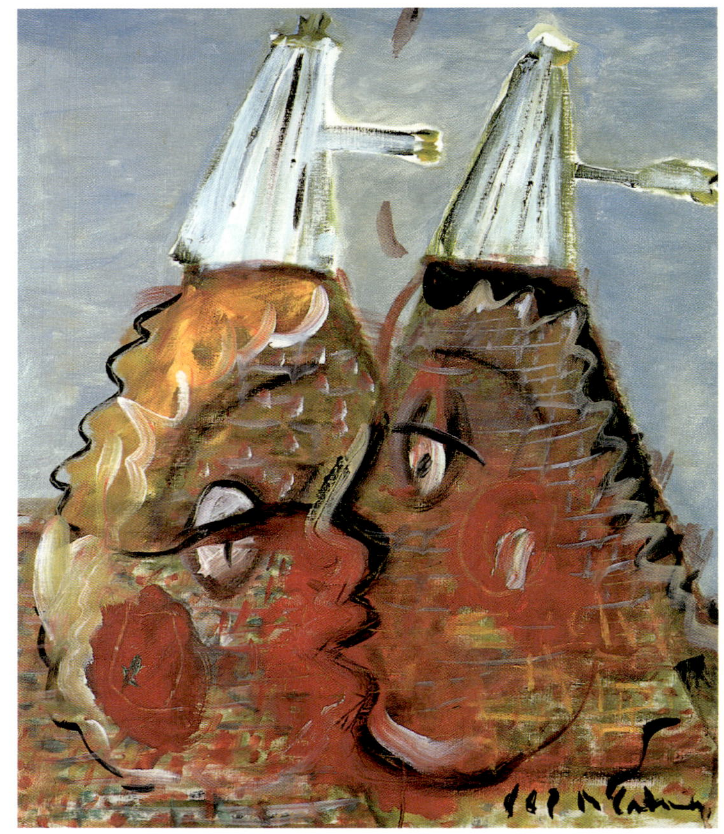

Oast kiss, 1988

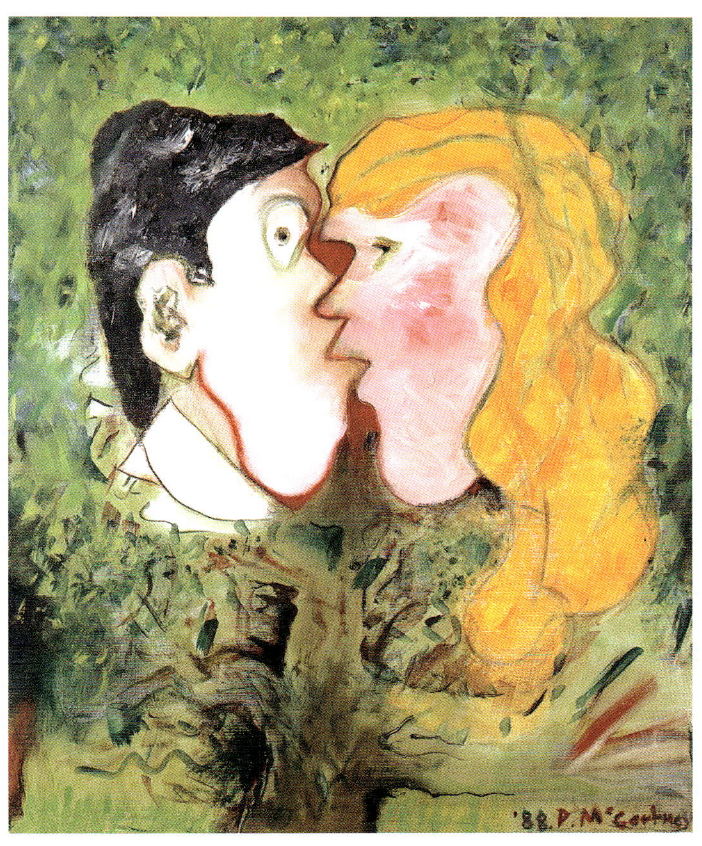

The kiss, 1988

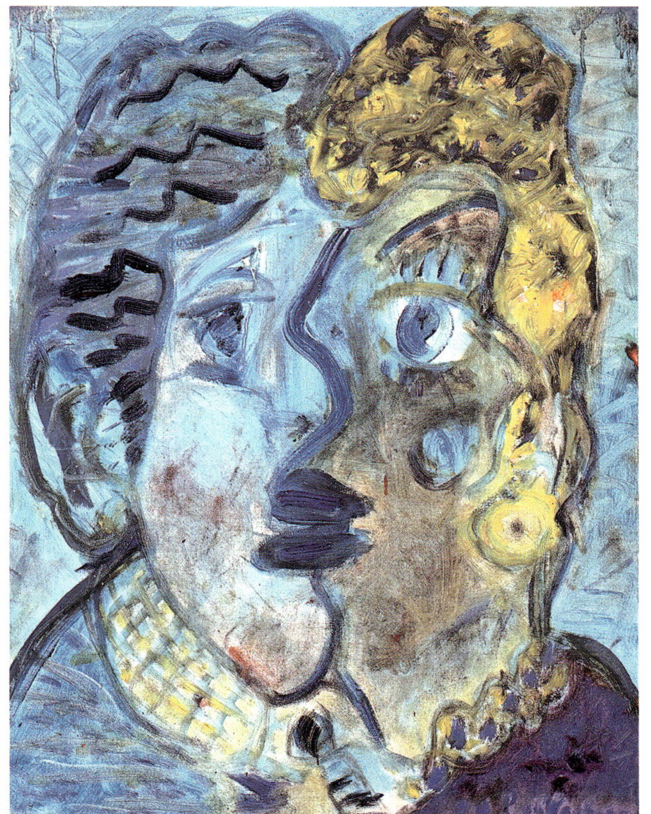

Blue kiss, 1988

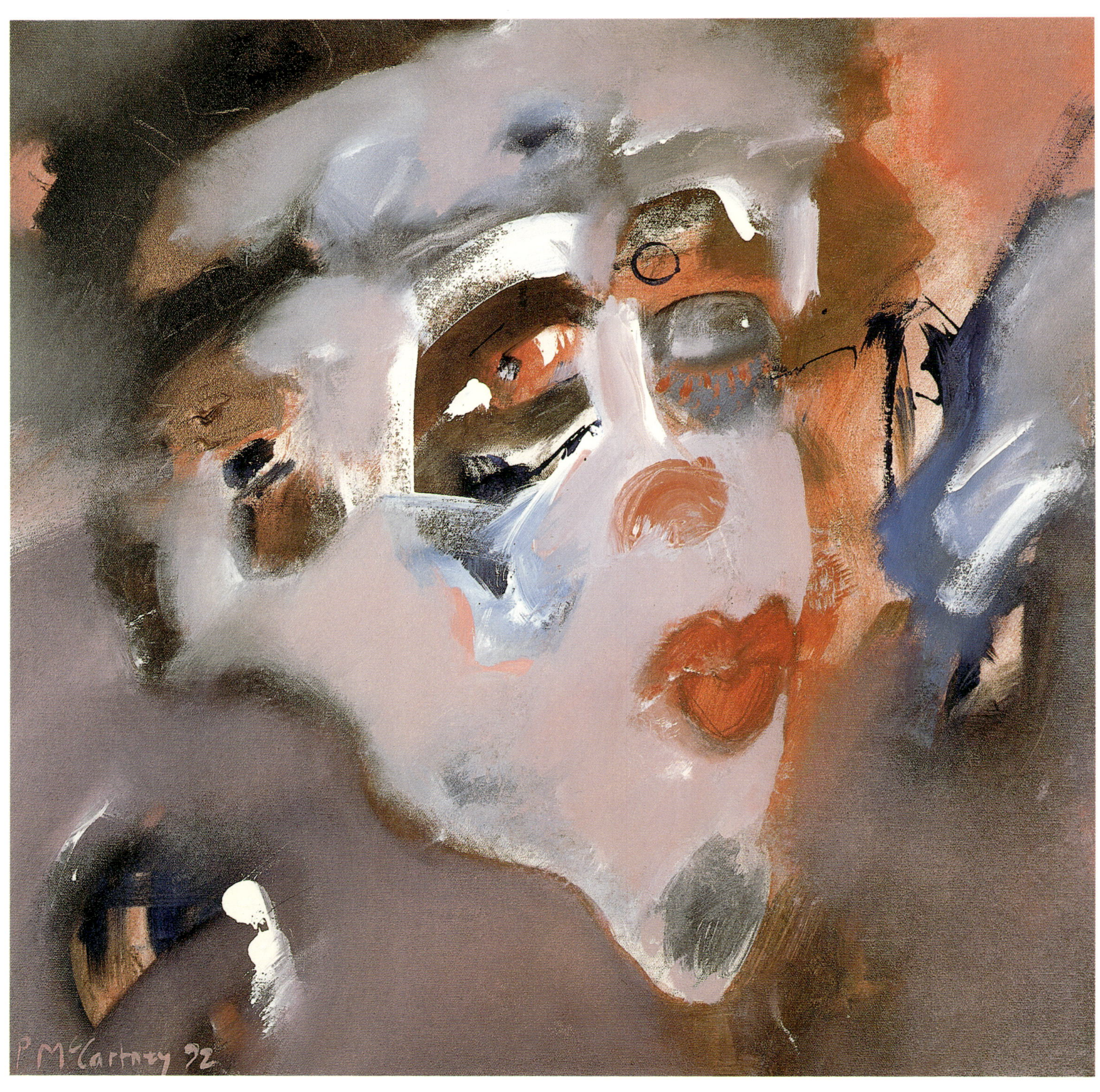

Grey head vision, 1992

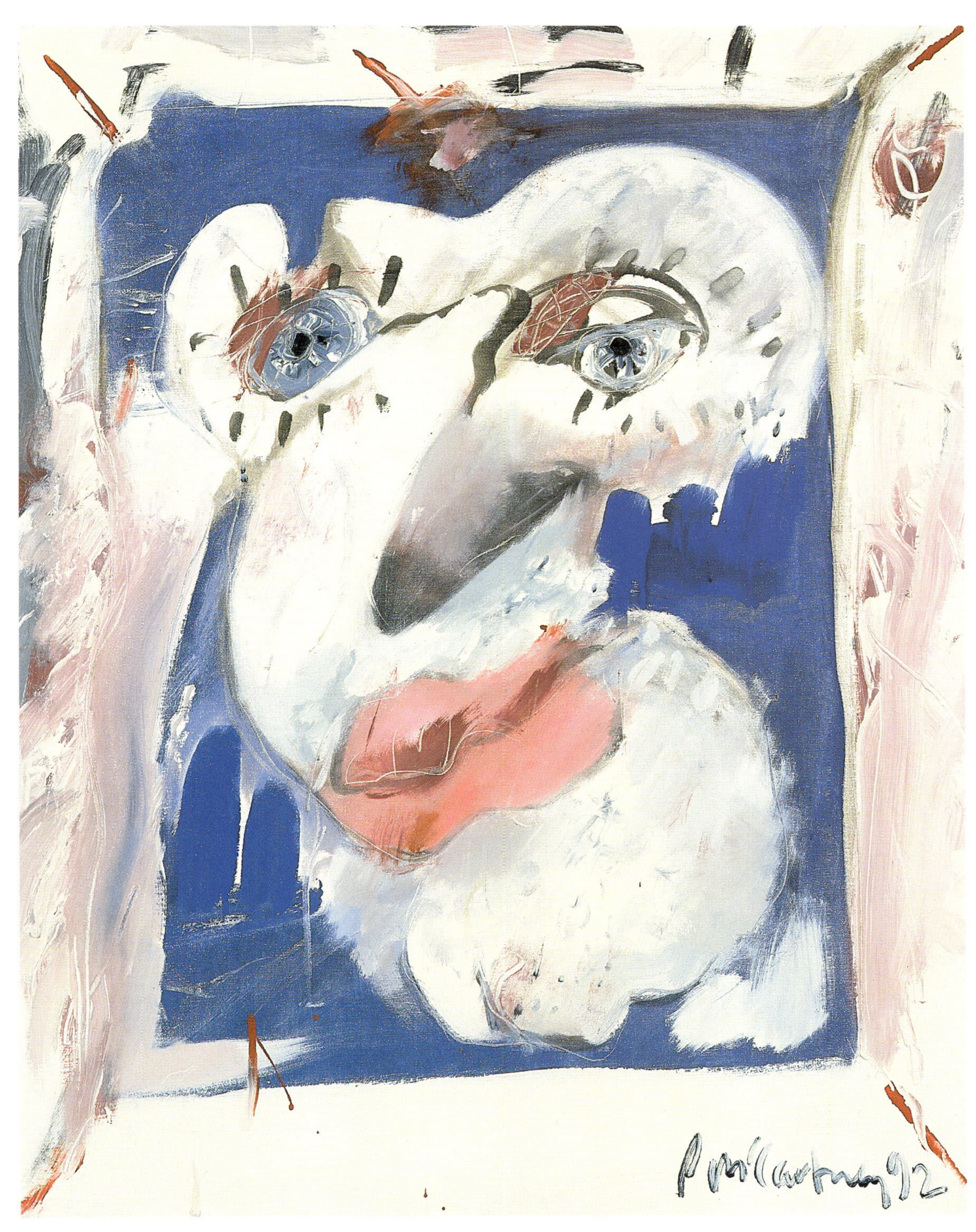

Housepaint down, 1992

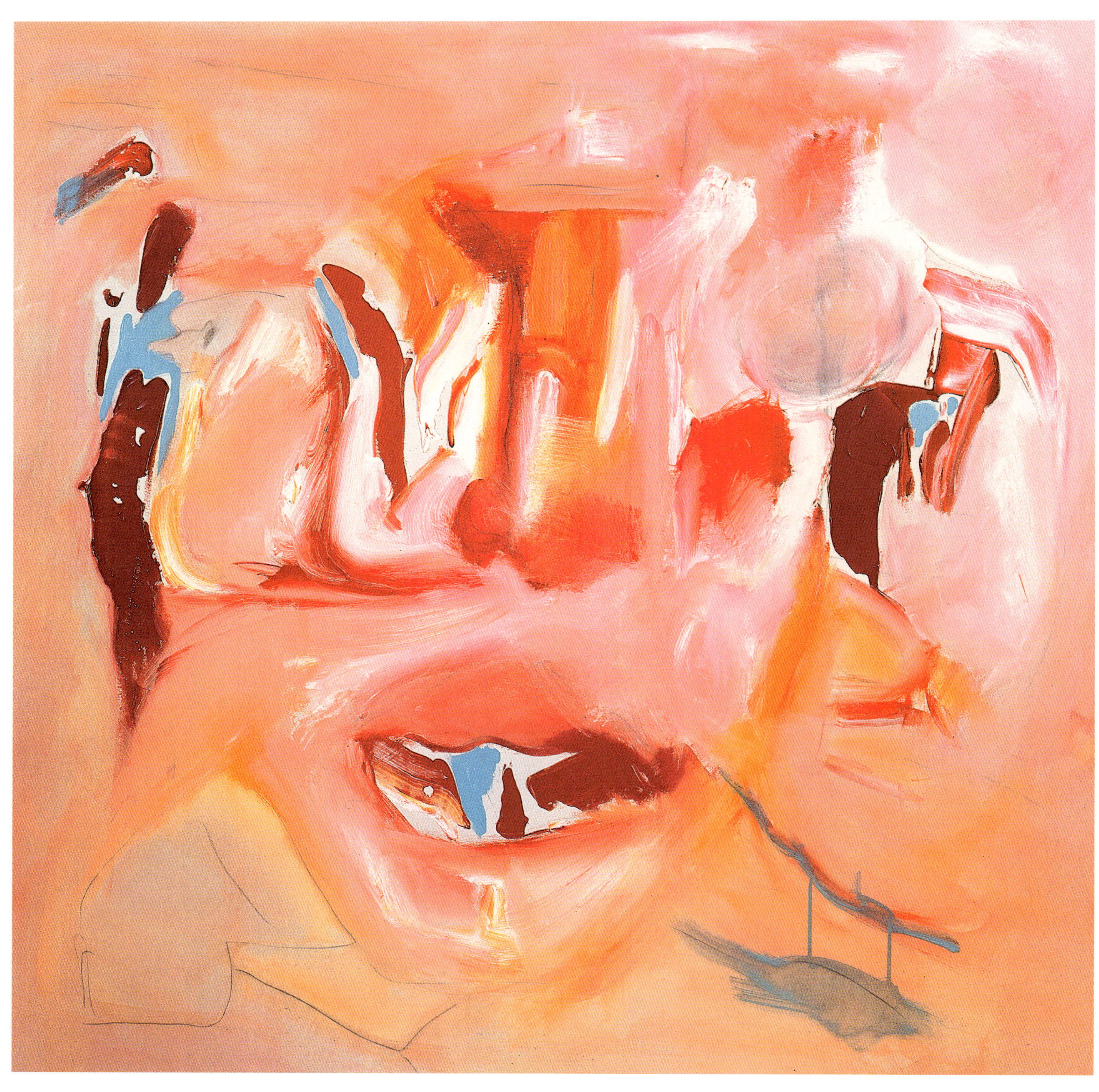

Blue tooth, 1991

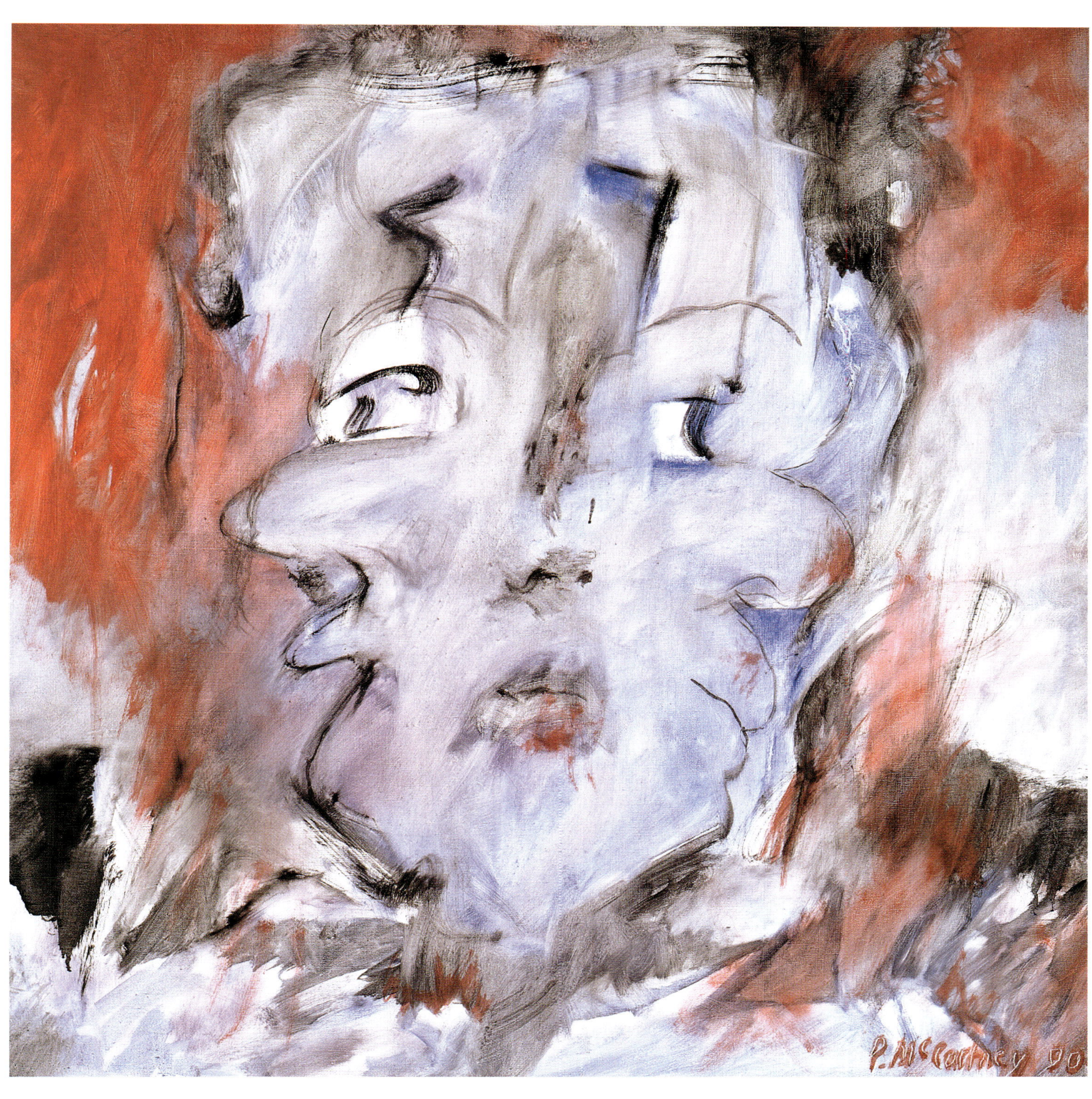

Three blue faces in red sky, 1990

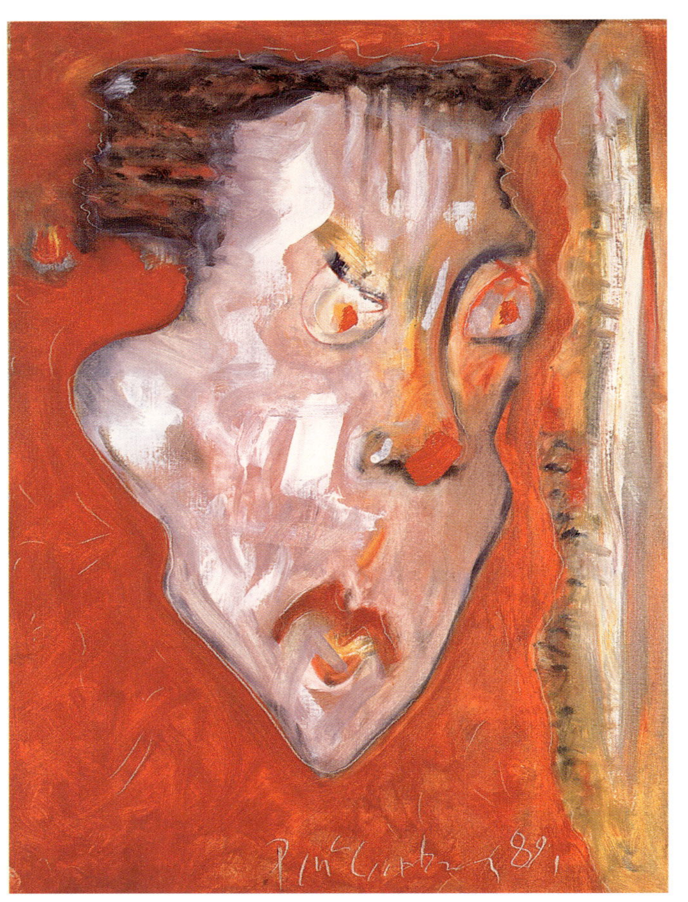

Angry red face, 1989

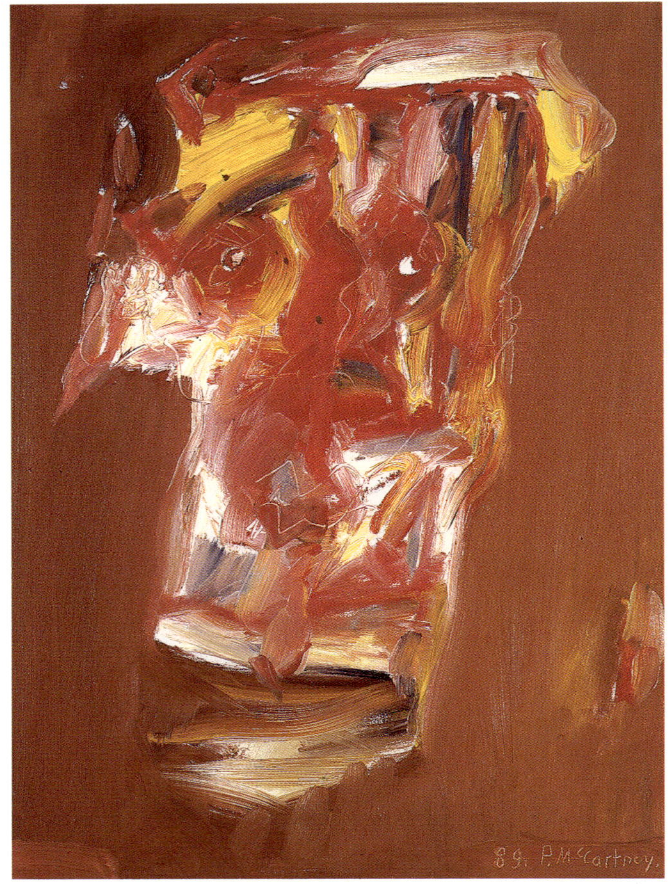

Skull face, 1989

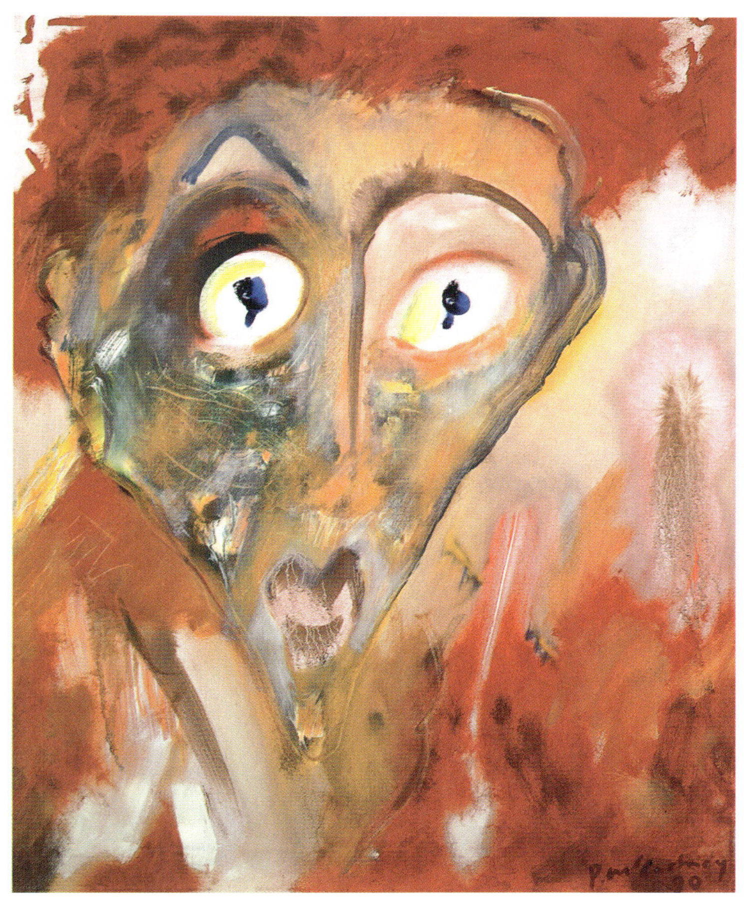

Scared red head, 1990

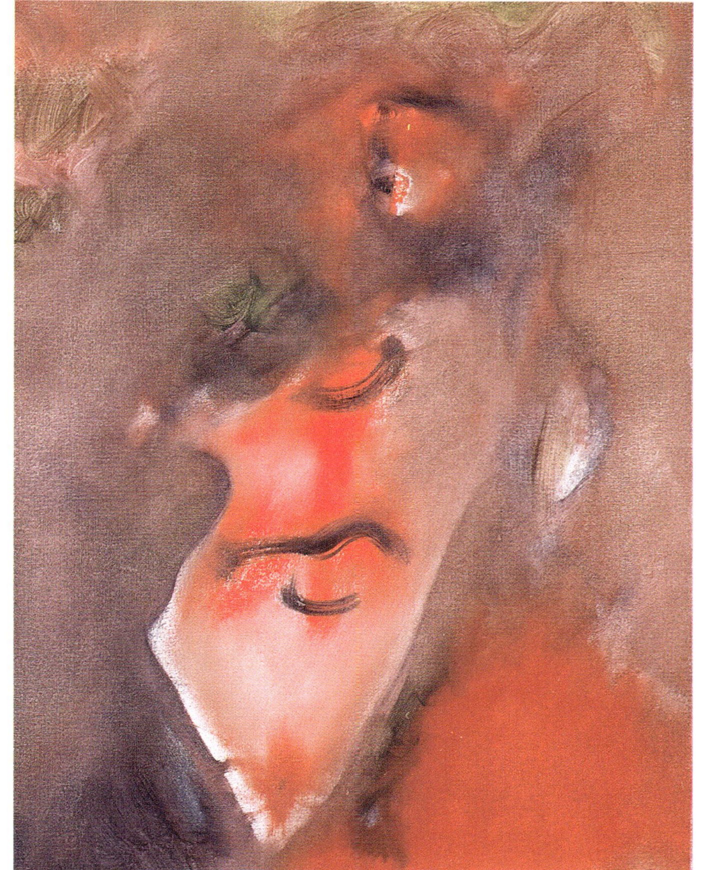

Half red fog face, 1990

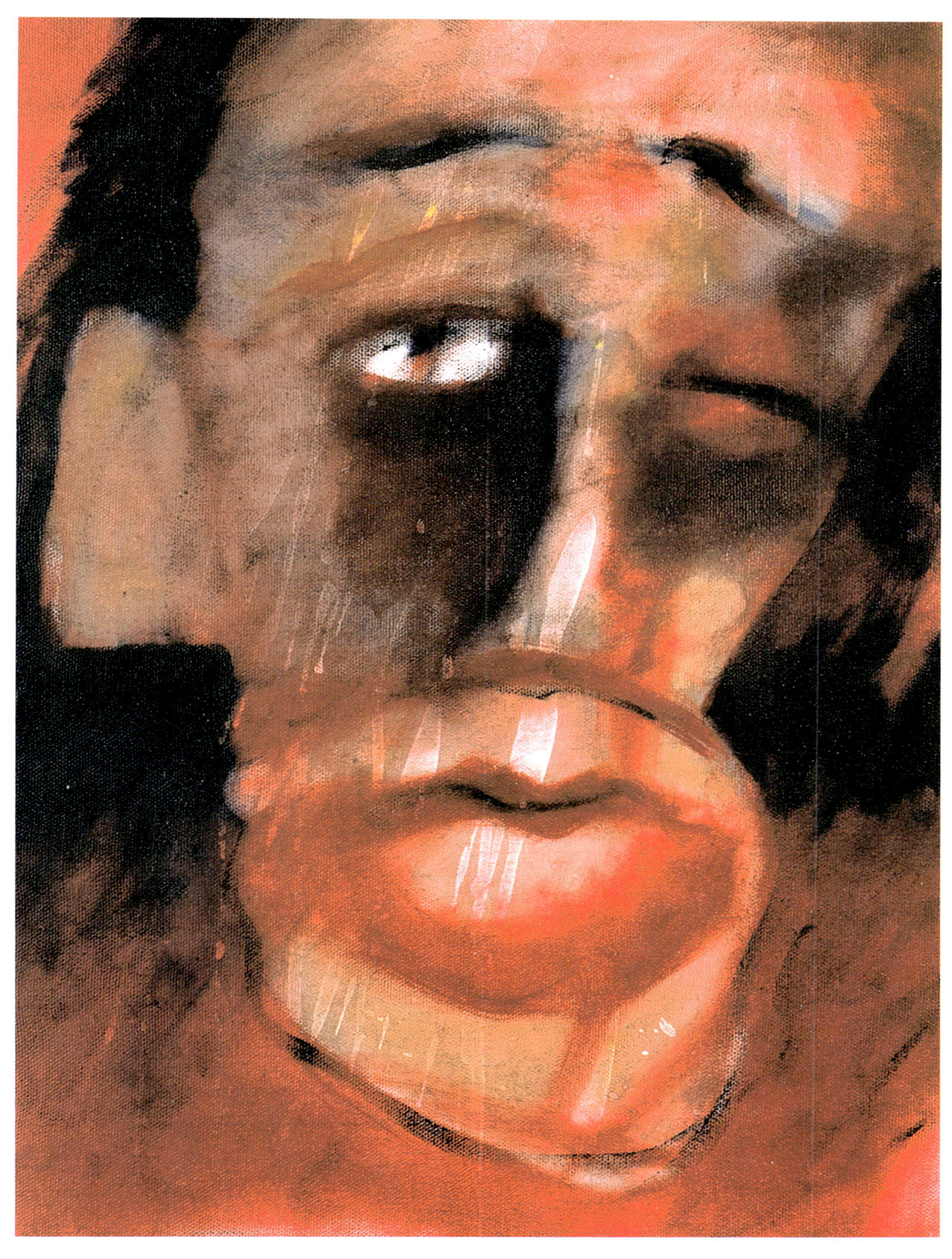

Boxer lips, 1990

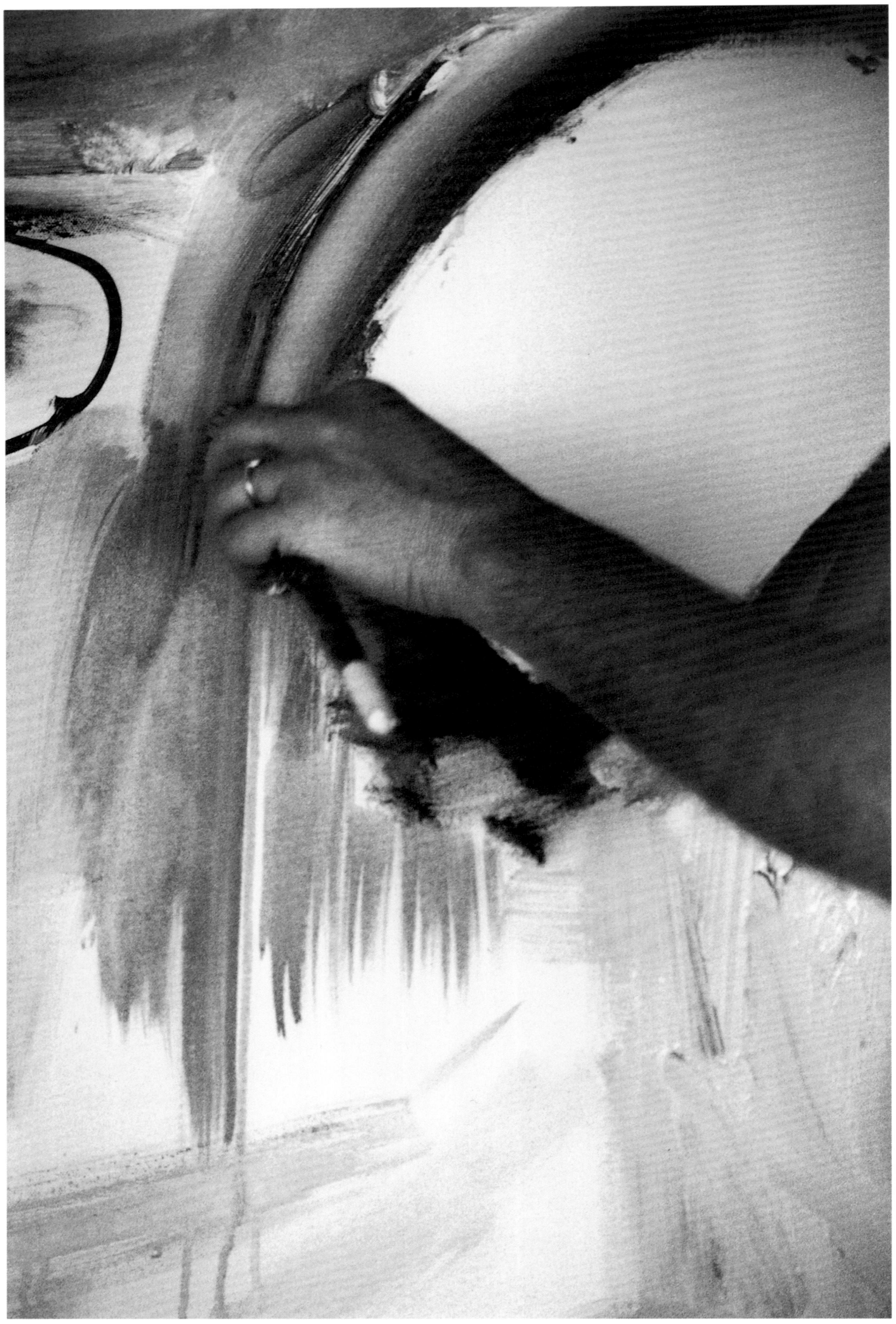

Paul McCartney: Reverses and Other Advances

CHRISTOPH TANNERT

Arm/painting, brushstroke
Sussex, 1992

Anyone who feels part of the current great "rave-o-lotion" — disco fever to confound the zealots — cultivates crossover, combining no-matter-what from wherever. No art exhibition without megaparty, no catwalk without elemental techno-show, every street parade a triumphal procession of artistic transcendence.

Anyone who wants to be part of the "situational transglobality" [1] of the 90s sets out in pursuit of the right mix of "love, sex, screenplays, photography, video, social Utopias on dance-floor planets, painting, studies in democracy, analyses of language and communication, electronic music, dance, parties and last but not least the night-culture techno revolution." [2] Woodstock was never that.

Was yesterday somehow better? The present flood of revivals and the ever expanding retro-culture might seem to imply so. In any case, the revolution proclaimed by the bards in 1968 seems to have been absorbed into the everyday. And now an ecstatic peace has set in like electronic icing on our Big Brother society. The weight of reality is negated by the weightless mindlessness of "We are the move." In the silence of speechlessness, millions of young people disport themselves, shrilly clad and lulled into insensitivity by a constant beat. Rock culture has become club culture, with party animals and dance acrobats to set the tone. That is the norm in popular culture today.

Against this background comes the news that Paul McCartney — whom some might see as the classic feel-good figure — has decided to exhibit and publish his paintings. Of course, there have been others who are now reputed to be wielding a paintbrush. But Paul McCartney? Yet when you think about it, Captain Beefheart's (Don Van Vliet) and David Bowie's paintings and David Byrne's photos are fine in fact, and the overlap of music and the visual arts in the twentieth century is by no means a rarity.

Up until now Paul McCartney has been very hesitant about letting others see his work as a painter, making exceptions only in response to requests and recommendations from his friends. In the book by Barry Miles, McCartney clearly expressed his reticence about having a show of his paintings: "It's just a question of looking for something that feels comfortable. I could hire a gallery and have an exhibition, but I wouldn't want to do that because . . . I'm trying to avoid the [performer]-turned-painter syndrome. I was thinking something quieter, a little German gallery might be nice." [3] The fact that he agreed to an exhibition of his paintings may have had to do with the particular situation, namely the trust he had in Wolfgang Suttner and the exhibition space in the Siegener Kunstforum LŸZ, which is where he first exhibited the work; this space has something of a test-bed quality to it. Nevertheless, in the course of the preparations for the exhibition, what started as perhaps a tentative exploration became a self-confident exercise in presenting art on its own terms. And, in fact, the work in this exhibition and in this book takes on a completely unexpected dimension. Paul McCartney crosses two life-forces: perfect songwriting and intensely coloristic field studies. Now the music — including the overpowering weight of the songs of the Beatles period — no longer takes first place. There is a shift in emphasis in that McCartney is now publicly extending his sphere of activity. Quite astonishingly, a process of relativization has been set in motion that takes the hitherto dominant songs and relocates them next to the formal aesthetics of the paintings.

Unlike pop music, art is not dependent on the entertainment world, even if the juvenile, soppy "boyism" of some young artists today might lead one to think the opposite. Painting can survive without the art market. It is precisely that individual relish in experiment which cares nothing for the outside world and which leads to something that is not "made" but just "comes into being." Identity and authenticity in art have to be generated in those hidden corners that we all have somewhere. As an art form, this is deregulation in action and has no need to explain itself.

Anyone who has been captivated by "Blackbird" — unsurpassed in its simplicity as it balances the harsher lyrics by Lennon on the "white album" — will find after coming face-to-face with McCartney's paintings that he or she has landed up right at the other end of his or her emotions. For McCartney the musician, painting adds new force to his expressive output, a new accent. And for this emotional experience alone, one would want to see these paintings by McCartney the Romantic — of course, not in the sense of tear-drenched outpourings but (particularly in view of the powerful "Give Ireland Back to the Irish") with that deeper, Romantic vision of the advance of humankind toward an ideal world, all the more vital in an age when indecision is celebrated as a virtue and songs disintegrate into no more than "tracks."

McCartney, who has been expending his musical talent for decades onstage, for the recording industry and the public, finds in painting the opposite of his daily round — a place to withdraw into, which can offer him respite from everywhere and nowhere.[4]

The pictures that come into being in these moments of peace and contemplation — but also of explosive emotion, tumbling somewhere between articulacy and inarticulacy — stand in contrast to the reality of McCartney's everyday life and transport him into a place beyond, where images and sound may mingle. That is what makes these paintings so not-normal. And the figurations in them must strike the viewer as particularly individual (completely self-sufficient in their individuality and materiality), because — unlike McCartney's songs — they are more like emotional spirals, whereas the songs flow in an ultimately well-tempered manner subject only to the subtlest of interruptions.

Art always goes beyond the norm; that is to say, it is abnormal. As far as the distinction between normal and abnormal is concerned, I think that one could draw a line between art that keeps within a certain framework and art that is imbued with an extreme, joyful waywardness. True creativity must always be extreme; it must have something feverishly expressive about it.

McCartney's pictures combine art and provocation, dilettantism and banality. They embrace the apparently deranged, demonstrating the need to disarrange the familiar and to re-arrange, to advance into the unfamiliar, to see and expect the new and unknown.

McCartney's "simultaneous heads," his *Shock head* (page 71), and people wearing masks of course are not in need of hospitalization. On the contrary, there is a structure to their lives, albeit only the structure of the frame of the picture; for the artist McCartney, going beyond the borders of ordinary reason does not involve potential humiliation but rather an increase in one's understanding and awareness.

The visionary heads glowing with color in *Yellow bow tie* (page 70) and in *Large yellow face* (page 80), or the inward-looking *Is this a self-portrait?* (page 66), look into the past, into the history of art, and into the future. They link psy-

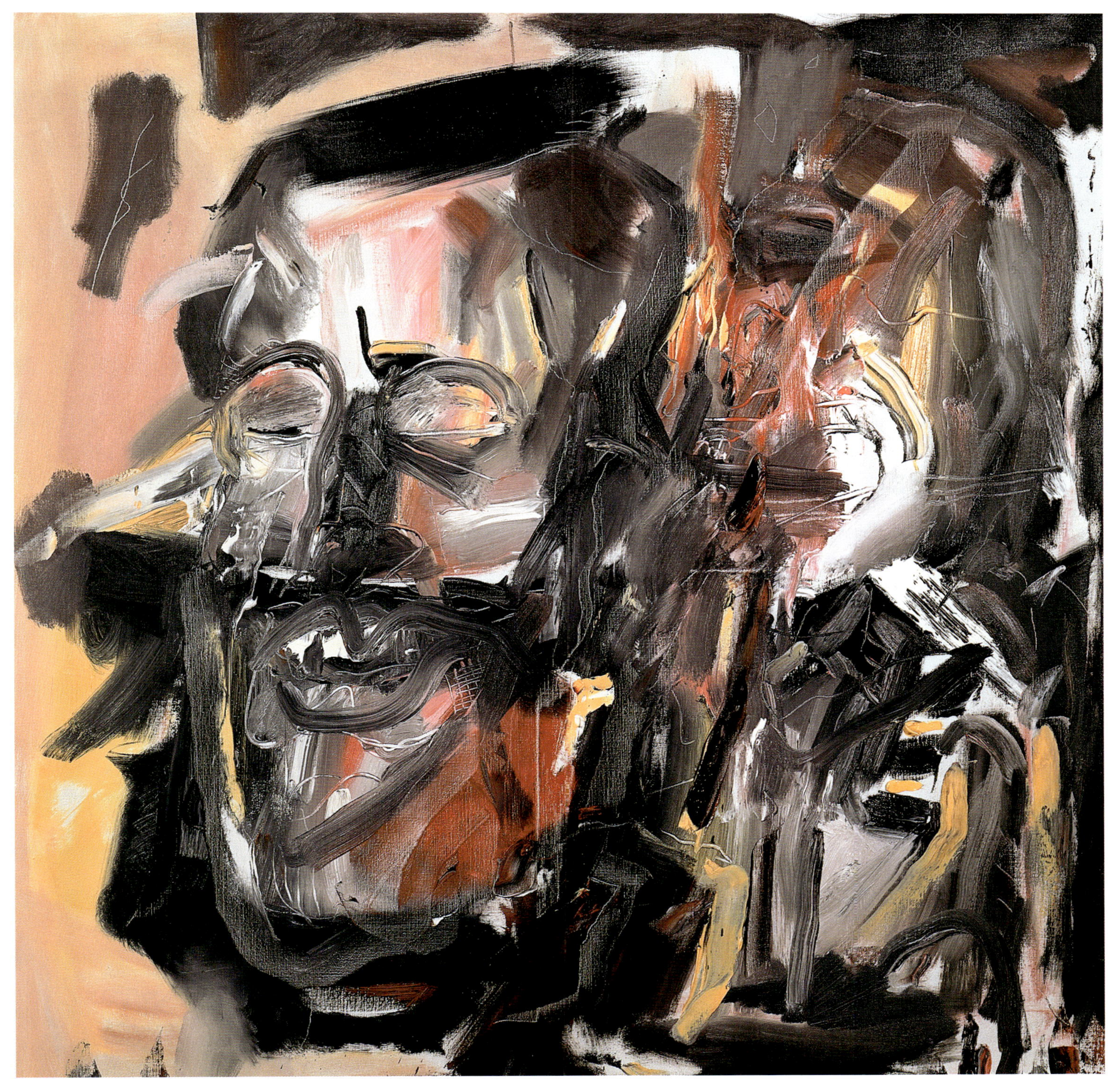

Brains on fire, 1994

chosis to basic forms of creativity. They draw on the fundamentals of existence. They look further. They look more deeply. And at the same time they intensify and deepen the artistic qualities of the compositions of McCartney the musician.

McCartney's paintings are the as-yet-unseen side of his artistic being. That is what makes this work so highly individual. And in it McCartney goes back to expressive — or rather to abstract expressionist — roots that lend voice to the archaic and the wild, and suddenly underpin Paul McCartney's songs with "non-entertaining-noises." [5] It is as though one can hear the movement and the grating of the brush and the palette knife on the canvas.[6]

And that is the crucial point. Humility and audacity are in the ring together. In his paintings McCartney advances into realms that he never entered in his songs.

Where McCartney makes his disturbing, sawlike frontal attacks on the canvas, he is, if anything, closest to the experiments of the cutting-edge electronauts of the present.

But this perfectly normal situation is also paradoxical: what McCartney does in paint cuts right across what he does in sound. Even in his autobiographically colored *Liverpool Oratorio,*[7] which could be seen as a projection screen showing all the various coordinates of the McCartney sound world and, as the critics have said, tends in its acoustic innovation toward the surreal — even in this work there is far less physically overwhelming experiment than in a number of his pictures that function like "normality traps" because the viewer is completely taken in by their casually insolent yet relentless brushwork.

Pictures like *Brains on fire* (page 133) or *Robot and star* (page 110) and *Unfinished symphony* (page 77) breathe new life into tradition. In an aesthetic quantum leap McCartney defends the wondrous and the power of the imagination against the carefully calculated positioning of expressionism in art history. McCartney sets fire to the canvas with colors, beats out a rhythm with his brush, and applies layer upon layer, only to partially remove them again as he returns to the canvas below. In *Brains on fire* it seems that the ratio evaporates and the pelvis rotates. *Robot and star* transmits a sense of energy and restlessness to the viewer, as though one were right in the middle of the solid steel, hectically steaming world of Fritz Lang's *Metropolis,* reflecting more than just the mood of the person behind the paintbrush. McCartney successfully manages to walk the tightrope above these roaring, pulsating fireworks into the beyond: he never loses his footing and never descends into the merely chic or exotic. However heavy his own heart may be.

Much like the COBRA artists, including Carl-Henning Pedersen, who wanted "to catch the arms of the fire and detach them one by one so that they could take up a new life in the four-cornered world of the canvas," [8] so too McCartney, with childlike enthusiasm, mobilizes the colors and the stuttering forms, and each of his pictures becomes a self-contained world of its own that defies and contradicts language. Carl-Henning Pedersen, who wrote numerous art-historical and lyrical texts that greatly inspired the COBRA members, once said: "We must try to attain a general understanding of the wonderful and the beautiful which is color — the red, the yellow, the green, the violet, the white, the black. These colors are our world, to the painter they are an orchestra, both earthly and heavenly, that he plays with." [9]

In *Unfinished symphony* McCartney accompanies the trumpets of Jericho with brush-point staccato and allows the sub/unconscious to run free. In one fell swoop he captures the image of a mood as though it were a natural phenomenon. In pictures such as *C minor* (page 135) and *Key of F* (page 136) McCartney had already been creating a color picture combining nature, sounds, and their effect. These were clearly chamber works. In *Unfinished symphony* a whole orchestra seems to have marched past his inner ear, with avalanches of sound locked into chaos until they were reigned in and calmed as though by the tender touch of a hand on the temple.

Paul McCartney has been involved with art and artists since the days of the Beatles. Peter

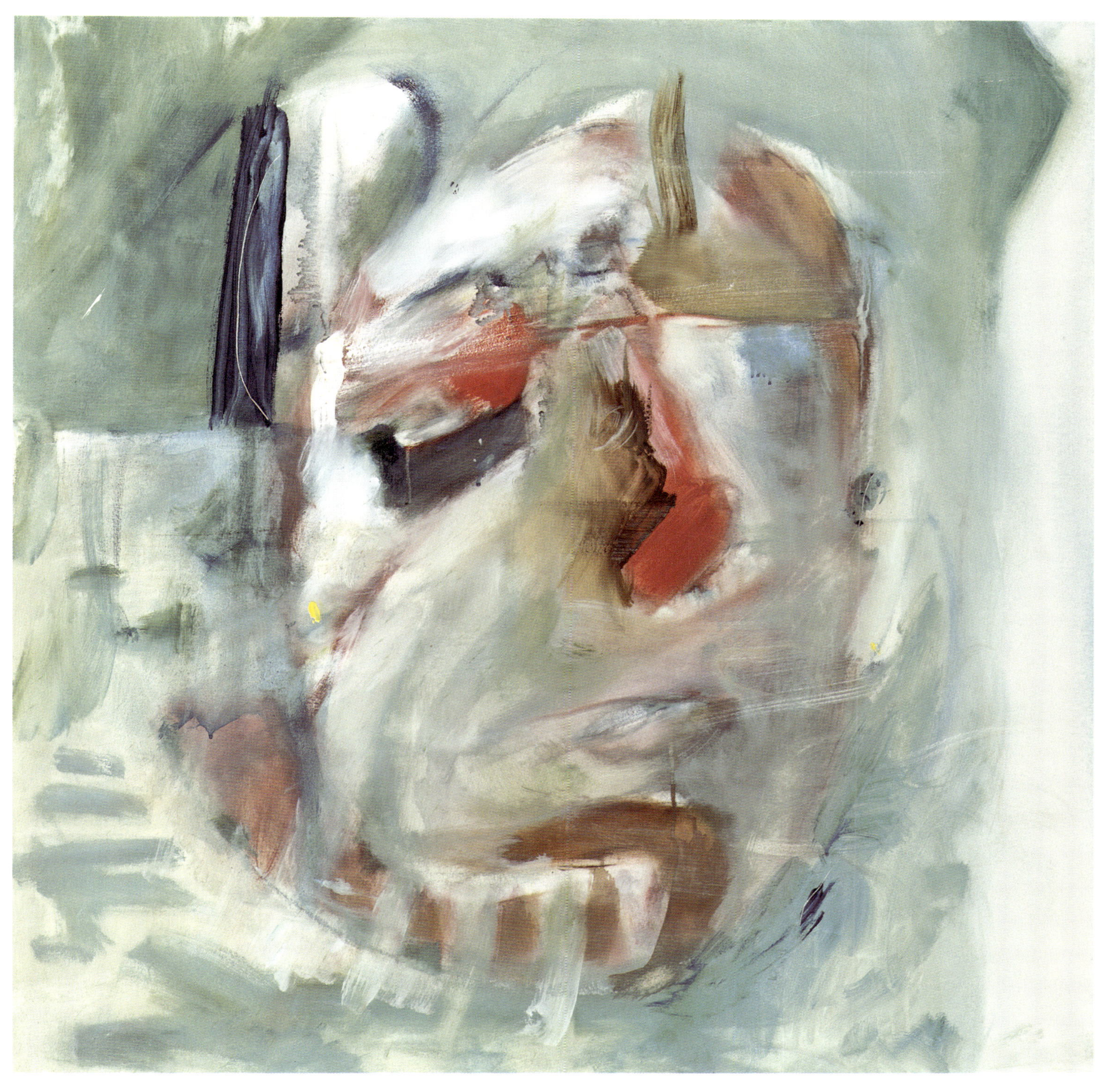

C minor, 1993

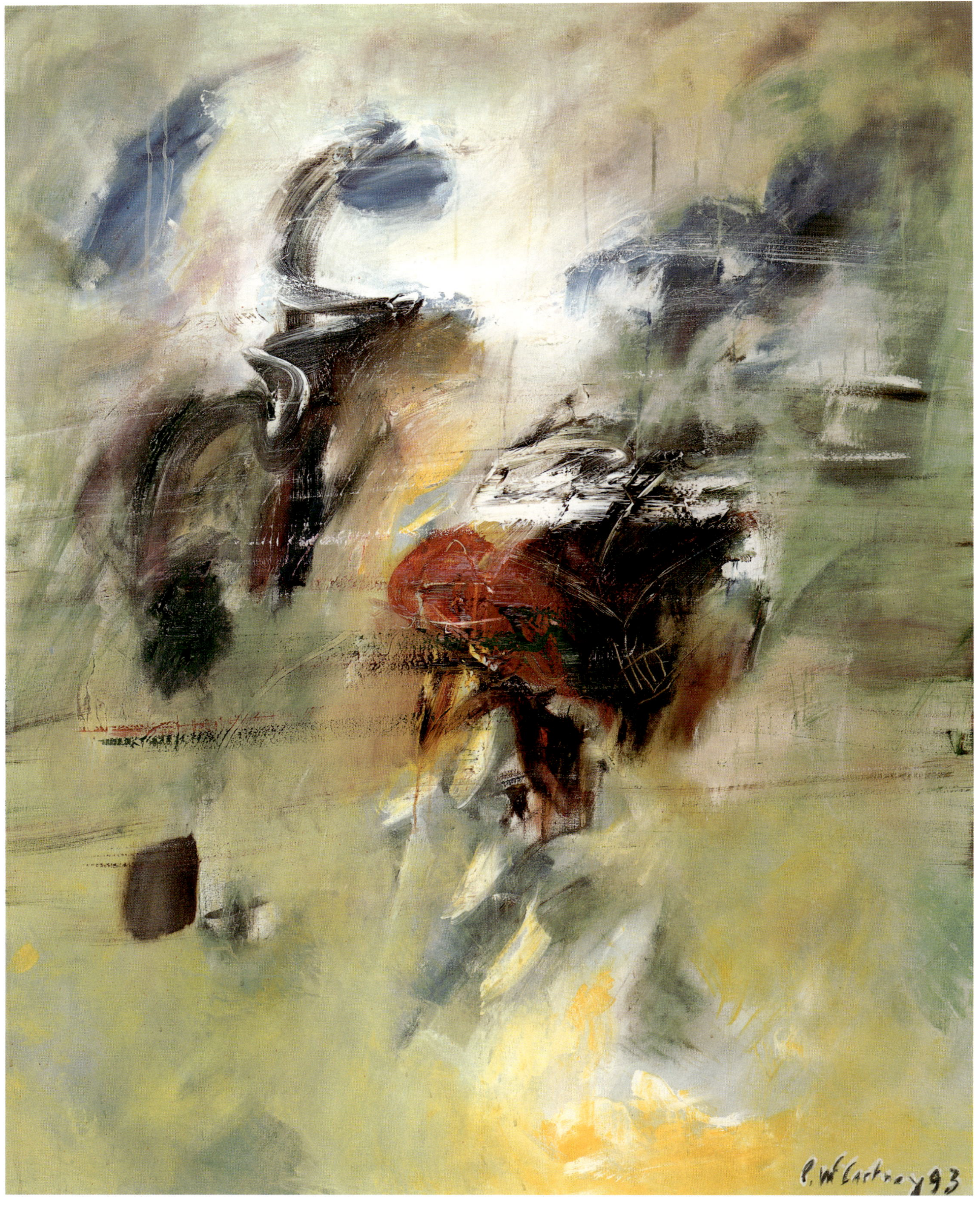

Blake designed the cover for *Sgt. Pepper* (based on an idea by McCartney), and Richard Hamilton came up with the idea for a white sleeve with only a serial number and the embossed name of the group for another album, which led to its later simply being known as the "white album."

One of the artists who has most inspired McCartney is Willem de Kooning; like him, McCartney sticks to "the principle of styleless-ness" and views painting as a "way of living" [10] — but McCartney's work is less concerned with the differences between abstract and representational painting: his is about the appropriation of external reality and the metamorphosis of his own inner worlds along the twin tracks of song-writing and painting. In his music McCartney varies the style of his hits by means of homogenously structured gradations. But as an art-aware painter, he allows himself the license to recognize no rules and to deploy uncertainty as a pictorial force. Resisting any hint of nostalgia, McCartney faced the canvas and began to carve out a new path into the future, without paying heed to the aesthetic trends of the time. De Kooning, typically polemic and stubbornly opposing the notion of "inventing a style," once declared: "An artist is someone who also makes art. He didn't invent it. How it started — 'what the hell.' It is clear that art knows no progress." [11] And these sentiments support Paul McCartney's more relaxed line of argument: "It is just to have a go with paint, to play with it, to juxtapose the yellow against the blue, to learn what happens when the red comes in with the yellow and the blue, and to deal with all these colors as one harmonious unit. That is what I have been doing all those years." [12]

McCartney has chosen a good time to become involved with painting. Widespread references to the end of painting or to "painting after the end of painting" [13] point to a caesura in the history of art, meaning that painting is no longer part of the vanguard of art. It is now just one medium among many. It is as though the reverent "Oh, he is a painter" has turned into "How nice that the man with the briefcase also has artistic vision." The aesthetic paradigms of painting have been toppled. It has lost the aesthetic privileges of its traditional position of power. But it was only through this epoch-making process of disempowerment that it is possible to recognize painting and its materiality anew. McCartney the artist seems intuitively to have known right from the outset that painting is no longer about the illustration of reality but about the transformation and appropriation of that reality in a specific historical context. In *Brains on fire, Robot and star,* and *Unfinished symphony,* he proves beyond all doubt that he has little time for the "representative" function of painting that has been poisoning art schools and academies since the nineteenth century. His paintings are not about objects but about seeing and experiencing things, objects, landscapes (including emotional landscapes), events. . . . McCartney's own words are both dreamy and distinct when he says, "But I find, in music as well, I find the paradox, something you didn't expect to work, is what works. You know, I think that, otherwise, I would really be trying to paint motor cars, with chrome, exactly, exactly. But it isn't interesting to me. . . . It is like painting a dream." [14]

So not having attended art school turns out to be not the slightest hindrance at all. In McCartney's paintings, hints and calculated fractures create a mode of expression that consciously drives the viewer to doubt the picture as a medium for conveying some particular meaning. Meaning no longer attaches to a subject but is to be found instead in what is now the autonomy of the picture. We are dealing here with pictures that go down deep into the layers of their own contents. Furthermore, McCartney's work, with its cross-media references, demonstrates vividly how one aesthetic horizon (painting) is not negated by another (music), but how the two constitute a dialogue that first started in antiquity and is still far from coming to a conclusion, even in the idea of the *Gesamtkunstwerk.*

Small drawings, caricatures, and doodles by McCartney have survived from the Beatles era. He painted his first picture in the late 1970s inspired by having met de Kooning. After 1983 his

Key of F, 1993

involvement with painting became more serious, and from 1987 onward there was a marked increase in his output, particularly of acrylics and oils. Paul McCartney has built up an art collection of his own (of classical modernists) and some years ago his wife Linda bought him various items from Magritte's studio, including a ruler and easel that McCartney uses today. The painting *Mr. Magritte's ruler* (page 18), a wonderfully cloudy echo of Magritte, can readily be understood as a respectful invocation of surrealism.

When the authors of *Das neue Rock-Lexikon* talk of Paul McCartney as being "blessed with melody,"[15] they are not so wide of the mark, because the aesthetic fabric of his songs and pictures is not woven from discord. But at the same time it is a harmonic whirlpool that constantly releases new energies where lines of tension threaten to snap. Head wind? It simply flows along McCartney as though he were the new model in a wind tunnel. This ability to don his musical background as an aerodynamic protective covering into which the pictures now have to be incorporated in itself answers one of the problems of contemporary painting — its sheer obviousness. Now there is a line that McCartney can cross in whichever direction he likes. Part of the purity of this formal divide is its intrinsic instability. It would be betraying its own principles if it sought durability for its own sake. Being simultaneously present in the art world and in the distribution channels of the music business is simply the logical outcome of this new situation and has nothing to do with lowering standards.

In his paintings it seems that McCartney has added certain flavor enhancers that sometimes taste strong and are sometimes much milder. McCartney's paintings are of the earthquake variety; he gets right in there, lets go, and comes up with various trumps. McCartney is not frightened of pressing certain sentimental buttons or of mannerist touches, although at the same time he can be distinctly irreverent regarding the rather more hallowed traditions of English portraiture, showing that smoke gets in the Queen's eyes, too.[16] Of course, this is not some antiroyalist tendency escaping onto the canvas via the artist's brush, but we do see here that tiny measure of cheerfully critical determination to survive, tinged with laughter that prevents his work from ever descending into kitsch. Every time the abyss gapes wide, at the last moment McCartney finds his balance again, reaches out for the rope, and turns round to head off in a different direction — never short of stamina and avoiding the many traps that he himself has laid. His paintings are constantly fending off foes on all sides.

It is only in the landscapes that he occasionally holds his breath for a moment. They could be a film, a "nouvelle vague" piece, perhaps bordered by Emil Nolde's summer-soaked flowers. McCartney's heart is expansive and particularly the landscapes, the "body landscapes," have gaps, holes, white patches that could have been painted in. But he let these be, and that was good; as they are, the fresh air of authenticity can blow freely through the exhibition space.

The interior and exterior landscapes (with their readily identifiable Celtic proportions and shapes), the bizarre paintings of heads, his extravagant use of paint and the relevant sensuality, and of course the moments of the all-too-human, like in *Bowie spewing* (page 97) — all these throw a spotlight on Paul McCartney as he moves through his own alchemical narrative, hand in hand with the bizarre figures he invokes in *Insect face* (page 118) and *Sea god* (page 68), which might easily have escaped from the "Octopus's Garden."

It would be completely false to interpret McCartney's paintings as illustrations to songs, those by the Beatles or anyone else. Of course, as always, exceptions make the rule. Naturally McCartney's music is in there, a life force; naturally the secret foundation, the basic outline of the material of the songs, is recast in the subconscious (of the artist, listener, and viewer alike). Yet McCartney's paintings are not some sort of contrived artwork to go with long-familiar songs; it is not a matter of generating or destroying some kind of euphoria around the songs or of revamping them altogether. If, as Michael

Wetzel suggests,[17] painting in the 1990s can be categorized as photographic, filmic, or digital, then McCartney's work might be counted as part of the "acoustic substratum." The intensity and independence with which Paul McCartney creates sound interfaces in his own freestyle process bears witness to the complexity of his potential to reinvent himself.

When the vibrations from a painting such as *Red abstract white moon* (page 64) rush out toward us, when an infinite cosmos of variations takes a Bach-like turn, then we are dealing with a Paul McCartney who — with no trace of the coquette — is deeply engaged in the experiment to paint his own unique refuge for the senses and the soul.

1 Transl. from Theo Altenberg, "Situationistische Transglobale. Ein retrovisionärer Dialog von Paolo Bianchi," *KUNSTFORUM INTERNATIONAL* 135 (1997), pp. 97–129.

2 Ibid., p. 98

3 Quoted in Barry Miles, *Paul McCartney: Many Years from Now* (New York: Henry Holt and Co., 1997), p. 609.

4 Paul McCartney talks about the relationship between painting and music, and his own motivation to paint in conversation with Wolfgang Suttner in this book about the picture *Brains on fire:* "I decided, I know some people think about painters that if they don't paint every day, it isn't right, that's not considered right. But if you do paint every day and you don't enjoy it, or you don't paint well, I think it's probably better not to paint. I don't think it is any great heroic act in going in slavishly every day and saying, 'I must do this.' So what I find is that I do it when I am inspired. And it's how I can combine it with music. Some days the inspiration is a musical one and other days it has just got to be painting."

5 The author is fully aware of the risky use of the term coined by Throbbing Gristle with reference to their cacophonous industrial collages.

6 In conversation with Wolfgang Suttner, McCartney repeatedly refers to the fact that he loves to work with a palette knife, to scrape off layers of paint, to paint with his ears, as though he were listening under the surface of things, as for instance in connection with *Brains on fire:* "Another thing I enjoy, you can see in that fire, to the right of it, I have scraped off a bunch of paint with a palette knife. And it is as if I have put sticky tape on things, like when they wax women's legs [makes whooshing sound] and pulled it off, and it reveals a millimeter beneath that layer. It is that sort of contrast to this, just with a palette knife I just lift off that thickness."

7 Paul McCartney's *Liverpool Oratorio* was performed on June 28, 1991, by the Royal Liverpool Philharmonic Orchestra in the Anglican Cathedral in Liverpool, "where, at the age of eleven Paul once failed an audition to sing in the choir. It was written as a repertory piece to commemorate the 150th anniversary of the founding of the Royal Liverpool Philharmonic Society and was the culmination of a three-year collaboration with the American composer Carl Davis, who had made three previous albums with the RLPO." See Barry Miles, op. cit., pp. 610–11.

8 Carl-Henning Pedersen, "Das Licht der Sonne, 1950," *COBRA. 1948–1951*, exh. cat., Kunstverein in Hamburg, September 25–November 7, 1982, p. 170.

9 Carl-Henning Pedersen, op. cit.

10 Jörn Merkert, "Stillosigkeit als Prinzip. Zur Malerei von Willem de Kooning," *Willem de Kooning. Retrospective,* exh. cat, Whitney Museum of American Art, New York, December 15, 1983–February 26, 1984; Akademie der Künste, Berlin, March 11–May 6, 1984; Musée National d'Art Moderne, Centre Georges Pompidou, Paris, June 26–September 24, 1984; Munich: Prestel Verlag (1984), pp. 115–132.

11 Willem de Kooning in a lecture held on February 18, 1949, "The Subjects of the Artist: A New School," in New York, published in *Willem de Kooning. Retrospective,* exh. cat., op. cit., p. 271.

12 McCartney in conversation with Wolfgang Suttner, June 1995, on the painting *Yellow cool thumb,* unpublished manuscript.

13 Thus the title in *KUNSTFORUM INTERNATIONAL* 131 (1995).

14 McCartney in conversation with Wolfgang Suttner on the painting *Mountain landscrape,* 1991, unpublished manuscript, December 1995.

15 Barry Graves, Siegfried Schmidt-Joos, Bernward Halbscheffel, *Das neue Rock-Lexikon,* vol. 2, Reinbek bei Hamburg, Rowohlt Taschenbuch Verlag (1998), p. 587.

16 See McCartney's paintings *The Queen after her first cigarette, The Queen getting a joke,* and *A greener Queen* (pages 94–95), all from 1991.

17 An interview with Michael Wetzel of *Texte zur Kunst,* "Vor der Malerei," *Texte zur Kunst,* part 31, Cologne (1998), pp. 89–93. See also: Michael Wetzei, *Die Wahrheit nach der Malerei,* Munich: Wilhelm Fink Verlag (1997).

Biographies

Paul McCartney Paul McCartney was born in Liverpool on June 18, 1942, and attended school at the Liverpool Institute. While at the institute, he won an art contest and also became involved with the Walker Art Gallery, whose collection includes Renaissance and Pre-Raphaelite art as well as some of Turner's paintings. In the mid-1950s McCartney acquainted himself with the work of artists who were popular in England at that time. Among these artists were Picasso, Jackson Pollock, de Staël, the cubists, and the surrealists.

At fourteen years of age, McCartney wrote his first song, and there began what was to be a long and celebrated music career. As a part of the Beatles in the 1960s, he revolutionized the music world, and when the Beatles separated in 1970, he created the music group Wings. Later he recorded as a solo artist and exerted a strong influence on international music trends.

During the 1960s, as the Beatles were enjoying ever-increasing success, McCartney deepened his involvement with the visual arts. Through his friendship with the London art dealer Robert Fraser, McCartney became acquainted with pop art and met an array of contemporary artists, including Peter Blake, Richard Hamilton, David Hockney, Allen Jones, Eduardo Paolozzi, Andy Warhol, and Claes Oldenburg. It was at this time that McCartney developed a strong interest in surrealism and the works of de Chirico, Dalí, Max Ernst and, above all, René Magritte, from whom he acquired some paintings.

The Indica Bookshop and Gallery was founded by John Dunbar, Peter Asher, and Barry Miles in the mid-1960s. McCartney maintained friendly contact with the gallery as it quickly became the center of the London avant-garde, and he often assisted with exhibition installation at the gallery. McCartney designed the gallery's brochure and wrapping paper using his own drawings.

In 1966 the Beatles' *Sgt. Pepper* album appeared with Peter Blake's design for the cover. Blake based this design on previous sketches by McCartney. In 1968 *The Beatles,* also known as the White Album, was released with a cover and poster designed by Richard Hamilton. Hamilton's design inspired McCartney, and in 1969 *Abbey Road* appeared with a cover design based on McCartney's concept. During his time with Wings, McCartney designed all the album covers in collaboration with his wife, Linda.

After his marriage in 1969, McCartney became familiar with his father-in-law's art collection. This collection included Picasso prints, drawings by Matisse, and paintings by Rothko, Lindner, de Kooning, and Philip Guston. A few years later McCartney met Willem de Kooning and began an important friendship that lasted for many years. In the early 1980s McCartney began to paint, and de Kooning was a significant influence on this work.

Paul McCartney is an honorary citizen of the city of Liverpool and patron of the Liverpool Institute for the Performing Arts. In 1995 Prince

Charles named McCartney a member of the Royal College of Music and in 1996 he was knighted by Queen Elizabeth II for his contribution to music.

Since 1990 McCartney has been composing orchestral and choral music, and his *Liverpool Oratorio,* commissioned by the Royal Liverpool Philharmonic Society, has been performed more than 100 times in twenty countries since its premiere in 1991. McCartney's other classical compositions are *A Leaf, Stately Horn, Inebriation, Spiral,* and *Standing Stone*.

Approximately forty years after Paul McCartney's passion for the visual arts was awakened, he exhibited his work for the first time in Siegen, Germany, in early 1999.

Brian Clarke Born in 1953, Brian Clarke is a painter and creator of large-scale colored glass works for architectural projects. *Time* magazine has said about him that he "collaborates with some of the most internationally recognized architects as one of the world's leading glass artists." He lives and works in London, New York, and Munich.

Linda McCartney Born in Scarsdale, New York, on September 24, 1941, Linda McCartney began taking photographs in the early sixties while studying art at the University of Arizona. From the mid-sixties on, her pictures accompanied the musical revolution of the decade. She photographed, among others, the Rolling Stones, B. B. King, the Doors, the Grateful Dead, the Who, Jimi Hendrix, and — above all — the Beatles. In 1969 she and Paul McCartney were married. Linda then experimented successfully with photograms. In the 1990s she collaborated more and more with Brian Clarke, and as a result her snapshots found their way into his glass projects. Her photographic publications include *Sixties, Portrait of an Era* (1992), *Roadworks* (1996), and *Wide Open* (1998).

Linda McCartney died in April 1998.

Barry Miles Born in 1943, Barry Miles is a freelance writer living in England and France. He is cofounder and editor of the *International Times,* an underground British magazine. Supported by McCartney, he created the Indica Bookshop and Gallery in London, a center for artistic and avant-garde literature. Later he led Zapple, the experimental literary label from Apple Records. Miles is author of the McCartney biography *Many Years from Now* and works about Allen Ginsburg and William S. Burroughs.

Wolfgang Suttner Born in 1951, Wolfgang Suttner, head of the cultural department of the county council district of Siegen-Wittgenstein, Germany, studied art, psychology, and German philology and has been organizing exhibitions and art shows for twenty years. He also founded the Siegen Art Society, is a board member of the Association of German Art Societies, and has been publishing and lecturing for the past twenty years on twentieth-century art and artists.

Wolfgang Suttner collaborated with Paul McCartney on cataloging and documenting the latter's artistic oeuvre and directed the world's first exhibition of McCartney's paintings in the Lÿz Art Forum, Siegen, Germany

Christoph Tannert Born in 1955 in Leipzig, Christoph Tannert studied art history and archaeology at the Humboldt University in Berlin. An art critic and exhibition curator, he lives in Berlin and writes regularly for the newspaper *Berliner Zeitung.* Since 1991 he has been project leader for the Bethany artists' house in Berlin.

Julian Treuherz Julian Treuherz is Keeper of Art Galleries for the National Museums & Galleries on Merseyside, responsible for the Walker Art Gallery, Sudley House, and the Lady Lever Art Gallery. He was previously Keeper of Fine Art at Manchester City Art Gallery. He is the author of numerous books and articles, with a concentration on aspects of nineteenth-century British art.

List of Paintings

The following A-numbers are the inventory numbers from the McCartney Archives.

Page 2
Pintos in the sky with desert poppy
1991
Acrylic on canvas
152 x 120.5 cm
A 152

Page 14
Home territory
1990
Acrylic on canvas
101.5 x 86.5 cm
A 124

Page 18
Mr. Magritte's ruler
1995
Oil on canvas
121.5 x 121.5 cm
A 582

Page 20
Reclining woman
1987
Acrylic on paper
30 x 25 cm
A 509

Page 21
Pigtail
1988
Acrylic on paper
30 x 25 cm
A 574

Page 21
Red eye
1988
Acrylic on paper
30 x 25 cm
A 573

Page 21
A handbag?
1988
Acrylic on paper
30 x 25 cm
A 569

Page 21
Is this Bernard Miles?
1988
Acrylic on paper
61 x 46 cm
A 568

Page 21
Blue face
1988
Acrylic on paper
61 x 46 cm
A 567

Page 25
White dream
1990
Oil on canvas
101.5 x 127 cm
A 339

Page 26
Father figure
1992
Acrylic on canvas
121.5 x 91.5 cm
A 157

Page 63
Big mountain face
1991
Acrylic on canvas
152.5 x 120.5 cm
A 176

Page 64
Red abstract white moon
1991
Acrylic on canvas
121.5 x 90.5 cm
A 175

Page 65
Mountain landscrape
1991
Acrylic on canvas
60.5 x 50.5 cm
A 326

Page 66
Is this a self-portrait?
1988
Oil on canvas
35.5 x 28 cm
A 556

Page 67
Andy in the garden
1990
Oil on canvas
60.5 x 90.5 cm
A 106

Page 68
Sea god
1990
Oil on canvas
76 x 61 cm
A 081

Page 69
Twin freaks
1990
Oil on canvas
121.5 x 121.5 cm
A 125

Page 70
Yellow bow tie
1989
Oil on canvas
56 x 40.5 cm
A 094

Page 70
Scratch man
1989
Oil on canvas
51 x 40.5 cm
A 550

Page 71
Shock head
1989
Oil on canvas
46 x 35.5 cm
A 370

Page 71
Red yellow face
1989
Oil on canvas
56 x 40.5 cm
A 352

Page 73
Black scratch I
1994
Oil on canvas
121.5 x 121.5 cm
A 231

Page 74
Black scratch II
1994
Oil on canvas
151 x 121 cm
A 229

Page 75
Black scratch III
1994
Oil on canvas
151.5 x 121 cm
A 240

Page 76
Tara's plastic skirt
1992
Acrylic on canvas
121.5 x 186 cm
A 220

Page 77
Unfinished symphony
1993
Oil on canvas
151.5 x 120.5 cm
A 210

Page 79
Yellow Linda with piano
1988
Oil on canvas
56 x 41 cm
A 020

Page 80
Large yellow face
1990
Oil on canvas
121.5 x 121.5 cm
A 196

Page 81
Chinaman
1990
Oil on canvas
121.5 x 75.3 cm
A 211

Page 82
Oak apple twenties man
1988
Acrylic on canvas
35 x 45 cm
A 577

Page 83
Prehistoric antelope
1989
Acrylic on canvas
61 x 50.5 cm
A 090

Page 84
Egypt station
1988
Acrylic on canvas
40.5 x 51 cm
A 171

Page 85
Linda yellow red cross
1991
Oil on canvas
127 x 101.6 cm
A 128

Page 86
Standing Stone story
1994
Oil on canvas
121.5 x 121.5 cm
A 233

Page 87
Chief rug
1994
Oil on canvas
121.5 x 121.5 cm
A 186

Page 88
Celtic eloquence
1994
Oil on canvas
121.5 x 121.5 cm
A 183

Page 89
Ancient connections
1994
Oil on canvas
121.5 x 121.5 cm
A 180

Page 90
White Celts
1994
Oil on canvas
121.5 x 121.5 cm
A 184

Page 91
Celts
1994
Oil on canvas
121.5 x 121.5 cm
A 188

Page 92
Celtic fertility
1994
Oil on canvas
121.5 x 121.5 cm
A 190

Page 93
Yellow Celt
1994
Oil on canvas
121.5 x 121.5 cm
A 185

Page 95
Black singer
1991
Acrylic on canvas
152.5 x 120.5 cm
A 154

Page 96
Upturned critic framed
1988
Oil on canvas
61 x 45.5 cm
A 004

Page 97
Bowie spewing
1990
Oil on canvas
50.5 x 41 cm
A 089

Page 98
The Queen after her first cigarette
1991
Acrylic on canvas
56 x 46.5 cm
A 391

Page 99
The Queen getting a joke
1991
Acrylic on canvas
51 x 40.7 cm
A 392

Page 99
A greener Queen
1991
Acrylic on canvas
56 x 45.5 cm
A 393

Page 100
Patti Boyd
1989
Acrylic on canvas
91 x 70.5 cm
A 103

Page 100
Mr. Kipps
1988
Oil on canvas
61 x 64 cm
A 008

Page 101
Man o' the sea
1988
Acrylic on canvas
76 x 61 cm
A 544

Page 102
Elvish me
1989
Oil on canvas
91.5 x 91.5 cm
A 130

Page 103
Beach boy
1988
Acrylic on canvas
76 x 61 cm
A 546

Page 105
Red triangle sand
1992
Acrylic on canvas
101.5 x 101.5 cm
A 309

Page 106
Beach towels
1990
Acrylic on canvas
101.5 x 101.5 cm
A 310

Page 107
Shark on Georgica
1993
Acrylic on canvas
91.5 x 92 cm
A 318

Page 108
Unspoken words
1994
Oil on canvas
121.5 x 121.5 cm
A 242

Page 109
Dark faces
1991
Oil on canvas
121.5 x 121.5 cm
A 191

Page 110
Robot and star
1995
Oil on canvas
121.5 x 121.5 cm
A 579

Page 111
Abstract coloured twenties man
1989
Oil on canvas
121.5 x 121.5 cm
A 202

Page 112
Blue mask
1989
Acrylic on canvas
61 x 50.5 cm
A 048

Page 113
White cross face
1990
Oil on canvas
121.5 x 61 cm
A 147

Page 115
John's room
1990
Oil on canvas
121.5 x 121.5 cm
A 066

Page 116
Green jacket with cross on shoulder
1989
Oil on canvas
81.5 x 81.5 cm
A 101

Page 117
Bald head
1990
Oil on canvas
121.5 x 121.5 cm
A 067

Page 118
Insect face
1989
Oil on canvas
61 x 45.5
A 013

Page 119
Green head
1988
Acrylic on canvas
101.5 x 76 cm
A 541

Page 120
Green kiss
1988
Acrylic on canvas
61 x 49.5 cm
A 504

Page 120
Oast kiss
1988
Acrylic on canvas
61 x 51 cm
A 505

Page 121
The kiss
1988
Acrylic on canvas
61 x 49.5 cm
A 503

Page 121
Blue kiss
1988
Oil on canvas
61 x 49.5 cm
A 506

Page 122
Grey head vision
1992
Acrylic on canvas
60.5 x 60.5 cm
A 332

Page 123
Housepaint clown
1992
Oil on canvas
91.5 x 71 cm
A 367

Page 124
Blue tooth
1991
Oil on canvas
121.5 x 121.5 cm
A 206

Page 125
Three blue faces in red sky
1990
Oil on canvas
91 x 91 cm
A 119

Page 126
Angry red face
1989
Oil on canvas
56 x 40.5 cm
A 095

Page 126
Skull face
1989
Oil on canvas
56 x 40.5 cm
A 093

Page 127
Scared red head
1990
Oil on canvas
76.2 x 60.9
A 114

Page 127
Half red fog face
1990
Oil on canvas
51 x 46 cm
A 109

Page 129
Boxer lips
1990
Oil on canvas
40 x 30 cm
A 078

Page 133
Brains on fire
1994
Oil on canvas
121.5 x 121.5 cm
A 181

Page 135
C minor
1993
Oil on canvas
122 x 122 cm
A 224

Page 136
Key of F
1993
Oil on canvas
152 x 122 cm
A 219

List of Photographs by Linda McCartney

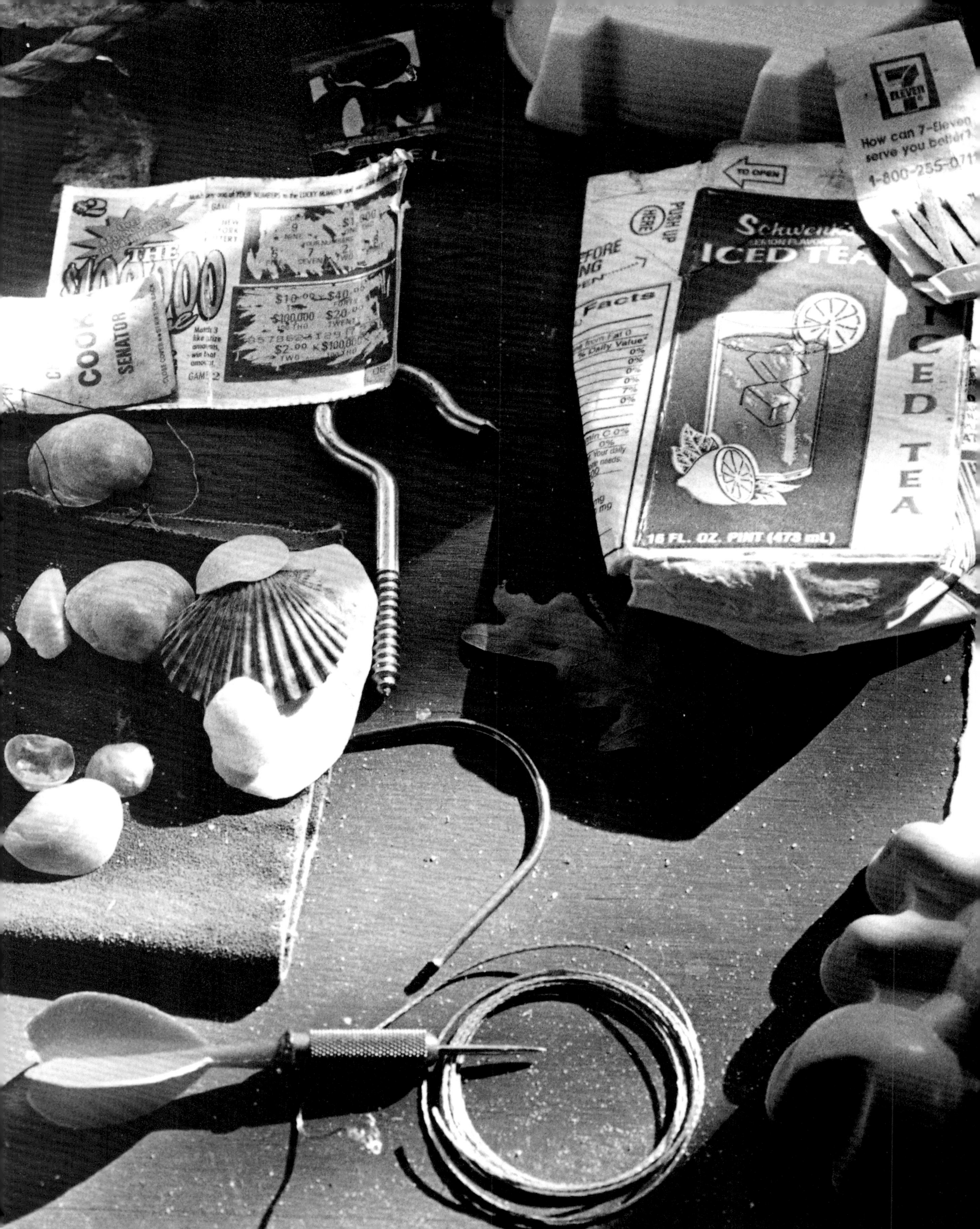

How can 7-Eleven serve you better?
TO OPEN
PUSH UP HERE
ICED TEA
16 FL. OZ. PINT (473 mL)
ICED TEA
SENATOR
NEW YORK LOTTERY

Paul McCartney thanks:

Linda McCartney

Mary McCartney

Brian Clarke

Wolfgang Suttner

Robert Montgomery

Roger Huggett

Shelagh Jones

Paul B. Winn

Terry Reece Hackford

Carol Judy Leslie

Designed by Susan Marsh

Typeset in Scala Sans

Printed by Dr. Cantz'sche Druckerei

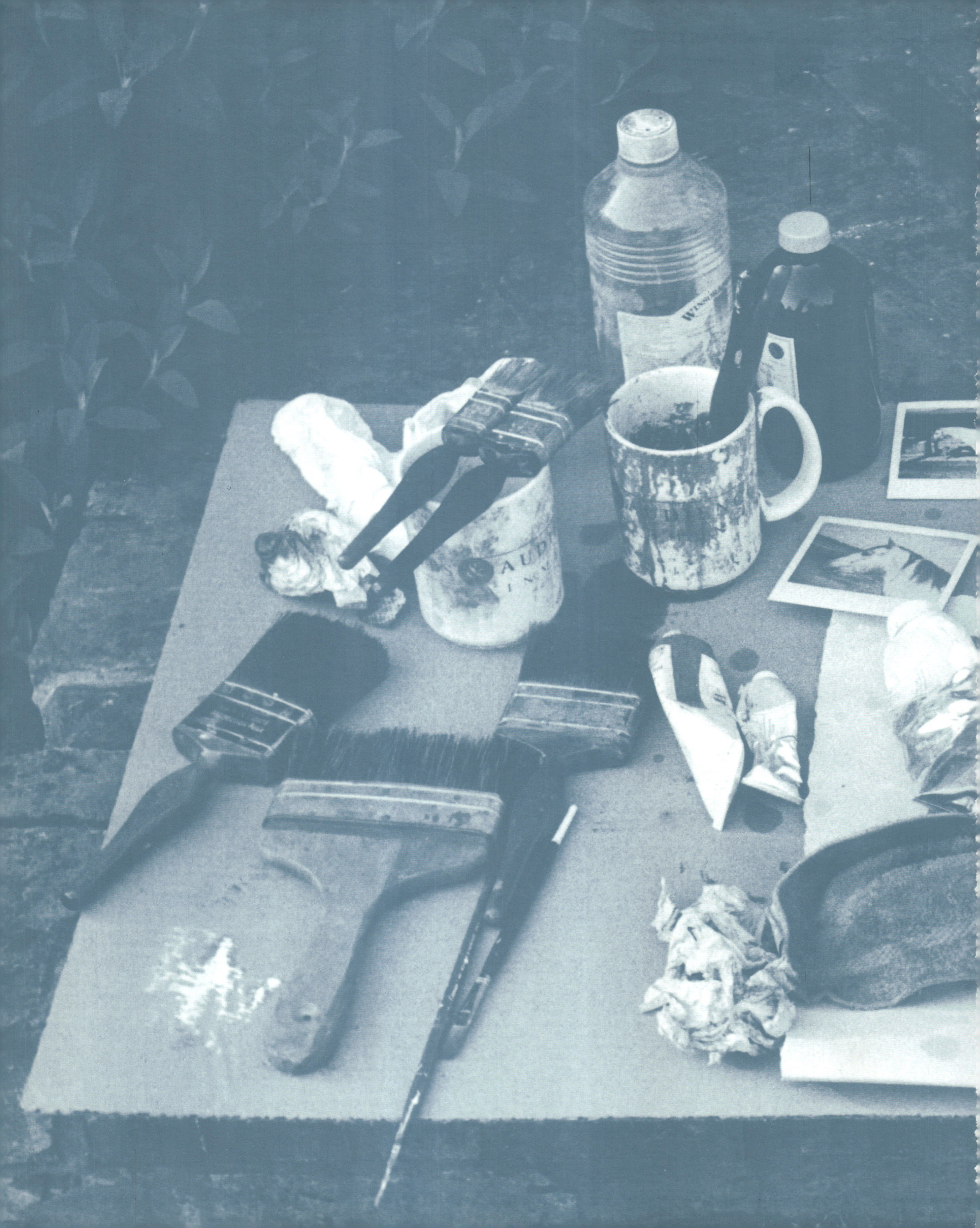